T0006430

CRoWS
AND
RAVEnS

© Rick de Yampert

ABOUT THE AUTHOR

Rick de Yampert is a Florida resident and longtime journalist who spent twenty-three years as the arts and entertainment writer for the *Daytona Beach News-Journal*. He presents workshops and performs on sitar and Native American flutes at Pagan festivals in the Southeast. He also presents lectures on metaphysical topics at non-Pagan events and venues, including Unitarian Universalist churches. Rick has studied Hindu sacred sound, shamanic drumming, Goddess worship, Taoism, and more. His crow art has been displayed at galleries and art festivals around Florida. Visit him at RickdeYampert.com or mistercrowart.com.

RICK DE YAMPERT

CROWS
AND
RAVENS

MYSTERY, MYTH,
AND MAGIC OF
SACRED CORVIDS

LLEWELLYN PUBLICATIONS
WOODBURY, MINNESOTA

FIRST EDITION
First Printing, 2024

Book design by R. Brasington
Cover design by Shannon McKuhen
Interior illustrations by Llewellyn Art Department: pages 22, 57

Photography is used for illustrative purposes only. The persons depicted may not endorse or represent the book's subject.

Llewellyn Publications is a registered trademark of Llewellyn Worldwide Ltd.

Library of Congress Cataloging-in-Publication Data (Pending)
ISBN: 978-0-7387-6387-3

Llewellyn Worldwide Ltd. does not participate in, endorse, or have any authority or responsibility concerning private business transactions between our authors and the public.

All mail addressed to the author is forwarded but the publisher cannot, unless specifically instructed by the author, give out an address or phone number.

Any internet references contained in this work are current at publication time, but the publisher cannot guarantee that a specific location will continue to be maintained. Please refer to the publisher's website for links to authors' websites and other sources.

Llewellyn Publications
A Division of Llewellyn Worldwide Ltd.
2143 Wooddale Drive
Woodbury, MN 55125-2989
www.llewellyn.com

Printed in the United States of America

For my sweet Michelle LaBella,
whose love has led me deeper into Magic and Spirit.

Contents

FOREWORD

There is a family of crows who live in the back garden—or maybe I live in their front garden. I have loved crows my whole life. When I read that a group of crows was called a "murder," I refused to use it. They form lasting bonds and vibrant families, so I refer to a group of crows as a "family." In fact, as I write this, a few of them are outside the window chatting. No alarm cries; no calling the stragglers in for the evening roost. Just chatting.

When I go out to my car later, one of them will probably greet me from the old maple tree with a harsh cry. I respond with a cheery "good morning," which is often answered by a softer sound. We converse until I am out of sight. Sometimes another will greet me at the back of the driveway as I get into my car and drive away. Throughout the day, the sight of a crow and a quick analysis of its actions makes me think that they have a particular fondness for me. I don't feed them, as some people do. For many years, we had cats, and it seemed cruel to lure birds to the yard.

But my grandmother, from whom I inherited my toughness and my witchery, kept a crow as a pet during the Depression. I don't remember how she acquired such a companion but likely one of her brothers found a fallen nestling and brought it to her. The crow was known for stealing hairpins out of ladies' coiffures, pilfering shiny trinkets, and depositing all of the loot between the keys of the family's player piano. At heart, I'd love to have a pet crow, but I'd feel bad about the family that lost her. I'll keep enjoying my happy interactions with these friendly, thoughtful birds and leave it at that.

All corvids are smart and charismatic, and Rick's love and admiration for them shines through every page. Whether you are here to learn about the ravens, the jackdaws, the blue jays, and the magpies or you are here to celebrate this group of clever and friendly birds, you have come to the right place.

—H. Byron Ballard

Introduction

AS THE CROW FLIES

I was on my daily, three-mile sunset walk around my former neighborhood one summer day when I saw three crows flying directly overhead. I was about five blocks from my home in Palm Coast, Florida, and curiously the crows were headed—ahem, as the crow flies—directly toward my place.

Even more curiously, as I gazed skyward, the trio suddenly but gracefully pirouetted in a circle some thirty feet right above me, then continued on their way in the direction of my home.

They recognized me, I thought, recalling scientific research that has proven crows indeed distinguish and remember individual human faces. They especially remember humans who have tried to do them harm, and those who have favored them—and crows will react to each accordingly.

My home backs up to woodlands, and the menagerie that has sauntered into my backyard over the past decade has included deer, otters, raccoons, black racer snakes, ibises, and even an alligator and a bobcat.

But I see crows daily. My *National Audubon Society Field Guide to Florida* and other sources tell me that Florida is home to the American crow and the fish crow, but no ravens.

Anytime I have heard crows cawing in the slash pines behind my home, at both my previous Palm Coast residence and my new place, I have grabbed the tortilla chips, bread, and crackers I keep just for them and have gone outside to scatter them on my lawn. The crows finally seem to know that they have trained me to come outside at their command.

At my former Palm Coast home, Lord Valiant the Bold would swoop down from his pine perch and alight on the grass, even as I scattered their feast. As the largest of my crow visitors, he was also the only one brave enough to retrieve any chips that I tossed close to my living room window.

Ms. Skitta was skittish; she would dart down, snap up a cracker, and quickly crow-hop to safety behind the nearby bluejack oak tree. Mr. Piggy would wait until I was back inside and then take his time, stacking up three, four, or five crackers before clamping down on his pile with his beak and flying away to who knows where—perhaps sharing his feast with his family or flock.

Part of that crew also included a crow I named Rockette because of the peculiar high kick in her right leg as she walked, like one of those Radio City Music Hall dancers. Her step, I surmised, was the result of some past injury. She was one of the few crows that didn't mind dining alone. Rounding out my clan of five was Shada (a derivation of *Shadow*). She was an infrequent visitor to my former home—so much so that I considered it an auspicious occasion when she would come by and the entire group would appear at once.

That summer day as the initial trio of crows performed their circle greeting above me, I intuited they were part of the flock of crows who felt at home near my place. Without my seeking to initiate it, at least not directly, a moment of Crow Magic had been visited upon me, a Pagan who finds divinity manifested in nature.

Anyone who chooses—or is chosen—to pursue Crow or Raven Magic will find favor. Likewise, birders, naturalists, and amateur wildlife biologists who come under the enchantment of corvids—the bird family that includes crows and ravens—will be richly rewarded.

Crows and ravens are almost everywhere—quite literally. The geography of ornithology, the scientific study of birds, tells us that crows and/or ravens inhabit every continent except Antarctica. Crows, by the way, are far less people-shy and more human gregarious (my term) than ravens. You may certainly spot crows on a foray into deep woods, but—somewhat ironically—you are more likely to see them in your backyard, while you stroll through a slightly woodsy, urban playground park as kids frolic on monkey bars, or when you visit a city burger joint, as one will swoop down onto the parking lot to snatch up a fumbled French fry.

Crows and ravens are omnivores and will eat just about anything, from smaller birds to human food. That these birds willfully snack on people food has played a role in bringing crow populations into the city, where opportunities abound to scavenge the littered food of wasteful humans. Like coyotes, corvids, especially crows, have adapted to urban living—although, of course, our black, winged friends are much more ubiquitous.

That's the thing about becoming a corvid-phile, whether you are a Pagan practicing Crow-Raven Magic or an amateur naturalist looking to get your bird-jones on, opportunities will present themselves to you often and seemingly everywhere. (One of the practices detailed in this book, a tarot method fused with augury or ornithomancy—divination by the numbers or actions of birds—will involve counting crows or their caws over a short period of time.)

Thus are corvids' intelligence and behaviors well documented, whether by scientific study or, given their ubiquity, by ample anecdotal evidence. Just check out the myriad YouTube videos where you can see corvids devising ingenious ways of getting to food or water, or crows heeding their dead via what are intriguingly but misleadingly called "crow funerals." Likewise, corvids' sense of play is well-known. Again, the YouTube thing: Corvids prank dogs, cats, and many other animals by tugging their tails. They intentionally swing on tree limbs and play tug-of-war with twigs. I am still gobsmacked when I recall the time I witnessed a crow hanging upside down on a tree branch in my backyard.

Given such uncanny, readily observable behaviors—I mean, crow funerals!—it's no wonder that millennia ago humans began to sense that corvids possess a preternatural, even supernatural nature. *These creatures, above and beyond other animals, have magical abilities! They must be favored by the gods and goddesses!*

That assessment played out in the myths and legends of many ancient cultures in ways at once enlightening, astonishing, playful, ... and spooky.

Corvids' omnivorous appetites included—gulp!—feasting on human corpses scattered upon ancient battlefields. That historically observed fact, which so many of us humans find disturbing, gave rise to numerous myths in various cultures about these birds' roles as harbingers of death and their special place as companions to gods and goddesses who hold dominion over death.

Indeed, the Morrigan, the ancient Irish battle goddess, will often shape-shift into the form of a crow or raven—a dire omen for any warrior who sees her in that guise before combat. The Morrigan's triple goddess aspect sometimes finds her manifesting as Badb (also rendered as Badbh or Badhbh), which in the Irish language means "crow," or Badb Catha, Irish for "battle crow." Badb's ominous nature is heightened by her appearance as a hooded crow, whose black head, set off by gray body plumage, eerily and unnervingly resembles the executioner's hood of ancient lore.

CUCHULAINN AND THE RAVEN—SO IT BEGINS

Before beginning this book, I had been practicing Crow-Raven Magic in various ways and to various degrees for many years as part of my Pagan path— incorporating Crow Spirit and Raven Spirit into my practice intuitively at first but gradually with more and more intent.

I trace the roots of my crow-raven alliance to my first visit to Ireland in 1995—a trip that, inexplicably, I did not see at the time as reconnecting to my Irish heritage. Nevertheless, at the General Post Office in Dublin, I found myself transfixed as I stared at *The Death of Cuchulainn*, a bronze sculpture by Oliver Sheppard of the great mythic Irish warrior whose exploits are immortalized in the millennium-old epic *Táin Bó Cuailnge* (The Cattle Raid of Cooley).

As recounted in the *Táin*, Cuchulainn (pronounced *koo-HUL-in*), fixated on an impending battle, had rebuffed the amorous advances of the Morrigan when she appeared to him in the disguise of a beautiful young woman, and he further spurned her offer to aid him in his coming clash. The angered goddess thus vowed to bring about Cuchulainn's doom. Wounded later in another battle, Cuchulainn strapped himself to a stone pillar so that he could die standing upright. Despite his apparent death, Cuchulainn's enemies feared the fierce warrior might still be alive three days later, and they dared to approach him only after witnessing a raven—the Morrigan in shape-shifted form—landing on his shoulder and noting that the great warrior's lifeless body didn't move.

It was not only Cuchulainn but the raven—I had no clue about the Morrigan then—that entranced me that day in Dublin. I began to study crow and raven lore over the ensuing years and became something of a crow-obsessed naturalist. Along with ample opportunities for "field research"—crows in my backyard, crows on roadsides, and crows across the cityscape everywhere I venture—there is a rich body of worldwide lore, mythology, and recorded history concerning crows and their cousins the ravens. Along with tales of the Morrigan, other myths of ancient Ireland and the nearby British Isles are populated by corvids. One of the more curious tales is *The Dream of Rhonabwy*, in which the Welsh prince Owain and his army of ravens, although allied with King Arthur, have a battle of nerves that leads to a bloody run-in with the fabled monarch and his men. Two ravens, Hugin and Munin, serve as the world-traversing eyes and ears of Odin, the Norse god associated with wisdom, war, and death—although some writers less generously refer to Odin's two ravens as spies who report back to their master. (Such a view is bolstered by the fact that the coat of arms of the modern-day Norwegian Intelligence Service features the two ravens.) The exploits of Raven—usually a trickster—and Crow feature in many Native American tales, especially those told by tribes of the Pacific Northwest. Those tales serve as wisdom teachings or as stories that explain how the world came to be the way it is.

A Journey into Crow-Raven Magic

This book's journey into Crow and Raven Magic will begin with the science of crows and ravens—an examination of findings by animal behaviorists and wildlife biologists who have documented the stunning intelligence and abilities of corvids. Some scientists have even studied the brains of crows using MRI procedures!

Chapters headed "Lore" will explore myths and legends, as well as historical writings, artifacts, folklore, and more, from the millennia-old paleolithic Lascaux Cave paintings and the mythologies of the ancient Norse, Celts, and Native American tribes to Poe's "The Raven" and modern-day Pagans' veneration of the Morrigan.

In chapters headed "Grimoire," we will delve into ways to bring Crow and Raven Magic into our lives and spiritual work, the better to help us enter non-ordinary realities, access sacred space-time, and explore the divine Mysteries. These methods include ritual, meditation, divination, mind-body-spirit exercises, scientific knowledge, and shamanic practices that religion scholar Mircea Eliade called "archaic techniques of ecstasy."[1]

Scattered throughout our journey will be "Lessons"—simple, or perhaps intricate, life lessons that can be learned from mere everyday observation of and engagement with these magical, mystical creatures who readily share this planet with us.

---

1 Eliade, *Shamanism.*

A NOTE TO NON-PAGANS, THE MYSTICALLY CURIOUS, AND PAGAN NEWBIES

This book was spawned because crows naturally, organically became part of my Pagan path. In turn, it is the practices of modern Paganism and the paths that fall under its umbrella, such as Wicca and Witchcraft, that spawned the grimoire chapters.

Grimoire is an Old French term for a book containing how-to knowledge about magical practices: crafting spells, making amulets and talismans, performing rituals to contact and commune with deities, methods of divination, etc. The chapter "A Path into Corvid Magic" will explore the how and why behind magical methods and the ways those curious corvids have forged a bridge between science and magic.

If you are not Pagan, if you are non-Pagan but embrace adventures into the mystical realms, or if you are new to Paganism, the grimoire workings in this book are exercises that, for the most part, make use of basic shamanic techniques that are doable by anyone. Such terms as *amulet, talisman, tarot, scrying*, and so on are briefly explained in the text, while numerous resources for further knowledge—even on the most esoteric of subjects—can be found in bookstores or on the internet.

A few of the grimoire workings—the Crow-Meets-Tarot spread, candle shadow scrying, and therianthropy—are more complex. By all means, don't hesitate to pursue them, but know that having some prior personal experience in those realms will be greatly beneficial.

FORGING CORVID COMMUNION

Whether you are a non-Pagan birder, a corvid-phile, or a seasoned Wiccan, Witch, or Pagan, the goal is the same: to forge a deeper communion with these fascinating creatures.

For you on a Pagan path, you will learn ways to alter your consciousness, to shake free of what the Buddhists call the chattering monkey mind and what philosopher Colin Wilson calls the "robot" mind, so that you can "altar" your consciousness—commune with God-Goddess-Spirit.[2]

---

2 Wilson, *Super Consciousness*, 86–87.

Follow the path of Crow and Raven Magic and you will create an empathic connection to these intelligent, winged beings as you take deeper notice of their daily rhythms, their deliberate behaviors, their sense of community, their sense of play, their astonishing vocabulary, and their uncanny, seemingly supernatural intelligence. Yes, their presence—beautiful and wild and mythic and mundane all at the same time, a part of the everydayness of our lives—will teach you factoids and lessons about the natural world, or at least a part of it. But also, even your most casual (yet dedicated and persistent) efforts will summon corvid encounters, synchronicities, and phenomena that will forge new connections between you and the sweet arcana of Gaia, the great Earth Mother Goddess. You will find yourself living that universal law that operates within any spiritual path, any journey into the mystical realms, any magical exploration: "When you change the way you look at things, the things you look at change."

For any corvid-curious Pagan, Wiccan, Witch, Heathen, shamanic practitioner, or follower of an earth-based spirituality, or for any amateur naturalist intrigued by these creatures, discovering the ways of crows and ravens, as well as the myths and magic-infused legends that have surrounded them through the ages, will leave you glamoured. Whether you seek to incorporate crows or ravens into your spiritual path or you are merely curious about what those three crows in your backyard are up to—and yes, they really are up to something!—corvids offer palpable ways to peek behind the veil that separates us humans from the natural world. They offer portals into directly experiencing the sacredness of nature and open us into deeper relationship with Gaia.

Chapter 1

CANNY CORVIDS

When Roman author Pliny the Elder completed his *Naturalis Historia* (Natural History) in 77 CE, he noted that "the Corvus for the most part layeth five Eggs, and the Vulgar [the masses] are of opinion that they conceive and lay Eggs at the Bill; and therefore if Women with Child eat a Raven's Egg, they shall be delivered of their Children at the Mouth: and generally they have difficult Labour if such an Egg be brought into the House."[3]

Before embarking on a path of Crow-Raven Magic, one should be well versed in the scientific basics of corvidology, for modern science indeed has learned much about these exceptional creatures, and some of that knowledge is so astonishing that one will come away believing that yes, these are supernaturally endowed beings—and one doesn't need the misinformation and misunderstandings propagated by Pliny and other ancient scholars, however well intentioned, to be so convinced.

Elsewhere in his *Naturalis Historia*, Pliny seems to throw in his lot with the "vulgar" and wander into gullibility when discussing the supposed astonishing longevity of crows and ravens. He even cites a report written almost eight centuries earlier by the Greek poet Hesiod (circa 700 BCE):

> The extent and duration of Man's Life are rendered uncertain, not only by the Situation of Places, but also from Examples, and the peculiar lot of his Nativity. Hesiod, the first Writer who has treated on this Subject, in his Fabulous Discourse (as I regard it)

---

3 Pliny the Elder, *Pliny's Natural History in Thirty-Seven Books*, book 10, 198.

embracing many things about the Age of Man, saith that a Crow lives nine times as long as we; the Stags four times as long as the Crow; and the Ravens thrice as long as they.[4]

Pliny (23–79 CE) is credited with creating the world's first encyclopedia—of a sort—and his massive text (720 pages in the English translation cited here) covers anthropology, human physiology, zoology, geography, meteorology, astronomy, botany, pharmacology, art, and more—including his skeptical accounts of magic and astrology.

While Pliny writes "to be alive is to be watchful," and the term *naturalist* certainly applies to him (he was also a writer and naval officer), he doesn't claim to have observed all he chronicles. Rather, he meticulously cites his sources, noting his compendium of knowledge was drawn from 2,000 works by more than 100 Greek and Roman writers—although modern scholars say many of Pliny's sources no longer exist.

However, to say that Pliny and his source scholars were reporting on astronomy, zoology, or any of the other disciplines cited means something vastly different from the way we conceive of those scientific fields today. Along with insightful descriptions of, say, the earth as a sphere or of the effects of opium, these chroniclers recorded fantastic entries besides those ravens who gave birth through their mouths and could cause humans to do the same. Consider the mountain-dwelling "men with Heads like Dogs ... above 120,000 in number" and the humans known as "Monoscelli, which have but one Leg but they are exceedingly Swift" and are "not far from the Trogloditae."[5]

While the *Naturalis Historia* is a substantive portrait of the state of purported knowledge during Pliny's time, by the 1490s scholars were questioning the accuracy of its more fanciful accounts—and perhaps we modern readers should be cognizant of our own hubris before thinking, *What took humankind so long to dismiss dog-headed men and raven-glamoured women who give birth through their mouths?*

While today we regard Pliny's *Naturalis Historia* with a sense of bemusement, the Roman's writings nevertheless give us a glimpse of how the ancients

---

4 Pliny, *Pliny's Natural History in Thirty-Seven Books*, book 7, 234.

5 Pliny, *Pliny's Natural History in Thirty-Seven Books*, book 7, 184.

beheld crows and ravens—a subject to be explored further in the chapter "Corvid Magic Takes Root."

It's easy for us twenty-first-century folks to feel superior to what we perceive as the gullibility of the ancients, but even we moderns may be startled to encounter a certain crow photo on the internet—a depiction that looks like it could be a scene from some sequel to the 1963 Alfred Hitchcock horror film *The Birds*.

The photo shows a hapless crow being fed into a hole in some sort of giant machine. The corvid's upper torso has already vanished into the maw of the device, while the bird's still-visible tail feathers and legs are fiendishly bound by a red strap.

What's going on here?

Sorry, Alfred. It's not corvid torture. It's quite the opposite—it's the state of corvid science today.

In 2016, the Audubon Society posted on their website an article by Kat McGowan titled "Meet the Bird Brainiacs: American Crow." It includes a photo by Andy Reynolds, with a caption noting that the crow, anesthetized and unharmed, is being ushered into a PET scan machine. John Marzluff, a University of Washington wildlife biologist, is about to take a deep peek into this bird's brain.[6]

Yes, corvid science has come a long way since Pliny the Elder's *Naturalis Historia*.

CROW BEHAVIOR

In the books *In the Company of Crows and Ravens* and *Gifts of the Crow: How Perception, Emotion, and Thought Allow Smart Birds to Behave Like Humans*, both by John Marzluff and Tony Angell, the authors are fond of drawing comparisons, however fleeting, between corvids and apes. "Mentally, crows and ravens are more like flying monkeys than they are like other birds," they write in *Company*.[7] In *Gifts of the Crow*, they affectionately note the birds have been described as "feathered apes."[8]

---

6 McGowan, "Meet the Bird Brainiacs."

7 Marzluff and Angell, *In the Company of Crows and Ravens*, 40.

8 Marzluff and Angell, *Gifts of the Crow*, 2.

Biologists and raven specialists Bernd Heinrich and Thomas Bugnyar conducted several food-related experiments on ravens and concluded the birds' abilities to solve problems goes beyond mere instinct and involves logic—a capacity that is nonexistent or very limited in most animals. Heinrich and Bugnyar noted some raven abilities approach or surpass those of the "great apes."[9]

Given the pop culture–fed knowledge that most people have of the intelligence of apes, whether through vintage episodes of the TV show *Mutual of Omaha's Wild Kingdom*, current programs on the National Geographic cable channel, or the research of Jane Goodall, perhaps nothing further need be remarked about the scientifically documented evidence of the smarts of corvids. They are as smart as apes—enough said.

But even a short cataloging of corvids' many specific intelligent behaviors is illuminating.

Crows Calculate

Crows understand cause and effect. They deliberate and calculate and know to approach potentially dangerous situations with far more caution than allowed by the mere instinct of other animals. Crows have been observed using and even making tools to collect insects. In one experiment, crows used a stick to poke a plastic snake in a box to see if it was dangerous.

Crows Learn

Crows learn from their experiences. They remember. They use deception to distract other birds and mammals—an otter, say—in order to steal their food.

Crows Give Gifts

Crows have been known to bring gifts to people who feed them—as with the renowned case of a Seattle girl named Gabi Mann, who received buttons, earrings, paper clips, glass baubles, and even the odd crab leg from crows after the times she brought them food.[10]

---

9 Heinrich and Bugnyar, "Just How Smart Are Ravens?"

10 Marzluff and Angell, *Gifts of the Crow*, 108–13.

Corvids Play

Crows and ravens engage in behaviors that not only everyday people but also biologists describe as play. That's evidenced in numerous YouTube videos taken by astonished humans—of a crow riding a car's windshield wiper or repeatedly sliding down a snow-covered roof. Ravens have been witnessed performing random aerial acrobatics and even "windsurfing" using pieces of tree bark.

Crows Hold "Funerals"

Numerous crows will gather around a dead crow in what even biologists call "crow funerals." While ornithologists note such a term is somewhat misleading—the birds likely are not paying homage to their deceased—scientists add that such gatherings are further evidence of crows' intelligence. Research suggests the birds may be assessing imminent dangers in the area and attempting to learn what predators may be nearby.

Crows Remember Faces

Perhaps most astonishing is that crows recognize and remember human faces. Put another way: crows seem to hold grudges.

Marzluff and Angell humorously and somewhat ruefully note that their many years of research activities at the University of Washington, which involved trapping crows for study before releasing them, caused the corvids at the campus to literally single them out. The two researchers were mystified that they would be scolded and dive-bombed by the birds while walking across campus, while other people nearby were left alone as they casually strolled about their business.[11]

In the Company of Crows and Ravens was published in 2005. A year later, Marzluff devised an experiment: He and two student assistant researchers donned a caveman rubber mask and then trapped and banded seven crows. During the following year, the researchers, as well as volunteers who were not involved in the banding process, would put on the caveman mask and merely walk around the university campus, displaying no threatening behavior whatsoever toward the crows.

---

11 Marzluff and Angell, *In the Company of Crows and Ravens*, 24.

But significant numbers of crows, far more than the seven that had been banded by the caveman or had witnessed that intrusion, would become agitated and emit harsh cawing to scold the caveman walking in their midst.

As a control, Marzluff also had research volunteers walk around campus in a mask of former Vice President Dick Chaney—a mask that had not been used in the banding process. Thus researchers could check whether the crows might be alerting to the smell of the latex rubber or to the surreal, not-quite-truly-human look of any mask. But the crows virtually ignored Chaney.

In a New York Times article published more than two years after the initial experiment, Marzluff reported that he had recently donned the caveman mask and walked across the university campus and was scolded by forty-seven of the fifty-three crows he encountered.[12]

Marzluff and company concluded that crows learn to recognize humans and, even more significantly, that such knowledge is shared with offspring and others in their flock. Crows share intelligence (my term) in the military sense of the word, whether it's intel about humans who have harmed or threatened crow kind or about humans who feed and otherwise benefit them. And crows will behave accordingly, whether scolding and diving at people who have proved themselves to be threatening or approaching and forming relationships with people who have favored them.[13]

To put it another way: humans—the Lascaux Cave artist, the ancient Greeks and Romans, the Celts, the Norse, Native Americans, modern-day biologists, backyard amateur naturalists, the Seattle girl—have been observing crows and ravens, and taking note of their uncanny intelligence and abilities, for millennia.

And all the while, crows and ravens have been observing us!

Crows remember human faces!

---

12 Nijhuis, "Friend or Foe?"

13 Marzluff and Angell, *Gifts of the Crow*, 2–3, 175–77.

Chapter 2

A Path into Corvid Magic

That scientifically documented fact that crows and ravens recognize us humans—never mind the other corvid findings of modern science and, yes, even neuroscience—is not only astonishing but enlightening. The Paleolithic cave painters of Lascaux, who created the world's first crow art almost 20,000 years ago; the ancient Celts with their battle goddess, the Morrigan; the ancient Norse with their raven god, Odin; and the Native Americans with their tales of Raven the trickster were not merely "making it up" or letting their imaginations run wild. They not only felt and intuited but also observed and experienced the uncanny ways of corvids. Indeed, it would be puzzling if these cultures and others around the world failed to incorporate crows and ravens into their myths, legends, and magical weltanschauung.

The widening body of corvid knowledge brings many positive implications for any Pagan, Witch, Wiccan, Heathen, shamanic practitioner, or follower of any earth-based spirituality.

Simply put, corvids offer spiritual seekers a unique opportunity.

As noted, corvid researchers are fond of comparing the birds' intelligence to that of apes. Far less common are references comparing corvids to dolphins, even though the scientific literature on dolphins and their intelligence is extensive. However, due to the obvious constraints of geography, forging close, natural relationships with dolphins or monkeys are possible only for a

privileged few. That's also true for many other wild animals that Witches or shamans traditionally feel called to choose as one's spirit ally: wolf, fox, bear, coyote, eagle, and on and on.

But crows or ravens are almost everywhere. As many corvid-philes have noted, crows and ravens not only tolerate human encroachment onto their turf. In Native American trickster tradition, Raven and Crow giddily turn human activities and human foibles to their advantage: You drop a Snickers, you feed a crow who has learned where careless, silly humans are likely to fumble their food. Drive a car down a boulevard and you may run over a walnut that an intrepid crow couldn't break open with her beak, and so she deposited it on a road expressly for the purpose of being cracked open by a human's auto, thus unleashing the delicious food morsels inside.

Such a trick has been documented by the 1998 BBC Earth series *The Life of Birds*, narrated by David Attenborough. While the tactic of dropping prey or food from heights onto a hard surface is common among many bird species, the BBC segment states that carrion crows (also known as Eurasian crows) in a Japanese city learned not only to drop nuts specifically in front of cars, but also to do so onto a crosswalk, the latter ploy making it safer to retrieve the nut-meat when traffic stops there.[14]

While the film footage in the BBC documentary is convincing, a 1997 study at the University of California, Davis disputed such a corvid capability. Titled "Crows Do Not Use Automobiles as Nutcrackers: Putting an Anecdote to the Test," the study's researchers concluded that the crows they observed were merely employing the common avian technique of dropping food onto hard surfaces, and any interaction with cars was coincidental.[15]

Perhaps there is a third interpretation. Given that biologists, amateur naturalists, and corvid aficionados alike have observed that crows and ravens possess a spirited and sophisticated sense of play, maybe the auto-nutcracker feat is a game for corvids as well as a dinner strategy.

Even a brief survey of the lives of crows and ravens may lead one to think, *It's the corvids' world—we just live in it.*

One might be tempted to compare Marzluff's high-tech neurological research on that hapless PET-scanned crow to accounts of extraterrestrials

14 Davis, "Bird Brains," *The Life of Birds*.
15 Cristol et al., "Crows Do Not Use Automobiles as Nutcrackers," 296–98.

abducting humans and conducting eldritch experiments on us. But consider the converse: corvid research has already established that crows and ravens know—indeed have *learned*—quite a bit about humankind and our ways.

Thus, for anyone practicing Crow-Raven Magic, the question may be: are crows and ravens the spirit allies of us humans, or is it that we humans are the spirit allies of the corvids?

Whichever direction that portal works (I would say it's both ways), the fact that corvids so readily share their world with us humans is propitious for pursuing Crow-Raven Magic.

A primer on modern Paganism and magic should be noted here. While it has no one-size-fits-all, definitive definition, Paganism revolves around three basic tenets:

- Divinity expresses and manifests itself through nature. Paganism, and those paths that fall under its umbrella, such as Wicca and Witchcraft, are thus called earth-based religions or practices.
- Paganism is polytheistic, and divine feminine entities/essences exist as well as divine masculine entities/essences—goddesses as well as gods.
- Magic happens.

It is this last tenet that forms the heart of the grimoire chapters in this work.

In fifth-grade science class we learned that our universe is in constant motion, constant flux. That's true not only of the Earth, stars, and planets, but also of that chair sitting in your living room. Physics tells us it's a swirl of energy, a mass of speeding electrons, protons, and neutrons, and that even its apparently solid structure is a deception, that this chair is composed mostly of space and energy.

Magic by my definition is the art and science of discovering, focusing upon, and attuning ourselves to the energy of the elements, the rhythms of nature, the behaviors of fauna and flora, the flux of the universe. The result is not so much that we change reality—rather, we change the ways we are able to *perceive* and *experience* reality (or *realities*, really) so that we have a truer understanding of the Mysteries of the universe that are masked by our mundane, workaday lives.

No matter if you are a corvid-curious birder or a seasoned Pagan or Witch, following the path of Crow-Raven Magic will take you into deeper communion with corvid kind, and you will discover a great secret hiding in plain sight: the mundane and the magical walk—and "caw" and fly—side by side.

Yes, that crow in your backyard and those three ravens in the maple tree at the park are watching you. Time to watch back.

Chapter 3

WATCHING THE WATCHERS

Given that crows recall the faces of humans who have harmed or favored them, perhaps it's ironic that humans have difficulty distinguishing crows and ravens. They do indeed differ.

Before venturing out on your first encounter—your first *conscious, magical* encounter—with corvids, knowing some scientifically certified basics will heighten your awareness and help you establish a baseline of corvid behaviors. Thus you can recognize those actions that are commonplace compared with those that are truly preternatural and that may be signs or omens, or happenstances indicative of deep synchronicities. This will be essential as you move deeper and deeper into Crow-Raven Magic.

CAWS AND CROAKS

Is that a crow or raven you see? The world—except Antarctica—is home to more than fifty species of crows and ravens, including the nine crow species and two raven species found in North America.

Crows and ravens belong to the family Corvidae, which also includes jays, magpies, and nutcrackers, and they belong to the genus *Corvus*, which also includes jackdaws and rooks. It is the family name Corvidae that gave rise to the term "corvids." The American crow, the most common crow in the Western Hemisphere, gets its scientific name, *Corvus brachyrhynchos*, from the Latin word *corvus*, which means either "raven" or, as corvid experts Marzluff and Angell translate it, "crow,"[16] while *brachyrhynchos* comes from the Greek words *brachys*,

---

16 Marzluff and Angell, *In the Company of Crows and Ravens*, 56.

meaning "short," and *rhynchos*, meaning "bill." Taxonomists have designated four subspecies of the American crow, including the Florida crow.

The common raven gets its scientific name, *Corvus corax*, from the Latin *corvus* and the Greek word *corax*, meaning "croaker."

Note that for scientific names, the genus name *Corvus* is used whether the bird in question is a crow, raven, rook, or jackdaw. So, for example, *Corvus splendens* will have the common name "house crow" and *Corvus cryptoleucus* is the "Chihuahuan raven."

That "croaker" part of the common raven's name points out one of the most evident distinguishing characteristics of these birds: typically, a raven croaks and a crow caws.

Anyone who has heard the familiar caw of a crow (and who hasn't?) or the croak of a raven might be surprised that both are scientifically classified as songbirds, of the order Passeriformes, which means they have feet that are adapted for perching.

A short but very informative primer on crow and ravens calls—with corvid sound bites!—is presented by biologist and crow specialist Kevin J. McGowan of the Cornell Lab of Ornithology. See his video "Caw vs. Croak: Inside the Calls of Crows and Ravens" on the Cornell Lab's excellent website, allaboutbirds.org. Crows, McGowan notes, emit not only the familiar "caw" but also "have a large repertoire of rattles and clicks and even clear bell-like notes." He refers to the common sound of the common raven as a "grunk kind of call" and mentions "little chuckling notes" and other raven vocalizations.[17]

As he and other wildlife biologists note, the vocal repertoire of crows and ravens includes far more than caws and croaks. It includes more than thirty distinct calls, in fact, and scientists readily confess they have not deciphered the precise meanings of many corvid communications.

The calls of individual crows and ravens are distinct enough that these corvids can recognize one another within their own pair, family, or even their "neighborhood," McGowan says. And yes, crows and ravens mate for life—

---

17 McGowan and Rodriguez, "Caw vs. Croak."

although biologists note some pair-bond transgressions occur. That fact led corvid researcher Kaeli Swift, who earned her doctorate from the School of Environmental and Forest Sciences at the University of Washington, to label crows as "monogamish."[18]

I routinely hear six to eight different vocalizations by the Florida subspecies of American crows that visit my backyard, and only half of those sounds would I characterize as caws or caw-like. Thus, the caw-croak divide is reliable as a corvid identifier only in a limited sense. Crows never voice a call that resembles the croak or "grunk" of a common raven, McGowan says. If you hear a croak-grunk, or what some term a "gronk" or "cr-r-ruck," it's a raven. Lack of a croak-grunk in a corvid call, however, does not necessarily indicate the presence of a crow.

I was utterly discombobulated the first time I heard a corvid voice a guttural, caterwauling call that sounded like a cat gargling and meowing at the same time. If my Audubon field guide hadn't schooled me that ravens currently do not inhabit Florida, I would have thought a cousin of Odin's Hugin had stopped by to visit me. However, it was a member of the American crow's Florida subspecies (*Corvus brachyrhynchos pascuus*, the latter word being Latin for "pasture" or "grazing"), emitting the catlike caterwaul—very distinct from the everyday caw.

OTHER DISTINCTIONS

Besides their respective caws and croaks, crows and ravens differ in other ways. Swift's website has a thorough guide in the section titled "The definitive guide for distinguishing American crows & common ravens."

Appearance

Ravens are noticeably larger. They can weigh two and a half pounds with wingspans exceeding four and a half feet, while crows typically weigh about a pound and have a wingspan of about three feet. Ravens' bills are larger—many biologists and birders use the term "Roman nose" to describe the size and shape. Ravens' tail feathers are shaped like the head of a shovel or a wedge when fanned, forming a curve at their edge, as opposed to the straight edge formed by a crow's tail when fanned.

---

18 Swift, "FAQs about Crows."

On a more subtle level, Roger Tory Peterson's *A Field Guide to the Birds* reports that ravens have a "goiter" look—that is, "shaggy throat feathers."[19]

Raven   *Crow*

Raven and Crow in Profile

Raven   *Crow*

Raven and Crow Body Comparison

---

19 Peterson, *A Field Guide to the Birds*, 206.

Long before I encountered that factoid, I was able to photograph a crow—not a raven—perched on a power line in my front yard. I captured the bird in perfect profile, and I was quite surprised by its shaggy throat. I rendered the image (viewable on my website, mistercrowart.com) in high-contrast black and white and titled it "Odin." If my authoritative Audubon field guide hadn't informed me otherwise, I would have believed I had witnessed a raven in my midst.

This recalls what McGowan and other corvid experts advise. Despite the documented differences between crows and ravens, identifying one in the wild may be difficult without having its opposite nearby for comparison—at least until you have gained some bird-watching experience via real life, the internet, books, or documentaries. Yes, the Audubon and Peterson wildlife guides are a must-have for any follower of an earth-based spirituality, and for any serious naturalist.

Interactions

Crows and ravens don't get along, as documented by a Cornell Lab study and other researchers, as well as anecdotal evidence reported by birders.[20] Ravens are known to raid crows' nests, looking for young or eggs to eat. Also, in the *Journal of Field Ornithology*, Lawrence Kilham presented a 1985 article titled "Sustained Robbing of American Crows by Common Ravens at a Feeding Station."[21] Yet reports indicate that the considerably smaller crows are much more often proactively the aggressors and will gang up to harass or mob a solitary raven, though usually no physical contact occurs.

Some Native American folk tales, such as How Raven Stole Crow's Potlatch, depict the rivalry between Raven and Crow with the former usually getting the better of the confrontation.[22]

Territory

Geography can play a role in which corvid you may encounter. The Audubon website says the common raven (also called the northern raven) vanished from

---

20 Leonard, "Crows Have a Mob Mentality Toward Ravens."

21 Kilham, "Sustained Robbing of American Crows by Common Ravens at a Feeding Station," 425–26.

22 "How Raven Stole Crow's Potlatch."

most of eastern and Midwestern North America before 1900 but is now return-ing to that territory. The habitat of the American crow, however, blankets much of North America.[23]

Worldwide, the Cornell Lab notes that the common raven is almost exclu-sively a Northern Hemisphere bird and is found throughout Europe (but sparse in the area of France) and Asia (except its southeast region).[24] Crows inhabit much of the world, with the exception of southern South America and Antarctica.[25]

GENDER IDENTIFICATION

Determining a corvid's gender is, frankly, difficult. Unlike, say, cardinals or red-winged blackbirds (which, like many other blackbirds, are not corvids, by the way), there are no easily discernible visible differences between the male and female American crow or common raven. The somewhat larger size of males is not always a reliable indicator, and spotting the birds during flight or perched dozens of yards away in the foliage of trees will also obscure their relative sizes. Biologists and naturalists say that male crows will display typical dominant male behaviors, such as acrobatic flying maneuvers meant to attract females during courtship, and males will procure food for females during breeding sea-son and after eggs are laid.

As I repeatedly watched the first crow flock I ever encountered, during almost daily visits to my backyard, it quickly became apparent which one was the alpha male; he was bigger and braver than the other crows who appeared with him in groups of three, four, or sometimes six or eight. As I watched from my back patio or living room window, he dared to come closer than the others to my home—an adventurous maneuver I encouraged by scattering food ever closer to my human abode. Yes, there were other males in this group, but he was by far the most dominant and most magnificent creature. I named him Lord Valiant the Bold. He became my Spirit Crow. It was Valiant who taught me shape-shifting—a technique I'll share in chapter 25.

When I moved to my new hermitage by the woods, and sadly had to leave Lord Valiant, Rockette, Ms. Skittah, and the other crows of my old neighbor-hood behind, I was promptly greeted by a new crow couple that I named Boga

---

23 Kaufman, "American Crow."

24 Boarman and Heinrich, "Common Raven."

25 Montgomery, "Crow"; BirdNote, "A Wide World of Crows."

and Baca. Boga's more daring behaviors quickly revealed that he was the male, although he was not nearly as alpha as Valiant.

Regardless, don't become hung up on gendering the crows you encounter. Intuit their essence in one way or the other, and feel confident if you decide to name one, some, or many of them.

SPEECH AND LANGUAGE

One of the fun aspects of crow encounters is crow talk! Crow speech is, in fact, communication. While that's true of a broad spectrum of animal vocalizations, crows, as already noted, have an ample vocabulary beyond their common caws and beyond that of other creatures. In more than a decade of close observation of the crows that visit my backyard, it has been very, very rare that they arrive and depart in silence. They are chatter mouths—loud chatter mouths.

As you encounter crows, note how they seem to be conversing with other crows nearby—that's because they are. Once you hear a crow call, listen for a reply. Sometimes the distance of their call-and-response is astonishing. A crow will shout a staccato burst of caws, and a not-too-faint reply will echo from several blocks away or far across a nearby field, park, or patch of woods.

This is where pen and paper will come in handy. Keep a record—just brief notes unless you are motivated to write down more detailed accounts—of the crow conversations you hear, at least during your early days of pursuing Crow-Raven Magic. I'll share more detail on the importance of this activity in chapter 6.

Devise your own onomatopoeia for the corvid talk you hear. "Caw" is almost universal in denoting the most common cry of a crow. However, as we have seen, opinion differs on whether a raven's most common call is best described as a "croak," "cr-r-ruck," "gronk," "grunk," or even "grob."

To get a further grounding in the variety of corvid language, you may want to read the chapter "Corvid Augury" before beginning your search. That chapter details divination systems devised around corvid speech by the ancient Irish and Tibetans—sounds they rendered into human language via detailed onomatopoeia. Then again, you may want to begin devising your own dictionary beforehand and make a game of it: begin building your corvid vocab list, then compare your onomatopoeia with the terminology of those ancient Irish and Tibetan scribes referenced in that chapter.

But remember: the goal is to create a vocabulary list of corvid sounds that is convenient and readily discernible by you, however you choose to denote those vocalizations.

My own crow dictionary includes, of course, "caw"—the all-purpose, readily recognizable, stereotypical crow word…except that it's not. Spend some time with crow kind and you will quickly learn there are different types of caws. The typical one is a muscular, robust, even jarring burst that is a bit raspy or even guttural. But crows also frequently voice a less harsh sound that I call a "soft caw" and a third type that I call a "yip caw." No, a yip caw doesn't sound like a dog yipping. Rather, it has the same lack of gravitas as a dog's lighthearted "yip" compared to a canine's outright, often aggressive bark.

As may be discernible in my terminology, the difference between these crow caws is the level of apparent urgency in each one. Apart from sunrise, the only time I hear the sturdiest "caw" is when the crows are in an obvious state of alert—when, for example, I hear the piercing "Kee! Kee!" of a threatening red-shouldered hawk nearby or when a dozen or more traveling crows are flying through, cawing excitedly as they dart among the slash pines in the nearby woods, heading to some high-priority encounter. Even more astonishing to witness is a crow scramble. "Scramble" is my term for when a group of crows, of whatever number, is perched in nearby trees or fluttering casually from branch to branch, and then they suddenly erupt in a raucous chorus of "caws" and take off like jet fighter planes and are quickly gone. I have never discerned a threat in the immediate vicinity during these crow scrambles. Indeed, it seems the birds are responding telepathically to stimuli from some distance away.

Again, this is based on my observations and experiences and may not be universally true—the only crow language I hear while the birds are in flight is cawing. While crows love to play, and do so in flight as well as while perched or flittering from branch to branch, the crows I see flying about often seem possessed by a sense of purpose or determination, as if they have business to attend. "Caw" seems to be the sole language of that realm.

Meanwhile, hearing that startling, catlike caterwaul instantly and forever banished the notion that these corvids' conversation is limited to plain ol' cawing.

The caterwaul is always articulated, at least in my experience, in one single vocalization and never in a burst of two or three or more caterwauls. Having never heard a crow caterwaul while flying has led me to several theories: crows may be physiologically unable to vocalize that sound in fight, the sound's meaning is not appropriate at that time, or perhaps they merely choose not to voice that call then.

I have heard the caterwaul only when crows are in my presence or when they have strong reason to suspect I am nearby—that is, I have heard that call only from the crows visiting my backyard and never when I have encountered them on a nature trail or in a park or urban retail area. Yes, I suspect they are communicating to me because they seek food.

I sometimes wish I had a cat or that a neighbor's cat had wandered into my backyard when Boga or another crow was caterwauling. I have halfway convinced myself that any nearby felines would tilt their head in curious wonderment at these slightly strange cat-calls coming from the treetops. I imagine Kitty thinking, *Why, that's a strange cat accent!*

Another strange bird call greeted me one sunny, warm early February day here in near-coastal Florida: the low murmuring of a barred owl coming from the woods behind my home. Usually I hear the local barred owls forlornly hooting from deep in the woods during my late-night walks. For Gaia to treat me to this rare occurrence during broad daylight was even more spellbinding.

I was sitting on my patio, and the bird sound—a sort of muted hooting that begged to be called a hoot-murmuring—was coming from a distance, somewhere deep in the stands of slash pines or in the fields of the flatwoods.

Only it wasn't. A short time later, I heard Baca and Boga casually cawing and occasionally caterwauling, and I grabbed some crackers and ventured into my backyard for one of their daily feedings. I heard the owl sound and looked up at the pine branch where the two crows were perched, and I discovered the truth of the matter: it was Baca who was hoot-murmuring like some faraway owl!

I witnessed Baca hoot-murmuring several times, her body gently heaving and her wings opening ever so slightly with each call, before I convinced myself that this enchanting sound indeed was coming from her and not some distant owl.

Yet another new bird call, coming from the wilderness behind my home, reached me one early spring day: a repeated two-syllable call that had the rhythm and melody of a classic cuckoo clock but in a squawky voice that reminded me of the Burgess Meredith portrayal of the Penguin in the 1960s *Batman* TV series.

For days, each and every time I heard this oddly charming, wacky cuckoo chirp, I searched high in the pines and the Chinese tallow tree—a favorite that became my Crow Spirit Tree—at the edge of my backyard, wondering what strange bird was calling out to me. Then one day, much to my surprise and awe, I saw the source: a crow fledgling!

Just as important as naming, describing, and documenting the types of calls is noting their number and rhythms when you hear them. The ubiquitous caw is vocalized in a near-infinite number of patterns. For example, your backyard crow shouts a four-caw burst: was it four caws that were equally apart rhythmically, or was it two caws in quick succession, followed by the briefest hesitation before a final two quick caws? Denote such patterns in your magical journal in whatever manner makes sense to you.

The most caws I have heard in a single burst was seven, each one equally spaced apart. More typical is three or four caws, which can—and are—unleashed in a variety of rhythms.

When you are watching the watchers, and especially when you are tracking their language, it is also important to note the time of day, the locale, weather conditions, and any peculiar circumstances, such as an approaching thunderstorm or the presence of other wildlife.

For example, I have discovered that crows are attuned to the sunrise much more than the rooster that lives about three miles away. A typical morning crow salutation is a hardy burst of two caws in quick succession, followed by the briefest pause and then a single muscular caw. I have heard this "sentence" so often from a crow in the first light of dawn that I am convinced it is keyed to the rising sun and the start of a new day. Perhaps it is literally a wake-up call or maybe a summoning to other crows that it is time to gather and forage for food; it might even be best described as a ritual. Or perhaps it's just a joyous shout of "Here comes the sun!"

The response to the "Caw-caw! Caw!" burst is often, but not always, an equally robust "Caw! Caw! Caw!" from a crow twenty to sixty yards away.

Diligently track the caws, caterwauls, and coo-coos, and note the circumstances surrounding those calls, and soon you will be comprehending the language of crow and raven kind.

HUMAN-CORVID INTERACTIONS

Peterson describes the American crow as "often gregarious,"[26] meaning among their own kind. Ravens tend to fly in pairs, crows in a multitude—although I frequently have witnessed crow couples, just the two of them, in my backyard over the years.

Ravens will soar or glide—that is, fly without flapping their wings—more than crows. Ravens will even playfully perform somersaults or barrel rolls in flight! An astonished friend of mine in the western United States once witnessed a raven somersaulting through the sky. Crows never perform such feats.

Researchers and ornithophiles report that crows thrive perfectly well in the company of humans, thank you, while ravens have adapted less well to our presence and are more people-shy. Note that crows and ravens that eat breakfast with humans on patios, leave sparkly baubles for kids, or ride around on people's shoulders are less common than YouTube would lead you to believe. While crows remain cautious around people, at least until they have assessed potential danger, they do not fly away at the mere sudden presence of a human. When I hear crows in my backyard and I go outside to feed them, the nearby crows in the slash pines will casually hop-fly up a few branches, just to put themselves at a safer distance from me. When I retreat to my patio, some will literally hop from branch to lower branch. Other, bolder crows will dare to alight on the grassy lawn to collect the treats I've tossed there.

But crows, more so than ravens, are comfortable in the presence of people, and a human typically—without coaxing or cultivating any sort of responsive behavior on the birds' part—can come within thirty or forty feet of crows in rural, suburban, or urban landscapes as they perch on trees, power lines, or lampposts or as they fly relatively low—a few stories high—overhead.

Except for those times in history where crows have been massacred by farming communities or cities that have perceived the birds' expanding populations as a danger to crops or a nuisance to people, human encroachment has aided their survival rather than threatened it. That's because the adaptable, malleable crows and their omnivorous appetites have learned where careless humans drop food.

Here are some tips for when you sally forth to encounter corvids or when they visit you in your own backyard.

---

26 Peterson, *A Field Guide to the Birds*, 206.

Use a Field Guide

Consult a field guide to determine whether crows or ravens, or both, are commonly found in your area. Also, research what species and subspecies may inhabit the landscape where you live.

For example, the hooded crow is quite striking due to its distinctive markings. Far from being the typical blackbird, hooded crows sport large areas of gray plumage artfully mixed with a black head, throat, wings, and tail. But you will see a hoodie, as they are sometimes called, only if you are in Europe or parts of the Middle East. One subspecies, the Mesopotamian crow, also known as the Iraq pied crow, is native to southern Iraq and southwest Iran, between the Tigris and Euphrates Rivers.

In Florida only the red-winged blackbird, boat-tail grackle, and common grackle come close to resembling a crow, so I rarely feel the need to carry my Audubon guide with me during my excursions—my memory serves me well. Also, while some field guides include the briefest of onomatopoetic descriptions of bird calls, I frankly don't find them helpful in identifying chattering birds hidden in trees or brush. That's especially true given the vast vocabulary of crows. Learn the basics from texts, then experience will be your best teacher.

Know Crows' Habitat, Roosting and Nesting Behaviors

The Cornell Lab of Ornithology notes that American crows "will live in any open place that offers a few trees to perch in and a reliable source of food," whether in natural areas or human-created spaces. However, crows shy away from vast forests.[27]

Crows are among the many birds that roost outside of the mating season. That is, they congregate in large numbers to sleep at night, in groups ranging from several hundred to the astonishing two million crows estimated to inhabit a roost in Fort Cobb, Oklahoma (as reported by Gerald Iams in 1972 in the State of Oklahoma Upland Game Inventory W-82-R-1).[28]

According to the Washington Department of Fish and Wildlife, crows—except during breeding season—may fly as far as forty miles each day from their nighttime roost site to their daytime feeding areas.[29] This likely explains why I

---

27 "American Crow," Cornell Lab of Ornithology.

28 McGowan, "Frequently Asked Questions about Crows."

29 Link, "Living with Wildlife."

rarely see crows after late afternoon or early evening, and why I have never seen nor heard a crow during or after twilight: my local crows are roosting far from my home.

Corvid researcher Kaeli Swift notes that crows will sleep in a nest only when incubating their young, will typically raise only one brood a year, and will abandon their nest once that task is complete, usually a period of eight weeks—although, she adds, crows may later build on top of an old nest.[30] So, be mindful that searching for a nesting crow may prove daunting.

Gather Supplies

All you need to interact with ravens and crows is your awareness, an observant eye, and alert ears. You may want to take a small notebook and pen for note taking or journaling—the better to document any encounters with, especially chatty corvids.

You don't need binoculars, but they can come in handy. Crows typically are not nervous or flittery like cardinals or Carolina wrens. When those latter birds stop by my backyard, they dart and dash about timidly, then quickly move on. Mourning doves will pause and rest, but they are easily spooked and will fly away at the slightest movement or noise they detect. Crows, on the other hand, will hang out a minute or two—or more—on sturdy tree branches, streetlights, or power lines. It's as if they are thinking, contemplating their next move or pondering some dilemma of existential philosophy. You likely will have a good opportunity to use binoculars to get an up-close view of a stationary crow.

If you take a camera, you will need one with a telephoto lens. A crow perched on a loblolly bay tree thirty feet away may seem close to the human eye, but you will capture only disappointing photos unless you can zoom in.

Attracting Corvids to Your Place

Food, glorious food! No surprise there—crows and ravens like to eat, just as we humans do. (The emphasis here, of course, is on crows because they have demonstrated they are far more human gregarious.)

Crows are veritable omnivores, and the Cornell Lab of Ornithology notes that their vast diet includes insects, grains, seeds, nuts, fruits, berries, mice, turtles, fish, and more, while adding that crows also are a "frequent nest predator"

---

30 Swift, *Corvid Research*.

and will devour the eggs and young of other birds. The Cornell Lab also states crows will eat "carrion and garbage."[31]

That word *garbage* is a documented observation, not a recommendation for feeding them.

Still, a 2001 study by Marzluff and other scientists revealed that half of the food intake of urban crows in Seattle was "human refuse." On the finnicky eater side of the spectrum, when crows in Manitoba, Canada, eat garter snakes, they deftly peck out only the serpents' livers.[32]

Crows love corn, numerous sources note. Yes, they will eat processed corn taken from a can, but their predilection is for the unprocessed, natural variety, which for centuries has raised the ire of farmers and long ago gave rise to the scarecrow.[33]

Kaeli Swift, corvid researcher, says crows love dried pet food; whole, unshelled peanuts and other nuts; eggs; meat scraps; and even tater tots.[34]

I feed my crow clan saltine crackers, tortilla chips, and pieces of bread—simple food for not-so-simple creatures.

Use your common sense and intuition to select corvid food. Just because a crow will wolf down a chunk of pepperoni pizza doesn't mean you should toss a slice into your backyard. Why feed crows sugary cereal or some other highly processed human food with a gaggle of artificial ingredients, when tortilla chips made from corn, vegetable oil, and salt will drive them giddy?

Crows will quickly learn whenever they have a new food benefactor and, in my experience, will return almost daily.

A WORD OF PRECAUTION

Given the ubiquity of bird feeding, it's one of the exceptions to that general rule that states "Don't feed the wildlife!" There are many sound reasons for such a protocol: Human food isn't gastronomically aligned with animals' digestive systems. Attracting wildlife out of their natural habitats and into human-infested places can wreak havoc on both animals and people—and be dangerous

---

31 "American Crow," Cornell Lab of Ornithology.

32 Marzluff and Angell, *In the Company of Crows and Ravens*, 223, 225.

33 Marzluff and Angell, *In the Company of Crows and Ravens*, 2, 140–43.

34 Swift, *Corvid Research*.

for both. Wild animals can be infected by rabies, a deadly viral infection that can easily be transmitted to humans by bite or scratch.

At the same time, crows and ravens are intelligent, very aware of their environment, adaptable, and cautious. It is very unlikely that you are going to inadvertently entice them into harm's way or bomb their digestive systems into oblivion.

In the end, always remember this one important fact: You are not trying to turn crows and ravens into your pets. You are seeking authentic, respectful communion with some of Gaia's most sentient creatures—beings that will be your messengers to the gods and goddess and reveal the Mysteries to you.

Chapter 4

LESSONS: GAIAN AGENCY

In the midst of writing this book, I received word from my landlords that they want their house back. After eleven years—the longest I have ever lived in one place in my life—I had to move.

"Do you think your crows will follow you?" one friend asked me.

"I don't think so," I told her. "From what I know about crows' territorial habits, I believe they stay close to wherever they roost or nest at night."

I was charmed by her notion that "my crows" might take a notion to magically hit the road and come with me. She was not alone in her concern. Many friends and family members expressed a similar empathy. Truth be told, I was also a bit distressed. I did not harbor any expectation that Lord Valiant and his clan would follow me, but I wondered, *What if there are no crows at my new place?*

During my exhaustive search for a new place, my main criteria was an environment that was as kissed by the great Mother Goddess—Gaia—as the home I was leaving.

After an exhaustive three-month search and with my moving deadline fast approaching, I became frustrated and was about to settle for a less-than-desirable abode. Then, a mere three miles away, I came across an available place that was a doppelgänger of my about-to-be-former home; tucked at the end of a cul-de-sac in a rural neighborhood, it had no canal or waterway nearby, but it backed up to wilderness with flatwoods beyond that.

I had a new place—one nestled next to Gaia's breast.

THE COMING OF THE CROWS

On a warm, breezy, mid-November day, I made the first of many trips in a rented moving truck packed with my late wife, Cheryl's, African doll collection, my 100-plus masks, my 70 boxes of books, my sitar, my Pagan altar, and other things. The windows were rolled down. Sun shining. A balmy day. Half a block from my new home, I heard a familiar sound: "Caw! Caw! Caw!"

I parked the truck and leaped out to search for the crows. I spied them—a crow couple—in one of the slash pines right at the border of my backyard and the woods beyond. They weren't Lord Valiant or Ms. Skitta or any of the other crows from my clan three miles north of my new place. But I was ecstatic.

Crow kind have a home in my new place!

I saw this crow couple during each and every moving-truck run I made to the place I dubbed my "hermitage by the woods."

Two days before I left my old home for the last time, I walked through the backyard near the canal. I spied two sizable branches that had fallen—recently, I surmised—onto my lawn from one of the slash pines favored by my crow clan. I smiled.

A Parting Gift from My Crows

I dutifully and gleefully picked up the two branches and loaded them into the truck. I was uncertain how I would make use of them, but I knew those pieces of wood favored by crows—my crows!—would one day manifest into Crow Magic.

On the morning of my first full day at my hermitage by the woods, I scattered cheap dollar-store crackers onto my backyard. A short time later I heard a "Caw! Caw!" I ventured onto my back patio, and I was able to see the crow couple high in a Chinese tallow tree—the one that would soon reveal itself to be my Crow Spirit Tree. After about ten minutes of casual cawing, the larger of the crows—the male—glided down to the earth and landed about ten feet from the light orange crackers I had spread for their feast. Much like Ms. Skitta—and much like a human approaching a lit firework that has failed to go off—this crow stepped toward the nearest cracker cautiously: his upper torso was literally, comically leaning away from this mysterious object that had suddenly appeared in his midst, while his crow feet were extended out from his body and toward the cracker as he tiptoed ever closer to it.

Finally he grabbed the cracker in his beak and flapped a hasty retreat to the upper branches of the pond cypress at the southeast corner of my backyard.

"This is the beginning of a beautiful friendship," I whispered to myself, quoting the last line spoken by Humphrey Bogart's character in *Casablanca*. I spontaneously dubbed my new crow companion Bogey, then shifted it to Boga. Rather than name Boga's mate after Ingrid Bergman, Bogart's costar in *Casablanca*, I instead named her Baca, after Bogart's frequent costar Lauren Bacall.

Boga and Baca returned to my backyard the next day, and the next, and the next. Just as I did with my old crow clan, each and every time I heard them caw in my backyard, I grabbed crackers and chips and spread a handful on my lawn. I wanted my new crow group to know that they could "train" me to come at their command, with a feast for them in my hands.

THE WAY OF CROW-RAVEN MAGIC

Aleister Crowley, the notorious twentieth-century British occultist, famously defined magic, or "magick," as he spelled it, as "the science and art of causing change to occur in conformity with will."[35] But that is not the way or the purpose of Crow-Raven Magic, mostly.

I will detail some techniques, such as shape-shifting, shadow scrying, and tarot readings, that will utilize your relationship with your neighborhood crows. As with any technique, whether physical, psychological, or metaphysical, these methods will become more effective as one practices and hones them with insights gained through repeated experiences.

But, with apologies to Uncle Al, the way of Crow-Raven Magic is not to master science. The "art" part of Crowley's equation might apply here, but any change involved will be the change within oneself, which any wise magus will realize was the sort of change that Crowley was referring to all along.

The way of Crow-Raven Magic is to seek and nurture communion with Gaia. The mysteries of the great Earth Goddess will unfold and be revealed— and your inner self, what the Irish poet William Butler Yeats called "the deep heart's core," will change, and your relationship to Gaia will change and will deepen. These magical, gifted birds are a portal to make that happen.[36]

---

35 Crowley, *Magick in Theory and Practice*, xii.

36 Yeats, "The Lake Isle of Innisfree," 39.

The lesson from Crow Spirit, imparted to me by my crows Boga and Baca, is that Gaia has agency. Even the most rational-pragmatic-brained, business-suited Wall Street banker hunkered down inside his office within some concrete megalopolis jungle knows that. The sun rises. The sun sets. Spring returns and Gaia's greenery is reborn, whether it's a field of wild sunflowers in the Smoky Mountains or a brave weed peeking out of a sidewalk crack in the heart of Manhattan.

Yet even followers of earth-centered spiritualities may become complacent and take Gaia's presence, vibrancy, and agency for granted. Poets and sages through the ages have tried to remind us of this, to shake us out of our mechanical, robotic, materialist existence. "There are more things in heaven and earth, Horatio, than are dreamt of in your philosophy," Shakespeare's Hamlet famously says.[37]

Spend time with crows and ravens and you will be reminded of Hamlet's dictum. The ancient Romans believed corvids were messengers of the gods and goddesses—and they are. Boga and Baca's greeting tells me I have been identified as a friend of crow kind, and they have delivered a message from Gaia: "My magic is afoot, wherever you may wander. It's as close as your backyard. Pay attention!"

37 Shakespeare, *Hamlet*, 22.

Chapter 5

GRIMOIRE: FIND YOUR SPIRIT CORVID

An initiation, whether performed with a Wiccan coven, with a Druidic group, with a Cub Scout troupe, with any organization, or as a solitary magical practitioner, is a demarcation—a purposeful, ceremonial marking of a beginning, of a "before" and an "after." While Gaia's energies, entities, and magic enfold us all—Pagan and non-Pagan alike—each and every day, this chapter's self-initiation of finding your spirit corvid will be a stark recognition of Gaia's presence and a stark, bold recognition of her emissaries, Crow and Raven.

As such, and assuming you are not already communing consciously and magically with corvids, your self-initiation will be your first official act of Crow-Raven Magic. Your initiation will mark the first time you use your intention to forge communion with Crow-Raven kind. You will be engaging crows or ravens not only with intention but also awareness and focus.

Initiate yourself into a relationship with your Spirit Crow or your Spirit Raven, and your relationship will all corvids will begin to change. Your relationship to nature, to Mother Earth, to Gaia will begin to change. As the Yaqui shaman don Juan Matus has it, you will begin to "see."

Carlos Castaneda, a writer, spiritual seeker, mystic, and chronicler of don Juan, wrote about one of his encounters with the shaman:

> Don Juan's particular interest in his second cycle of apprenticeship was to teach me to "see." Apparently in his system of knowledge there was the possibility of making a semantic difference between "seeing" and "looking" as two distinct manners of perceiving.

"Looking" referred to the ordinary way in which we are accustomed to perceive the world, while "seeing" entailed a very complex process by virtue of which a man of knowledge allegedly perceives the "essence" of the things of the world.[38]

The awareness and focus you bring to your initiation will change your future perception—your future awareness—and lay the foundation for further communion with Crow-Raven kind, with Gaia. You will never look at crows or ravens again in the same way because, above all, the greatest change will have begun to take place within your Self.

One important note about this work and all the rituals and techniques found in this book: they are rarely meant to be exact recipes. Doing any sort of metaphysical operation word for word or step-by-step is to some degree self-defeating, in both a practical and magical sense. For one, energy put toward memorizing a chant or ritual in great detail is energy that could be better applied in another manner. Consider a rock guitarist playing a song's solo in performance after performance. The more they try to replicate it note for note, the more the solo becomes robotic, even soulless. Even re-conjuring a solo precisely for just the second time introduces a mindset that is mechanical and more concerned about execution—hitting the "right" note—rather than conveying the intrinsic soul of the melodic phrase that is being communicated. It's the same with your magic.

As an example, my invocation, found in the following working, is composed of my words. They may or may not resonate with you. Your words may not resonate with someone else, nor need they do so. They need only resonate with your own heart, your own spirit.

Most importantly, words or actions that resonate with your own heart, your own spirit, will resonate more deeply with Spirit, Gaia, the goddess and gods ... and Crow and Raven kind. Remember that what you seek via communion with Crow and Raven—a parting of the veil to reveal glimpses of the Great Mysteries—has existed within Gaia's bosom since time out of mind. That impulse to seek the Mysteries has resided in the hearts of humans since the time of your ancestors' ancestors' ancestors—all the way back to the ancient

---

38 Castaneda, *A Separate Reality*, 8.

cave-painting artists of Lascaux and beyond. When you part that veil, you must ensure that it is your own heart that is being laid bare to Divinity.

WHAT YOU WILL NEED

- Awareness
- A quieting of your monkey mind
- A place, either rural, suburban, or urban, where you have witnessed corvids

BACKGROUND

Do your homework and acquire a basic understanding of corvid behaviors and their vocabulary. Study the preceding science chapters, and if you are ambitious, refer to some of the works cited in this book's bibliography, especially writings by John Marzluff. You will thus learn to discern between mundane crow behaviors and extraordinary, perhaps prophetic ones. For example, daily I hear my crows voice their "kitty-cat" call; it's a common cry that I intuit as an announcement of one's presence. However, during my twenty-plus years communing with crows, only once have I witnessed one hanging upside down from a tree branch, and only once have I witnessed a group of fifteen or so crows vehemently scolding a crow lying on its back.

PREPARATION

None. Forego any impulse to engage in meditation or breathwork. The efficacy and power of your initiation will come from spontaneity, serendipity, and synchronicity.

ACTIONS

First offer an invocation out loud and outdoors in a natural setting where you have witnessed corvids or where you intuit they might visit or congregate. This can be basically any spot with a few trees. Say:

> *Crow Spirit, Raven Spirit,*
> *Messengers between worlds,*
> *Gaia's creatures,*

whisperers to the goddess and gods,
flyers between worlds
caw, gronk, chatter
your sweet Arcana to me
who seeks your wisdom,
your knowledge,
your spirit
in this time, this place,
you whose ancestors
whispered to my ancestors
at Lascaux and beyond
in time almost out of mind.
Whisper your sweet Arcana
to me now
Crow Spirit, Raven Spirit.

Remember, use this invocation as a template only and borrow liberally from it. But it is important that you craft your own invocation, from your own heart.

Now, let's find a crow or raven.

Perhaps these birds already are frequent visitors to your backyard, your neighborhood, your village, your city. I always smile inwardly when a friend who lives in my corner of the universe—coastal East-Central Florida—tells me, "Well, there aren't any crows where I live." Maybe crows are not landing on their windowsills, but such friends are simply out of attunement with Gaia. Corvids populate every continent except Antarctica, and crows, much more than ravens, are ubiquitous throughout North America. They are there, in your neighborhood or at your local shopping center, cleverly continuing to adapt to human presence and human behaviors.

"But I live in the heart of the Big City," you say with a sigh. No matter. Consider an October 2016 article by David W. Dunlap in the *New York Times*. The story's headline says it all: "Crows and Ravens Make New York Comebacks to Caw (and Cr-r-ruck) About." The article notes that the species known as the common raven has always been uncommon, but not unheard of, in the Big

Apple. The city's American crow population was quite robust and on the rise throughout the 1990s, then was devastated in the early 2000s by the West Nile virus, but it has been making a return to pre-outbreak numbers ever since. And New Yorkers are now spotting ravens, too.[39]

If you already have established a relationship with crows or ravens—you see them often in your backyard or from your apartment balcony, you feed them crackers or bread, and/or perhaps you've even named some of your more frequent visitors—then simply rededicate and reinvigorate your Crow-Raven communion by chanting an invocation similar to the one just shared.

If you are just beginning your journey into discovering Crow-Raven Spirit, then, after chanting your invocation, go find a corvid. You may want to merely sit in your backyard, take a walk in your neighborhood or through an urban landscape, or venture to a city park or a nature trail beyond your concrete jungle. Don't be discouraged if a crow or raven does not readily appear. They are there. If your corvid-seeking adventure turns up corvid-less, or seemingly so, then merely restate your intention out loud, saying something to the effect of: "Crow Spirit, Raven Spirit—I seek communion with you and await your messengers." Then go about your day. Keep your heart, and your senses, open. Having set your intention, soon—maybe an hour later, the next day, or the day after that—a crow or raven, or perhaps many, will appear.

The first corvid that engages you, the first crow that you "see" in the don Juan sense—a corvid that engages your consciousness, that pings something inside you and makes your soul go "Wow!" or perhaps gives you a palpable sign via some unusual behavior—is your initiator, your Spirit Crow or Spirit Raven.

That corvid may not and need not be the very first one you encounter on your quest, especially if, say, you come across one during a drive by at seventy miles per hour down the highway. Then again, that roadside corvid very well could be your Spirit Crow or Spirit Raven—perhaps you are passing by or through what for you is sacred land or a "place of power" as described by don Juan in the writings of Castaneda.

Any crow or raven sighting commands my attention if I am driving along the desert highways or mountain roads of northern New Mexico, which is the land of my youth and which holds many places of power for me.

---

39 Dunlap, "Crows and Ravens Make New York Comebacks to Caw (and Cr-r-ruck) About."

Request Your Spirit Crow or Raven's Name

When your Spirit Crow or Spirit Raven has initiated you, has announced its presence undeniably, whether in a provocative or intuitive manner, then silently request its name. That name may arrive immediately or days later after intermittent reflection, meditation, or just plain mundane activities far from thoughts of Crow or Raven kind. Sometimes magic of any sort, as well as the muse, inspiration, or intuition, works that way: slowly, roiling around in one's subconscious until it bursts forth with some insight—and Spirit, magic, or the muse is no less spontaneous, serendipitous, or efficacious for having worked that way.

This corvid will be your Spirit Crow or Spirit Raven because it will be the first corvid that has communicated to you, whether brashly or subtly, since you embarked on your newfound journey. This bird has parted the veil that separates you from the Great Mysteries. This bird is a messenger from Gaia, an emissary of the goddess and gods.

This bird has initiated you into the path of Crow-Raven Magic.

Magic is afoot!

Speak aloud a simple acknowledgment of gratitude: "Thank you, Crow-Raven Spirit. Thank you, Gaia. Blessed be."

GOING FORWARD

By acknowledging this messenger, you have not only undergone an initiation—you have also performed a magical act. You have placed yourself in direct lineage of the Lascaux Cave artist and your ancestors beyond that time. Remember that, in the midsts of ancient, prehistoric times that are now indecipherable to us modern humans, one of our ancestors was the very first human to notice and acknowledge the preternatural abilities and behaviors of corvids. One of our ancestors was the very first human to not only intuit but to *witness* the otherworldly ways of crows and ravens. The Lascaux Cave artist, as far as modern archaeology has been able to reveal, was merely the first human so gobsmacked that they felt compelled to commemorate and immortalize such an encounter.

Now you have, too.

In my years of practicing Crow Magic, family and friends have noticed (with an assist from my Mister Crow art) my predilection for crows, all without my ever "proselytizing" them or subjecting them to a deep dive into my Pagan path. Inevitably, fam and friends have told me that, as they now go about their daily lives, they notice crows more often, and they share with me their stories of their encounters. All this from mere casual conversations, which I have come to view as unintentional, sort of verbal-contagious acts of magic.

Imagine the efficacy of putting your focus and magical intention into your initiation. You may never see or encounter your particular Spirit Crow or Spirit Raven in flesh-feather-blood-bone form again. But you will carry that encounter with you, and you will encounter Crow-Raven Spirit once more, over and over.

Chapter 6

GRIMOIRE: KEEP A MAGICAL JOURNAL

Grimoire is a term for a spell book or a collection of magical writings. Typically such writings are instructional and include passages on how to perform spells; create magical objects, such as talismans and amulets; work various methods of divination; and so forth.

A magical journal expands that concept. Along with any informative guidelines for performing spells, rituals, and workings, your journal may include general or detailed accounts of when, where, and exactly how you worked a spell, ritual, or tarot reading—while allowing space to record the results as they may (or may not) manifest in the following days, weeks, and even months.

And, of course, you will document your observations of corvids. This is essential. Corvids are complex, intelligent creatures, and their behaviors are vast, varied, and nuanced. Recording their activities will allow you to better see synchronicities and patterns with possible magical implications.

Also, consider adopting the traditional role of a journal, and record your own thoughts, reflections, emotions, and activities, whether directly related to Crow-Raven Magic or not. Revisiting past entries may reveal previously unnoticed synchronicities or correlations between your psychological states or physical circumstances and the efficacy of your magical activities.

WHAT YOU WILL NEED

- A paper notebook or bound journal. Choose one that is aesthetically pleasing to you and aligns with your magical sensibilities—or create your own cover illustration.
- Pens of various colors.

Background

Six weeks after my wife, Cheryl, died from breast cancer, I was in the music room in the back of our home when I heard a loud, sharp, cracking sound come from the kitchen. The noise sounded like a champagne glass shattering on the hard tile floor.

I was startled and instinctively called out Cheryl's name as I rushed to the kitchen—a holdover from her last months in this world when the spread of the disease had made her susceptible to blackouts and falls, leading me to call out to check on her anytime I heard a noise in our home. At the sound of breaking glass, my Rat-Prag Brain (Rational-Pragmatic Brain) assumed the air conditioning or something had vibrated a wineglass off its shelf and sent it crashing to the floor. But, in that same nanosecond, my Misty-Intu Brain (Mystical-Intuitive Brain) wondered if Cheryl's spirit was sending me a sign.

I arrived in the kitchen and—nothing. I could find no shattered glass, no sign of any disturbance, accidental or otherwise.

On a late night two months later, I slipped into a trance and a vision of Cheryl appeared; with her beautiful Isis smile and her cinnamon Nubian skin, Cheryl had metamorphosed into the comforting, shimmering form of the goddess.

That night I decided to write about my vision, as well as the shattered glass incident from three months earlier. That initial writing became the basis for my book *I Buried My Wife and Danced on Top of Her: A Pagan, Punkish, Sort-Of Spooky Grief Memoir.*

Reading the earliest pages of that memoir now, I am stunned. It's as if its narrative—my life story!—had been written by a novelist and I am reading a strange, unknown tale for the first time. I remember the broken glass, the Cheryl-Goddess vision, the shadowy shapes I began to see around our home out of the proverbial corner of my eye, and other eerie occurrences, but so many of the details of those happenings and others, as well as entire episodes, had lapsed from my memory.

In case my personal story is too subtle, the lesson is this: write it down!

Keeping a magical journal or diary—call it a Book of Shadows if you like—is so de rigueur for anyone seriously pursuing a Pagan path that this chapter should not be required in this book.

Writing is both my livelihood and my passion, so it's easy for me to trumpet the benefits of casting words onto paper or laptop. But for anyone who is not convinced of the magical efficacy of writing, consider these points:

Memory Is Faulty

You will not remember. Sure, you recall the time you turned that corner on that secluded woodland path and Pan jumped out and scared you shitless—and you lived to tell the tale. Yes, the next day, the next week, and the next month you still vividly recalled your encounter. This was, after all, one of the most profound moments you have experienced on your magical path. But how detailed and intimate are your memories now? Do you remember what Pan was wearing? Was a grin or a scowl on his face? What did he say? Did he have a Sasquatch-like stench?

In the early 1980s, long before I set upon my Pagan path, I saw the movie *Altered States*, which was based upon research by scientist John Lilly into the effects of sensory deprivation, via isolation tanks, on human consciousness. (Lily also is the scientist known for his research and efforts to communicate with dolphins.) An isolation tank typically is a cube-like structure that is filled with salt water and allows a person to be enclosed within and float in a pitch-black, soundproof environment. I had no access to any sort of isolation tank, but I was determined to conduct my own Lilly-esque experiment—sans the psychedelic drugs that he employed in his research.

And so I cleared out a small closet in my home, sealed off the cracks in the door with towels to block any and all light leakage, and prayed that any external noise, from my refrigerator's compressor kicking in to a garbage truck passing by my house, would be blessedly absent. I had my "isolation tank."

I breathed as quietly as possible and, unlike in a true sensory-deprivation tank, I was not floating in salt water and so I was cognizant of the weight of my body—or rather, I was unable to experience the absence of that weight.

Still, as expected, time melted. I have no idea how long I was so isolated and sensory-deprived when my first trance-vision arrived: Jim Morrison—the charismatic, Dionysian singer-poet of the rock band the Doors—appeared in a shadowy haze, his face and upper body illuminated by the faint, orangey glow of some sort of flame, perhaps a candle but I don't recall specifically.

I have nothing beyond that. My memory has faltered, and I didn't have the foresight at that time to chronicle my sensory-deprivation experiment in writing. Sure, that's no great loss for the history of research into altered states of consciousness, but years later I became so disappointed that I didn't write about my experience. Mr. Mojo Risin', feel free to visit me again anytime and remind me of what happened when I met you during that long-ago journey into an altered state.

Also, as a lifelong newspaper journalist, I have interviewed thousands of people and have been privy to the idiosyncrasies and shortfalls of human memory. Yes, your memories will corrode.

You Must Accurately Document Your Field Research

A second prime reason to keep a magical diary is that, like any good naturalist, you will want/need to document your field research, whether it's observing the behaviors of crows and ravens in your backyard or in your dreams, trance-visions, rituals, and tarot readings. For one thing, you will be aiding your sporadic memory and preserving your corvid adventures, in all their drama, for their own sake. Also, you will be creating a detailed chronicle that will enable you to discern patterns, anomalies, and synchronicities in the behaviors of these magical, intelligent birds that walk and fly between worlds.

For example, let's say you are scrying and you trance to a vision of a crow voicing a peculiar pattern of caws above a pack of wolves. Two days later in your backyard, a crow begins to speak in what seems to be a familiar burst of caws. Was it the same call pattern as the one in your vision?

Or maybe you do a Crow-Meets-Tarot reading (a guide follows in this book) and a number of cards from the suit of swords appear, and you recall that dream from three weeks ago in which a sword-wielding dragon showed up at your business meeting—but the vivid details of that dream have dissipated like a hinkypunk slinking away in the night. And so you are left floundering over what synchronicities may be afoot.

Keeping a well-maintained magical journal will eliminate guesswork in such instances.

Always keep a record of each and every tarot reading you do. The same applies to your magical path, whether your practice involves Crow-Raven

Magic, Druidry, Kitchen Witchery, spellcasting, candle magic, moon magic, attending workshops at festivals, dowsing, dream work, or celebrating the magic of Beltane and Samhain.

Writing Is a Magical Act

As a writer, I believe in the magical efficacy of words. No surprise there.

I tell stories of humans' experiences (my journalist side); I write for self-expression, pleasure, and the sheer joy of playing with words (personal essays, philosophical essays, and poetry); and I cast words onto paper to explore my own psyche (writing is my most common form of meditation).

And, as a Pagan who *mostly* eschews Wiccan cast-the-circle rituals and traditional Witchcraft spellcasting (not that there's anything wrong with that), I write to forge my non-ordinary realities into something tangible. Such chronicles will serve not only as a magical diary and a history of my own soul but as narratives with a utilitarian aspect apart from "field research." My accounts of breaking open my head, heart, and soul will become inspiration and guide me further and deeper into even more non-ordinary realties. Thus will my chronicles take me ever closer to the divine mystery, to deeper communion with the goddess and god, with Gaia and Cernunnos, and with Crow Spirit which, for me, is another manifestation of Gaia.

Sure, we each have our memories of our profound encounters with the other realms, but writing down your adventures will be transformative. Your life may not parallel Frodo in *The Lord of the Rings* or Morgaine in *The Mists of Avalon*. But writing down your soul's story, or writing any account, tends to uncover and conjure details lurking in one's subconscious and reveal previously hidden connections, synchronicities, and cause and effect. You may be surprised how much your story transcends the mundane.

However, Magical Writing Comes with a Cost

Writing is a vastly overlooked and underutilized magical tool. But it does come with a price.

Some observers will note, with just concern, that writing can be antithetical to the "experiencer" nature of shamanism, Paganism, or any nature-based spiritual path. Writing—or rather the process of writing, in which one begins to contemplate putting down in words what one is currently experiencing—takes us out of the moment. As a writer, I am incessantly in "writer mode," formulating my thoughts—"hammering my thoughts,"[40] as the Irish poet William Butler Yeats would say—for an essay or poem, even as I am standing in line at a grocery store, taking a neighborhood walk, or participating in a ritual at the Phoenix Phyre Pagan Festival in Florida.

I was quite cognizant of this during my two visits to the sacred sites of Ireland. Naturally I planned to chronicle my adventures in a journal and also to write a series of travel stories for my newspaper upon my return. But I also knew the writing process could suck me into an alternate universe, into a mere simulacrum of my current experience of space-time. That is, I was wary of being like the tourist who is more concerned about getting the perfect selfie photo with the Giza pyramid rather than being in the moment at such an epic, sacred place.

Still, writing is transformative. Writing is a magical act. Write it down!

ACTIONS

The most efficacious method of magical writing is good ol' pen and paper. Even if you prefer the speed and efficiency of a laptop keyboard, print out your writings (always date every entry!) and assemble them in a notebook or staple them to the pages of your bound journal. Then, when you reflect on your entries days or weeks later, you can annotate them in the margins, perhaps observing patterns, reflecting on how synchronicities played out over time, or noting how a particular encounter proved to be prophetic. Plus, a paper journal allows you to draw maps or doodle images, which can serve a Book of Shadows in ways that written text cannot. Also, a journal or notebook is more portable, allowing you to document your observations and insights in the field.

You may choose to create a color-coded system so that entries marked with a red asterisk denote the proverbial "red-letter days" of whatever sort of significance, a purple asterisk indicates details of crow sightings, etc.

You don't have to be Shakespeare, and you don't have to be Tolstoy and spin a thousand-word chronicle. Even a journal filled with brief, succinct, staccato, mnemonic phrases will prove quite fruitful.

---

40 Yeats, "If I Were Four-and-Twenty," 263.

GOING FORWARD

The more you document the who, what, when, and where of your magical life, the more you will be able to discern the how: the techniques, settings, and conditions that seem to produce the most dramatic and effective results in your ultimate quest for the why—the "why am I doing this?"

That why of Crow-Raven Magic is to part the veil and connect and commune with the higher realms, cosmic consciousness, divinity, the Mysteries of Gaia. Knowing the how will lead you deeper into the discovery of the why that inspired you to begin your search on your Pagan/Witch/magical path in the first place.

Through writing, you will become more adept—in both the mundane and magical sense.

Chapter 7

LORE: THE LASCAUX BIRD-MAN AND PREHISTORY

Who was the first human—or protohuman—to take notice of the peculiar ways of crows and ravens?

We *Homo sapiens*—we modern humans, who dubbed ourselves the Latin term for "wise men"—can readily see that corvids behave differently, behave with intent in ways beyond other birds and even many mammals and other wild creatures. While modern wildlife biologists say corvids' intelligence is on a par with dolphins and apes, you don't have to be even an amateur naturalist to be aware of, charmed by, and awed by the ways of crows and ravens.

As I gaze from my patio at the backyard of my Florida home and the woods beyond, I see cardinals and Carolina wrens going about their business of foraging for weed seeds, black berries, beetles, crickets, spiders, and other bug beasties that populate the grass. Sometimes the cardinals and wrens will chance upon the saltine crackers and tortilla chips I scatter on my lawn for the crows, but they do not seem to have a taste for those foods. Rather, the cardinals and wrens seem instinctual, even mindless as they feast. However honed their food-scouting instincts may be, they seem to find their dinner, to a large degree, by sheer randomness.

That's similarly true of the raccoons and black racer snakes that occasionally meander into my backyard. Serendipity, rather than refined Darwinian survival skills, seem to have brought them there. Given that my back patio is a virtual village for green anole and Cuban brown anole lizards,

Southern toads, and the occasional green tree frog, it's telling that black racers do not have dinner there more often. These snakes only feed there when they are lost.

The wild squirrels that make their home in my backyard and the adjacent woods do indeed exhibit some agency: they retreat to the trees when I walk out back, and once they see me spread crackers on my lawn, they cautiously descend the trees and wait for me to leave.

Contrast those animals' behaviors to the corvids. The American crows that visit my backyard frequently each day tend to announce their arrival with that familiar "caw-caw" as they alight on the low branches of the slash pines or their favored Chinese tallow tree.

Almost every time I hear a crow, I grab chips and crackers and my camera and head outside to feed and photograph them.

After I've scattered their food, the crows usually are patient as I stand nearby and snap photos of them. Sometimes it seems as if the crows are posing for me as time melts, and I photograph them for five or eight or ten minutes or more.

All this is to note that it's easy to see and hear that crows go about their ways with deliberation, intent, and intelligence far beyond most creatures. No doubt early humans—or protohumans—similarly took notice of the peculiar ways of crows and ravens.

Who was the first human to do so?

History will not give us the answer to that enigma. However, we do know that our ancestors very likely were practicing Crow Magic as long as 19,000 years ago. The startling evidence can be seen in a Paleolithic cave painting, among many other such astonishing works, discovered in southwestern France in 1940.

BIRD-MAN

Known as Lascaux Cave, the complex of caverns is home to some 1,400 engravings and 600 paintings. Archaeologists have debated the age of these ancient images, as well as the Paleolithic rock art at other caves around the world, but the most common assessment is that the Lascaux works were created between 17,000 BCE and 15,000 BCE, and likely were not all painted during the same (relatively) short time span.[41]

---

41 Clottes, "The Lascaux Cave Paintings."

The paintings at Lascaux include horses, bison, felines, a bear, and other animals—and a peculiar, mystifying scene in the strikingly named Shaft of the Dead Man. The Shaft tableaux depicts a seemingly wounded bison right beside a supine human figure with a bird's head, or it's a human wearing a bird mask. Interpretations vary. Many scholars refer to it as simply a human figure, although technically it's a therianthrope, or a being that combines human and animal forms. Archaeologists report it's the only human—or humanlike—creature portrayed at Lascaux.

Rendering of the Lascaux Bird-Man

The bird-man is prominently ithyphallic, and he is lying with arms splayed out at shoulder level, with hands that resemble bird feet. However, despite the obvious bird head, avian feet may not have been the intent of the artist. This human figure is, well, quite primitively drawn—a veritable stick figure—compared to the majestic bison and a rhinoceros nearby, even though a spear has pierced the bison's hindquarters and spilled out its entrails. It's as though Van Gogh had rendered the gracefully curved horns, head, back, and shanks of the beasts, while a kindergartner drew the bird-man. The crudity of this human figure, compared to the breathtaking gracefulness of the many animal paintings in Lascaux, is yet another mystery of the cave.

The scene includes another curiosity: an upright pole or staff that is shorter than the trunk of the stick figure bird-man and topped by a full-bodied bird slightly bigger than, and just as crudely rendered as, the human's bird head.

Numerous scholars invariably refer to a bird, bird-man, or birdlike head when discussing the Shaft of the Dead Man, but John Marzluff and Tony Angell don't shy away from suggesting the Lascaux ancient artist specifically sought to depict a crow or raven. They state that the scene shows the death of a hunter and theorize that both the bird head on the human body and the nearby bird on a stick are likely crows or ravens because, even at this point in human evolution, those corvids would have already become associated with death in the minds of Paleolithic people.[42] That association likely was fostered by crows and ravens' predilection for feeding on carrion.

Of course, there is no definitive proof that the Lascaux bird-man sports the head of a corvid or that his staff is topped by one. But, following the exhaustive research and observations by Marzluff and Angell, Bernd Heinrich, and other wildlife biologists—and given my own yearslong observations of the intelligence, deliberation, and agency exhibited by the American crows around my Florida home—I believe it's safe to theorize that it was crows or ravens who caught the fancy of the Lascaux artist.

Theories about the Lascaux Bird-Man

What is the true meaning behind the curious case of the bird-man and his bird staff? The succinct, to-the-point answer is that no one knows. The meaning of the bird-man and bison are left to speculation. Theories fall mainly, but not exclusively, into two main categories: The Shaft of the Dead Man indeed depicts a dead man—a Paleolithic hunter killed during a hunting incident—or, alternately, a wounded hunter. The second major theory suggests the Shaft scene portrays a human who is very much alive but has entered some sort of shamanic trance.

Hunting Magic

Even the dead hunter or wounded hunter theory is not an argument for some sort of mundane Stone Age account of a tragic moment in time, as if some ancient historian merely wanted to report the news or record a slice of history.

---

42 Marzluff and Angell, *In the Company of Crows and Ravens*, 2.

Rather, the dead/wounded hunter theory posits that the ancient artist was steeped in a supernatural/magical weltanschauung and their creation of the bird-man and dying bison was a magical operation.

Mario Ruspoli, an Italian filmmaker who was enlisted by the French Ministry of Culture to document Lascaux after it had been closed to the public due to deteriorating conditions caused by human traffic, visited the Shaft and was awestruck. He claimed the site was "charged with occult power."[43]

As a young child, Kenyan paleoanthropologist Richard Leakey was astonished when he visited Lascaux with his parents, renowned paleontologists Louis and Mary Leakey, and with equally renowned French archaeologist, anthropologist, and Catholic priest Henri Breuil. So, it's no wonder that Lascaux and other cave painting sites figure prominently in Richard Leakey and Roger Lewin's 1992 book *Origins Reconsidered: In Search of What Makes Us Human*.

In 1903, French archaeologist and religious historian Salomon Reinach, as well as other researchers before him, theorized the bird-man scene and other cave paintings depict instances of "sympathetic magic, or hunting magic" and were part of "magical and totemic rituals," Leakey and Lewin write.[44]

That theory came to be most famously embraced and championed, Leakey and numerous other researchers note, by Abbé Breuil, especially in his 1952 work *Four Hundred Centuries of Cave Art*.

A fuller explication of sympathetic magic, particularly that expounded by Scottish anthropologist Sir James George Frazer in *The Golden Bough*, follows in these pages, but here a succinct definition of Frazer's law of similarity and its resulting "imitative magic" will suffice: create an image or representation of a real-life being or object, and what is done within that image or to that likeness will affect its real-world counterpart.

Cave paintings were thus an act of hunting magic (a term used by many scholars of Paleolithic cultures)—an act of imitative magic in which both the fecundity of prey animals (witness the many herds pictured on cave walls) and the successful hunting of them were portrayed, reflecting the primitive peoples' belief, intent, and desire that such portrayals would manifest in actual life. Such a theory only makes sense, of course, if one views the supine bird-man as wounded but surviving rather than dead.

---

43 Ryan, *The Strong Eye of Shamanism*, 56.

44 Leakey and Lewin, *Origins Reconsidered*, 318.

As for the peculiarity of the bird-headed human and his bird staff, those details fit in nicely with the imitative magic theory if one views them as death-obsessed corvids.

Later cultures, particularly the ancient Celts and Norse, would readily note the eerie and unnerving appearance of crows and ravens swooping down in the immediate aftermath of a grisly battle and feasting on the human corpses. Such corvid behaviors (among many other activities of the birds) began to figure in the mythologies of those cultures and others. Scientists today have even named one species the carrion crow.

Biologist Bernd Heinrich, in his book *Mind of the Raven: Investigations and Adventures with Wolf-Birds*, documents how wolves and ravens have developed a sophisticated, symbiotic hunt-and-kill relationship that goes far beyond ravens merely pouncing on fresh kills by wolf packs.

But I have turned up no researchers who theorize that corvids' carrion feeding, which must have been quite apparent to Paleolithic *Homo sapiens*, may have played a role, whether magical (my belief) or mundane, in the creation of the Lascaux bird-man.

Masculine-Feminine Duality or Practical Geometry

Surveying the entirety of the Lascaux Cave complex, Joseph Campbell writes in *The Way of the Animal Powers* that the beauty and regal nature of the depicted creatures, their postures, and the aesthetic arrangements of both the animals and numerous geometric shapes points to more than some attempt at "crude" primitive magic.[45]

French paleontologist André Leroi-Gourhan's structuralist-systematic approach to ancient cave paintings explored what he saw as a masculine/feminine duality emphasized in the beasts, geometrical designs, and the Lascaux bird-man and other therianthropes elsewhere.[46] Other cave explorers saw more practical intentions at work. For example, the three vertical pairs of dots just below the tail of the rhinoceros in the Lascaux bird-man scene is merely representative of feces, some researchers said.[47]

---

45 Campbell, *The Way of Animal Powers*, 64.

46 "Rock Art Theories VI," Bradshaw Foundation; Campbell, *The Way of Animal Powers*, 64–66.

47 Campbell, *Primitive Mythology*, 301.

Leakey goes on to note that when Abbé Breuil died in 1961, the popularity of the hunting-magic hypothesis began to fall out of favor.[48]

Shamanic Trance, Spirit Animals

Over the next several decades, researchers began to proffer more complex, often shamanic interpretations of the Lascaux bird-man, the famous antlered "Sorcerer" at the Cave of the Trois-Frères in France, and other therianthropes, creatures, and scenes discovered in the seemingly ever-burgeoning world of cave paintings. Along with arch mythology master Joseph Campbell, these researchers included South African archaeologist David Lewis-Williams and French prehistorian Jean Clottes in their 1998 work *The Shamans of Prehistory: Trance & Magic in the Painted Caves*; Robert E. Ryan in his exhaustive (but not exhausting) 1999 book *The Strong Eye of Shamanism: A Journey into the Caves of Consciousness*; and others.

The Bradshaw Foundation website, a nonprofit organization based in Geneva, is a magnificent resource on ancient rock art around the world. The foundation works in collaboration with the United Nations Educational, Scientific, and Cultural Organization (UNESCO), the Royal Geographic Society, the National Geographic Society, the Rock Art Research Institute in South Africa, and the Trust for African Rock Art.

Its utterly comprehensive website includes sections on rock art theories, such as art for art's sake, hunting magic, fertility magic, shamanism, and more.

The shamanism entry notes that in hunter-gatherer societies, the shaman "was a very important figure: priest, magician, healer, artist. As a messenger, medium or emissary, the shaman's role was to make the 'extraordinary' ordinary. The shaman could liaise between this world—the natural world—and the spirit world."[49]

The segment goes on to cite the intriguing theory of some researchers that "the rock face itself was believed to be the interface—the veil—between these two worlds," and that shamans would procure "the life-force from the animals in the spirit world" and bring that mojo back to serve his people in the physical world.[50]

---

48 Leakey and Lewin, *Origins Reconsidered*, 319.

49 "Rock Art Theories V."

50 "Rock Art Theories V."

Thus, this theory says, all those cave paintings of animals are not meant to depict earthbound, flesh-and-blood creatures but instead are "spirit animals," while the various therianthropes "represent shamans or sorcerers with masks."[51]

The Geometry of Shamanic Trance

The somewhat controversial research of David Lewis-Williams and Jean Clottes delved into modern-day neuropsychological studies and led them to claim that the many geometric forms in cave paintings resemble the hallucinations conjured by the brain circuitry of modern humans, regardless of cultural background, when one is experiencing certain altered states of consciousness—that is, when one is experiencing a shamanic trance state. Other stages of hallucinations begin to draw upon the particular cultural milieu of the experiencer, Lewis-Williams and Clottes say.[52]

Shaman Shape-Shifters

Considering the Lascaux bird-man, Campbell notes, again in *The Way of the Animal Powers*, the frequency of bird imagery and motifs in shamanic contexts and that trancing shamans often ride birds to the otherworld realms. Shamans often shape-shift into bird forms. Campbell concludes that it is quite possible that the Lascaux bird-man is not a hunter killed by his would-be prey but instead is a shaman deep in trance.[53]

Similarly, Ryan writes in *The Strong Eye of Shamanism* that the Lascaux scene depicts a shaman in "trance-death and transformation" and the pierced bison is a sacred sacrifice, and that human and beast elsewhere become "one in ecstasy."[54]

The External Soul Theory

Hunting magic or an entranced shaman are not the only interpretations of the Lascaux bird-man.

Edward Allworthy Armstrong, British ornithologist and Church of England priest, theorizes an "external soul" interpretation of the Lascaux tableaux. The

---

51 "Rock Art Theories V."

52 Clottes and Lewis-Williams, *The Shamans of Prehistory.*

53 Campbell, *The Way of Animal Powers*, 65

54 Ryan, *The Strong Eye of Shamanism*, 255.

"parson-naturalist" (as one obituary called Armstrong) posits the existence of "bird cults" in the Upper Paleolithic period.[55] The bird on the staff is a "cult object," given that the Lascaux artist could have easily depicted a bird in a more realistic-looking tree if that had been their intent. The similarity between the bird-man's head and the bird on the post reveal a connection between the two. It is perhaps a "totemic" relationship, but more likely the scene is "a representation of the external soul—which in later cultures was so often visualized as a bird. If any particular bird is represented it may be the raven, for Basque legends still refer to this bird as the spirit of the prehistoric hunters' caves."[56]

Armstrong supports his external soul theory by citing the prevalence of the bird-on-a-pole motif in the magical, religious, and funeral art of such later cultures as ancient Egypt and Mesopotamia, and he notes the spectacular painted sarcophagus discovered in Hagia Triada on Crete in 1903. Archaeologists date the sarcophagus to 1400 BCE, when that island was under Mycenaean rule, and say the images on the limestone coffin combine features of both the Minoan and Mycenaean cultures.

One of the most striking images on the sarcophagus depicts a woman wearing a white top with a blue sash and belt and a long skirt accented with wavy, ochre-colored lines. Her attention is focused on two nearby pillars that are only slightly taller than her. Each pillar is topped by what looks like a giant bat with wings extended, which Armstrong identifies as "double axes, symbols of power." The birds perched atop each "axe," Armstrong says, are ravens, and the entire tableau "hints" that ravens were "connected with death."[57]

Armstrong goes on to note the many bird-on-a-pole images depicted by such shamanic cultures as the Tungus, Voguls, Yakuts, Dolgans, and Ostyak of Siberia and other areas of Asia and Eurasia. The Lascaux bird staff, he suggests, was the forerunner of them all.[58]

THE DEEP CONNECTEDNESS OF LASCAUX

Joseph Campbell lamented that "the animal envoys of the Unseen Power no longer serve, as in primeval times, to teach and to guide mankind. ... Memories

---

55 British Birds, "Obituary: Rev. Edward Allworthy Armstrong."

56 Armstrong, The Folklore of Birds, 12–14.

57 Armstrong, The Folklore of Birds, 116.

58 Armstrong, The Folklore of Birds, 4–24.

of … animal envoys still must sleep, somehow, within us; for they wake a little and stir when we venture into wilderness."[59]

And so modern humankind is left pondering the arcane beauty of that wall deep in the Shaft at Lascaux Cave. Does the scene depict hunting magic? Shamanic trance? A commemoration of a terrifying event? Some other mystery as yet undeciphered by science or mystics?

Those questions may never be definitively answered.

As Richard Leakey observes, Lascaux "is imbued with meaning, but we can't decipher what is being said. The potency is palpable, but we are culturally blind to its content." Yet, he concludes, anyone who engages Lascaux with an eye toward understanding the origins of humankind will emerge with "a deep conviction of connectedness."[60]

But we modern humans do know that when that ancient Lascaux artist cast pigments onto the cavern wall of the Shaft of the Dead Man some 17,000 to 19,000 years ago, they felt some sort of deep connection to the animal world, to the avian world—to the world of corvids. Anyone familiar with the lives and ways of corvids will nod in agreement with scientists or shamans who claim that the Lascaux man and his bird staff are, indeed, a *crow* man with a *crow* staff.

That interpretation carries weight whether one views Lascaux through the now-largely discarded lens of hunting magic or through the more contemporary, sophisticated theories that embrace shamanism. Indeed, the manner in which human cultures around the world, in the ensuing millennia, began to fashion crow and raven lore into their myths, their legends, their shamanic practices, and their spiritualities only re-enforces that it all began deep in the womb of the earth almost 20,000 years ago.

Deep in Lascaux Cave, we find what is likely the world's earliest known instance of Crow Magic.

---

59 Campbell, *The Way of the Animal Powers*, 7.

60 Leakey and Lewin, *Origins Reconsidered*, 334.

Chapter 8

GRIMOIRE: YOUR CROW-RAVEN SPIRIT TREE

Numerous cultures and mythologies around the world regard trees as sacred entities or as repositories of magical power. Pursue Crow-Raven Magic for even a short period of time and you will notice the corvids in your backyard, neighborhood, or local park tend to favor a certain tree—or perhaps several trees.

Finding such a tree to consecrate as your Crow-Raven Spirit Tree will enhance your communion with both corvids and Gaia—nature—simultaneously. This will work on both a mundane and a magical level. Repeatedly watching corvids in a specific locale will sharpen your observation skills, and you will begin to notice, say, which birds favor the greater safety of the higher branches and which ones dare to perch closer to human activity. Their respective behaviors, far more than their size or physical appearance, will help you distinguish the birds from each other.

Also, your Crow-Raven Spirit Tree will be the place where you bestow the gift of food, helping to ensure the birds' daily return and that they see you as their benefactor.

And then the magic will begin to happen: The corvids, having identified you as a friend of Crow-Raven kind, will begin to communicate with you, cawing loudly whenever your presence intersects with theirs. They will begin to see you as their genius loci—the protective spirit of their place.

This grimoire chapter includes two workings: seeking/finding your Crow-Raven Spirit Tree, and a meditation to consecrate the tree once you have discovered it.

What You Will Need

- Raw, unprocessed corn and two other natural foods, such as unshelled nuts, sunflower seeds, or pumpkin seeds
- A naturalists' field guide to identify trees and other flora in your area
- A magical field guide to trees and other flora in your area (optional)

Background

Who was the first human to climb a tree? More to the point: What was going through their mind when they first scaled the branches of a tree? Primitive human hunters could have become the hunted and were fleeing a rampaging bison or an attacking saber-tooth tiger, and thus one of our ancestors went up a tree for the first time. They may have become curious about whatever the birds were seeing when perched upon the lofty branches of trees.

Regardless, at some precise moment in prehistory, some human shimmied up a tree and realized that their kind—the earth's first beings with self-awareness—were no longer earthbound.

For millennia now, we humans have taken it for granted that we can scale our human-made structures and get a bird's-eye, or god-goddess's-eye, view of the earth below. But until the ancients constructed the Necropolis of Bougon around 4800 BCE in modern-day France, trees were the only means for humans to achieve—literally—an elevated consciousness. Such a literal elevation above the soil of our planet led to a metaphorical-intellectual-spiritual elevation for our ancestors. Those high-above vistas spawned newfound thoughts, however primitive, of humans and our place in the world and the cosmos.

As Pagans and devotees of other earth-based religions know, Gaia's literal geography can—and does—impact our spiritual insight.

Many cultures esteem specific trees as sacred: the asvattha, or sacred fig, of Hindu mythology; the bodhi tree, under which the Buddha attained enlightenment; the iroko tree of the Yoruba people of West Africa; and the hazel tree, considered to be a fairy abode and a magical source of wisdom by the ancient Celts of Ireland.

Disparate mythologies and religions have taken their reverence of trees deeper, depicting their spiritual cosmos symbolically as a World Tree. Typically, the trunk of a World Tree resides in our everyday terrestrial realm, the abode of humankind, fauna, flora, the oceans, rivers, savannas, and mountains. The roots of the World Tree extend deep into the earth, the Underworld, the abode of the chthonic deities, and the realm that receives the fleshy vessels of all creatures upon death. The branches of the World Tree arch skyward into the heavens, the divine realm, the Upperworld, the abode of the gods and goddesses, and in some belief systems, the spirits of our deceased beloveds.

For the ancient Maya, the World Tree is a ceiba tree known as Yaxche. Followers of the sky god Tengri in ancient Central Asia believed a World Tree bridged the abode of humans on earth with the spiritual realm of the Upperworld.

In Norse mythology, Yggdrasil is an ash or yew tree (scholars debate this) whose branches cover the Nine Worlds and extend beyond the heavens, while the tree's three roots run deep into sacred waters. The etymology of Yggdrasil is unclear but is often translated as "Odin's horse"—a reference to the time Odin hung himself in self-sacrifice among Yggdrasil's branches to seek knowledge of the runes. *Horse*, in this instance, scholars say, is a poetic reference to gallows, since the condemned ride the gallows out of this world and into the next.

Through the idea of a World Tree, we see one reason why so many cultures hold trees to be sacred. Rooting deep into Gaia's flesh and branching into the sky, trees are literally closer to the Other Realms and therefore spiritually-psychologically-symbolically closer to the ancestors and to the gods and goddesses of both the chthonic and the celestial worlds. Sure, you say, even the tallest trees in the world, the redwoods of California, rise less than 400 feet above the earth's surface, and in cosmic terms that's still a far distance from the beard of Odin. Yet trees remain Gaia's gentle, beautiful sentinels—a reminder that while we humans, confined to the Middle Realm, continue our race to construct often soulless tall buildings, the earth herself has been cradling our beloved dead and yearning for and growing toward the celestial realms since time immemorial.

Even in our urban-scapes, trees remind us of the joy and spirit-lift of that yearning and that arching toward the heavens. Perhaps the relative scarcity of trees in our cities makes their presence there even more valuable, while those of us who dwell among or close to woods may have become, through familiarity, indifferent to Tree Magic.

But Crow and Raven know.

Preparation

Plan to go on a quest specifically for the purpose of finding your Crow-Raven Spirit Tree. Prepare an offering, to be used in your tree's consecration, by putting raw, unprocessed corn and two other natural foods, such as unshelled nuts, berries, and sunflower or pumpkin seeds into a paper bag. Do not use any processed human food. The foods can vary, but be sure to include fresh corn, a crow favorite. You can get dried cracked corn—which is marketed as bird feed—from a farm supply store or where birdseed is sold, or you can procure the corn by cutting it from a cob.

Before embarking to find your Crow-Raven Tree, set your intention by chanting aloud a spontaneous invocation to Crow-Raven Spirit. Create your own chant, akin to this:

> *Crow Spirit, Raven Spirit,*
> *Guide me in my quest upon Gaia's breast*
> *To find a tree where you reside.*

Action

The only requirement for the tree is that you have witnessed a crow or raven perched among its branches—that is, you have seen this tree provide succor for Crow or Raven kind. Perhaps you already have a tree in mind and in your heart—a tree where you have seen crows or ravens perched or frolicking. If so, that is fine. Go to the tree and skip to the consecration and blessing part of this work.

Looking for the Tree

Your quest to find the tree may be as simple as stepping into your backyard or walking through your neighborhood and observing Gaia's flora and fauna. Perhaps you may visit a favorite park, nearby nature trail, or primitive wilderness.

If you are beginning your quest with no certainty where it will be fulfilled, don't be in a hurry to proclaim the first corvid-inhabited tree you encounter as your Spirit Tree. If that happens—if you feel a connection to the first tree you see with a crow or raven—so be it. However, don't rush to conclude your quest. If, after your initial foray, you have come upon no tree that embodies Crow-Raven Spirit for you, then merely reset your intention, and vow to be alert and aware as you wander in the days and weeks ahead. Your Crow-Raven Spirit Tree may be one in which you have noticed crows numerous times previously, when suddenly you are walking by it and you sense an aura or feel a burst of energy from it for the first time. Or perhaps one day you notice a specific number of crows in that tree and that is a number of importance or magic for you.

Each of my Crow Spirit Trees—the loblolly bay and slash pine trees at my former residence and the Chinese tallow tree at my new hermitage by the woods—did not reveal themselves to me in any sort of "aha" moment. Instead, the crows' love of these trees revealed itself over time, in the ways that the crows I named Valiant, Ms. Skitta, Boga, and Baca would alight on their branches, and even a muggle could see how at home they felt. The aura of these trees grew and grew until their Crow Magic was palpable and undeniable.

It will be a blessing to have your Crow Spirit Tree in your yard; the wooded, undeveloped lot three blocks down the street; or a nearby park, but it is not essential to have it nearby. Let Crow Spirit be your guide. If your tree is nearby, you will be blessed to have it as an easily accessible portal that will help you achieve communion with Crow kind and Gaia. If your Crow Spirit Tree is farther away, perhaps nestled deep along your favorite hiking trail beyond the city, then you will be blessed to visit it at Samhain, Beltane, or any time that is special to you as the Wheel of the Year turns. However, it absolutely must be a tree where you have spotted crows and/or ravens, and wherever it grows and nurtures the birds, you will be called to visit the tree and leave offerings to Crow or Raven.

Almost as important as discovering a tree where crows and ravens have appeared is finding one that exudes, for you, a magical vibe. The physical beauty of the tree—the color of its bark, the artful curve of its branches, the geometry of its leaves or needles, the fruit, nuts, or flowers it bears—may be what attracts you to it. If you are well versed in the magical properties of trees, you may want to search for such a tree—a yew, rowan, or oak, perhaps—until you find one that is hosting crows or ravens. Or, if you are unaware of the histories of magical trees, you may want to research them. Perhaps you will discover a kind of tree that speaks to you, and your quest will shape-shift and you will be looking for one that embodies both Crow Magic and a certain kind of Tree Magic.

As with all spellwork, metaphysical pursuits, and magical operations, set your intentions, then do the physical and mental work both in preparation and during the process, which will alter your consciousness away from your mundane robot mind and thus "altar" your consciousness and allow magic to happen. Then remain alert and aware.

The physical and mental work in this operation is "merely" engaging with heightened consciousness the natural world of trees, whether in deep woods, an urban landscape, suburbia, or your backyard.

Research Your Tree

As with all metaphysical work, some practical magic will come in handy during your quest. Along with researching Tree Magic in books or on the internet, this is yet another instance when an Audubon field guide will be handy. In fact, having such a guide is essential for anyone following a nature-based spiritual path. You may even want to take your field guide with you on your search.

Once you have found your Crow-Raven Spirit Tree, you will want to know—and need to know—what kind of tree it is. This is not only a magical matter but also a practical one; some plants are toxic to various degrees and in various ways, from causing skin rashes if touched to causing death if one ingests their fruits, nuts, sap, leaves, or needles. The tree known as the common yew, English yew, or European yew, for example—despite all of its magical properties and exalted place in mythology and folklore—is fatally toxic and has been known to cause the deaths of both humans and livestock. Birds, however, are unharmed by eating yew berries due to the nature of their digestive systems.

Need it be said that one should never eat any part of a plant unless one has absolute confidence those products of nature are safe.

I discovered my Crow Spirit Tree—a Chinese tallow tree—within a month of moving into my new hermitage by the woods. As I spread crackers on my back lawn upon hearing crows nearby, I soon noticed that the curious but cautious crow couple that came to investigate would inevitably land in the tallow. The couple, whom I named Boga and Baca, would spend a suitable time in the tallow's branches assessing the situation—five minutes or so in the early days—before one of them would glide down to the ground, casually crow-hop around, grasp a cracker, then fly up to a nearby slash pine or the lone pond cypress at the edge of the flatwoods to the east. Then the other crow would follow suit.

I had not found my Crow Spirit Tree at my new place—it had found me and revealed itself.

Consecration and Blessing

To consecrate and bless the tree, leave your offering of the three foods at the base of its trunk and say aloud a blessing of gratitude akin to this (as always, speak from your own heart):

> *Thank you, Gaia. Thank you, Crow Spirit. Thank you, Tree Spirit.*
> *I am blessed and blissed by your presence in this time, in this place.*
> *May you reveal your sweet mysteries to me. Blessed be.*

If you are confident of the tree's nature—that is, you know it's a pine, sycamore, oak, ash, sweetgum (a member of the witch-hazel family), or other common tree—then speak your blessing while touching its trunk with both palms. Mind you, the trees in the wilderness behind my home are overwhelmingly common and safe, as attested by my Audubon field guide, and the same is likely true for your area. Still, whenever one moves among Gaia's wild flora and fauna, one must do so with awareness and respect.

If your Crow Spirit Tree's nature is uncertain or unknown to you, simply hold your palms a few inches from its trunk as you murmur your blessing.

A Crow Spirit Tree Meditation

Once you have ascertained the nature of your tree, you will want to tactilely explore it, if possible, in preparation for a meditation-vision trance. Again, caution is advised if you harbor uncertainties about the species of your tree. Your first meditation-vision trance and any future work with your spirit tree can be done safely and effectively, without touch, beneath its branches and in near proximity to its aura.

Pursue whatever meditation-vision path you intuit. That is, you may want to initiate a meditation focused upon Samhain or Beltane, contact with your ancestors, or communion with your god or goddess. The following meditation, or one similar, is suggested as your first one as an introduction to your Crow Spirit Tree.

You likely will be embarking upon your vision in broad daylight or perhaps twilight, and yes, you will be outdoors, and unless you are in your backyard, you will be subject to the caprice of life flowing around you. If you are in a public park, for example, you likely will not have much solitude.

Entering a nemeton or some other sacred, often secluded space known to you, to part the veil and glimpse the mysteries, is one thing. Parting the veil in a public or semipublic space is another.

If you seek communion with Crow-Raven Spirit, Gaia, or goddess-god within what the Irish poet William Butler Yeats described as "the noisy set of bankers, schoolmasters, and clergymen the martyrs call the world,"[61] then know that the "monkey minds" of chattering passersby may swirl about you. Remind yourself that any such mundane intrusions ultimately do not negate Spirit; they merely interrupt our own abilities to focus and to "altar" our consciousness and enter into communion with Spirit at that time and place. And even the possibility of disruption is a maybe. Buddhists, including several personal friends of mine, seem quite adept at entering meditative states outside of ideal conditions. Cultivating such abilities—to be able to commune with the Divine far from the scared environs of Newgrange, Uluru, Chidambaram Nataraja, Glastonbury Tor, Tsankawi, or your favorite nature trail—is a useful tool for any spiritual seeker.

If your meditative trance at your newly consecrated Crow-Raven Spirit Tree is irrevocably disturbed, acknowledge that real-world magic, beyond the spell recipes in a book, can be messy and filled with the unexpected, and there are lessons to be learned from such experiences.

Begin Your Meditation

Sensually explore your spirit tree. Caress its trunk, leaves, or needles with your fingers, at first with your eyes closed so that touch becomes your main sensory input. When was the last time you touched a tree? Open your eyes and look closely at your tree's bark. You will see that Gaia is an abstract expressionist painter whose works are far more intricate and arresting than those of Jackson Pollock, Willem de Kooning, or Lee Krasner. Notice what animals find succor from the tree: ants or bugs or lizards crawling about its face, bees or butter-

---

61 Yeats, "Adam's Curse," 78.

flies fluttering among its branches. And, of course, take note if crows, ravens, or other birds are currently perched in the leafy world above you. Notice the scents of the tree and whether they emanate from its flowers, fruit, pollen, or branches. Listen for nearby sounds: the buzz of bees, the sitar of cicadas, the hum of other insects, the caws or gronks of nearby corvids.

Every single tree is its own ecosystem, its own little world, with all sorts of creatures—and their spirit—making their way and adding to Gaia's astonishing dance.

To begin your meditative trance, decide if you want to stand facing the tree with your palms touching its trunk or held up several inches away or if you want to stand or sit with your back leaning against the trunk. Close your eyes and take the proverbial three deep breaths, then murmur an invocation of your own creation. Something like:

> *Crow Spirit, Raven Spirit,*
> *May you find succor within*
> *The welcoming branches of this tree*
> *Upon Gaia's breast, now and forever more.*

When you intuit you are ready, envision a crow alighting on the upper branches of your Crow Spirit Tree, announcing her arrival with any number of caws. You are gazing upward at the tree's branches from beside its trunk, and among its limbs, leaves, or needles you can see Crow's rich black form. Welcome Crow and ask where she has come from—her reply may be a physical place or a mystical realm. Ask her what she has seen on her journey here. Remember to listen patiently; you are in no hurry.

Then and only then, tell Crow why you have come to be at this place, at this time. Tell Crow that you have dedicated this tree as your Crow Spirit Tree and that it will forever be a sacred place for Crow kind. Let Crow know that you will visit the tree to receive the wisdom of Crow kind and that you will leave offerings for her and her clan, such as the three foods you gifted the tree earlier.

Ask Crow to take you on a journey, to join her in flight to whatever destination she chooses, and then to bring you back again to your Crow Spirit Tree. Crow may choose a physical place near or distant, or she may choose a mystical, mythological, or otherworldly realm. You yourself will not be flying—Crow will be taking you on this journey upon her body and wings. Again, you and Crow are in no hurry.

Note the caress of the wind against your face. Listen to the murmur of Crow's heartbeat and the equally rhythmic swoosh-swoosh-swoosh of her flapping wings. Notice the way your heart begins to beat in sync with Crow's heart. Gaze at the tapestry of clouds spread before you on the turquoise-blue breast of Nuit, the Egyptian sky goddess. Turn your gaze downward to the green-brown-ochre flesh of Gaia below. Perhaps you recognize where you are. As Crow descends closer to Gaia's breasts, take note of the landscape and any distinguishing features: mountains, rivers, lakes, a cityscape, a castle, a tribal dance at the Taos Pueblo, the Sphinx, Victoria Falls, the Eiffel Tower, the lakeside cabin you visited as a child, the Place of Wisdom in Witch World's Estcarp, the woods of your first Beltane ritual.

Crows and ravens, remember, inhabit every earthly continent except Antarctica. Odin's ravens traverse the Nine Worlds. Crows can fly anywhere.

Ask Crow to return you to your Crow Spirit Tree. Thank her and bid her farewell.

Ending Your Meditation

Open your eyes and, whatever your position, focus your gaze upon the branches above you.

Ask the tree for permission to harvest a single leaf, a blossom, a twig, or one of its fruits or berries to place upon your home altar. If you intuit the tree's acceptance, then proceed to accept its gift. If you receive a sign that now is not the time, then wait until another day and repeat your gentle request. Promise your Crow Spirit Tree that you will visit again.

GOING FORWARD

At some point, a few days or even a few weeks after your initial consecration of your Crow-Raven Spirit Tree, return to further bless your newfound sacred space with a physical, sacred object. This could be a crystal or stone (know its magical attributes!), a goddess or god figurine, or even something playful, such as a toy gnome or fairy—or a crow! Something that brings you joy.

I honored my tree by placing the Blessing Sun, a treasured gift from my beloved late wife, Cheryl, at its trunk. The Blessing Sun is an olive-green ceramic sun face with cupped hands at its bottom—hands that both extend and receive offerings. I placed corn I cut from a cob, sunflower seeds, and a few pecans in the hands and murmured a brief blessing:

Thank you, Gaia, for the gifts of trees, the gift of Crow kind.

Since that initial offering, my tree is now home to a veritable fairy garden peopled with ceramic and plastic gnomes, dragons, unicorns, fairies, and more.

If your Crow-Raven Spirit Tree is in your yard or otherwise nearby, visit it whenever you hear the caws, gronks, or catlike caterwauls of corvids. You want them to "train" you to come at their beckoning.

I keep a "crow food" section in my pantry stocked with saltine crackers and any stale bread I have, and I spread their treats on my lawn or place a few crackers on the tree's lowest branches each and every time I hear "my" crows.

If you observe the eight Wiccan sabbats or the seasonal festivals of the Pagan Wheel of the Year, consider holding such rituals beneath or beside your Crow-Raven Spirit Tree. However, do not feel that such a practice is obligatory—performing any magical act by rote or obligation will deaden, not nurture, Spirit. For me, my daily crow feedings are times of ritual and communion, and given that I want my Beltane and Samhain rituals to honor the totality of Gaia and her creations, I don't make crows the centerpiece of those observances.

Chapter 9

LORE: CORVID MAGIC TAKES ROOT

What is the first mention of crows or ravens in writing?

That honor, as far as modern archaeology can assess, goes to *The Epic of Gilgamesh*, the ancient Mesopotamian epic poem that borrows its hero's name from a historical king who ruled the Sumerian city-state of Uruk between 2800 and 2500 BCE.

Gilgamesh is cited in what is known as the Sumerian King List, an account pieced together following the discovery of some twenty ancient stone fragments at various times in the twentieth century, with the oldest dating to circa 2100 BCE. These fragments appear to have sprung from the same unknown master source and are a mix of the fanciful and the factual—the writings detailing the earliest kings say they each reigned anywhere from 18,600 years to 43,200 years!

The Epic of Gilgamesh is a bit tricky to date precisely, given that the version we know today—and, indeed, the several ones that even the ancients came to know—were compiled from various sources over centuries. Five Gilgamesh poems, written in the Sumerian language and dating to around 2100 BCE, later became source material for an epic written in the Akkadian language, whose oldest surviving, but incomplete, version dates to around 1800 BCE. A later so-called standard version of *Gilgamesh* was compiled by Sîn-lēqi-unninni, a Babylonian priest, between 1300 and 1000 BCE. A copy of that work, dating to circa 600

CE, was discovered in 1853 on twelve clay tablets in Nineveh, in what is modern-day northern Iraq.

The epic tells us that Gilgamesh was born of the goddess Ninsun and was two-thirds god and one-third man. Gilgamesh builds a temple for Anu, the god of the earth, and Ishtar, the goddess of love and war. Gilgamesh and his friend Enkidu slay Humbaba, the lion-faced giant who guards the Cedar Forest. Gilgamesh rebuffs the romantic advances of Ishtar, knowing her reputation for mistreating her past lovers. Ishtar vows revenge and has her father, Anu, send Gugalanna, the Bull of Heaven, to wreak havoc on the city of Uruk. After much devastation, Gilgamesh and Endiku slay the bull, but Endiku dies soon after.

In his grief for his friend, and now fearing his own death, Gilgamesh sets out to learn the secret of immortality from Utnapishtim and his wife, who were the only humans to survive a great flood. The couple also had saved all animal life by building a giant ark and were granted eternal life by the gods for their efforts.

It is Utnapishtim who relates how a raven signaled the ordeal of the flood would soon be over:

> When the seventh day dawned I loosed a dove and let her go. She flew away, but finding no resting-place she returned. Then I loosed a swallow, and she flew away but finding no resting-place she returned. I loosed a raven, she saw that the waters had retreated, she ate, she flew around, she cawed, and she did not come back.[62]

Does this account of a deluge seem familiar? The Sumerian Gilgamesh poems contain a brief reference to a flood myth, as do several other ancient Babylonian texts roughly contemporary with the tale of Gilgamesh. Indeed, legends of ancient, massive floods feature in the stories of cultures around the world, almost to the point of being a universal myth.

NOAH AND THE RAVEN

Scholars, however, have noted particular connections between the tale of Gilgamesh and the story of Noah and the flood in the Hebrew scriptures—the Old Testament. In the popular consciousness of most people in Western soci-

---

62 Sanders, *The Epic of Gilgamesh*, 111.

ety, it was a dove that Noah released from the ark to find land. But the King James Version of the Christian Bible lets us know that a raven was sent forth first. Genesis 8: 6–8 reads:

> And it came to pass at the end of forty days, that Noah opened the window of the ark which he had made: And he sent forth a raven, which went forth to and fro, until the waters were dried up from off the earth. Also he sent forth a dove from him, to see if the waters were abated from off the face of the ground.

A far more lively, supernatural, and even randy account of the raven's ride upon Noah's ark is presented in *The Legends of the Jews*, a six-volume 1909 work by Lithuanian-born rabbi and scholar Louis Ginzberg.

"I have made the first attempt to gather from the original sources all Jewish legends, insofar as they refer to Biblical personages and events, and reproduce them with the greatest attainable completeness and accuracy," writes Ginzberg, who emigrated to America in 1899 at age twenty-six. "I use the expression Jewish, rather than Rabbinic, because the sources from which I have levied contributions are not limited to the Rabbinic literature." He notes that "the works of the Talmudic-Midrashic literature are of the first importance. Covering the period from the second to the fourteenth century, they contain the major part of the Jewish legendary material."[63]

Thus the tales of Ginzberg's *Legends of the Jews*, while covering some of the same turf as the Hebrew scriptures, were written considerably later than those biblical texts, which mostly date from approximately 1200 to 165 BCE.

The reputation of ravens did not fare well in those intervening years. As Ginzberg relates in one ancient Jewish legend, Noah decides to send the raven, rather than the dove, to determine whether the flood waters have diminished. In Ginzberg's telling, the insolent raven balks and accuses Noah of harboring ill intentions: "Thou sendest me forth only that I may meet my death, and thou wishest my death that my wife may be at thy service." Noah then curses the raven: "May thy mouth, which has spoken evil against me, be accursed, and thy intercourse with thy wife be only through it."[64]

---

63 Ginzberg, *The Legends of the Jews*, xi.
64 Ginzberg, *The Legends of the Jews*, 38–39.

Thus this ancient Jewish text provides an origin story for the archaic, erroneous belief that ravens copulate mouth to mouth.

Elsewhere Ginzberg relates a variant of the tale of Noah and the raven's search for dry land, with the sassy corvid accusing the human patriarch of lusting after his mate! In Ginzberg's telling, the raven says:

> The Lord, thy Master, hates me, and thou dost hate me, too.... Suppose, now, I should perish by reason of heat or cold, would not the world be the poorer by a whole species of animals? Or can it be that thou hast cast a lustful eye upon my mate, and desirest to rid thyself of me?[65]

Noah angrily rebukes the raven, and when the bird is sent out, he is distracted by a human corpse and "he set to work to devour it," abandoning his mission.[66]

Given the raven's suspicion that his mate was coveted by Noah, it's quite curious that a number of modern-day historians allege the ancient Hebrew texts say that Ham, Noah's second son, copulated with a raven. But such modern interpretations are the erroneous result of the mistranslation of an ancient text, says scholar David Mark Whitford.[67]

Elsewhere in Ginzberg's text, the ancient Hebrews ridicule ravens to the point of cruel pettiness, although, curiously, the Hebrew god favors the corvids on occasion. While the raven is called "an unattractive animal" and disdained because "from their own excrement maggots come forth" and they are "unkind toward [their] own young," the birds also are recognized for their love for one another, and the Hebrew god "therefore takes the young ravens under His special protection."[68]

Ancient ravens also faced more shaming. "The raven has himself to blame also for the awkward hop in his gait" because of his pathetic, unsuccessful

---

65 Ginzberg, *The Legends of the Jews*, 163–64.

66 Ginzberg, *The Legends of the Jews*, 163–64.

67 Whitford, *The Curse of Ham in the Early Modern Era*, 25 (footnote).

68 Ginzberg, *The Legends of the Jews*, 39.

attempts to emulate the dove, thus earning the scorn of the other animals. "His failure excited their ridicule."[69]

CORVIDS' "MAGICAL" MATING HABITS

Passages from Pliny, the Hebrew Bible, and rabbinic lore present intriguing evidence on three fronts for the increasing ubiquity of crow and raven lore in antiquity—and the burgeoning reputation among the ancients, in the many millennia since the creation of the Lascaux crow-man cave painting, of corvids as birds possessing eerie, even supernatural powers.

One of those three areas is the "magical" mating habits of corvids. These ancient Jewish tales of Noah's curse recall what Pliny the Elder wrote in his *Naturalis Historia* (Natural History) in 77 CE: "The Corvus for the most part layeth five Eggs, and the Vulgar are of opinion that they conceive and lay Eggs at the Bill."[70]

For the record, corvids do not copulate through their mouths or conceive "at the bill." Male crows and ravens, like most but not all birds, do not have a penis, but both male and female corvids have an orifice called a cloaca, which is used for both excretory and reproductive purposes. Copulating corvids touch their cloacas together. However, crows often will engage in beak-to-face and beak-to-beak touching, activities known as allopreening and allobilling, behaviors I have witnessed quite a bit in the apparently mated crow couples that frequent my backyard, especially in the pair I named Bola and Bella.

Given that corvids and numerous other bird species may share food beak-to-beak, and sometimes do so during mating rituals, it is not so ridiculous that the ancients believed corvids and other birds copulated by mouth.

It should be noted here that crows and ravens were not the only birds, much less the only animals, to be imbued with magical and supernatural qualities by the ancients and by human observers down through the ages. A quick browse through any number of works, from Pliny's *Naturalis Historia* up to such twentieth-century books as Edward A. Armstrong's *The Folklore of Birds* and Ernest Ingersoll's *Birds in Legend and Folklore*, will dispel the notion that corvids were accorded eldritch powers above and beyond other creatures.

---

69 Ginzberg, *The Legends of the Jews*, 39.

70 Pliny, *Pliny's Natural History in Thirty-Seven Books*, 198.

That said, crows and ravens do seem to be a special case, as is attested to by modern-day studies by numerous university-based researchers whose astonishing findings are published in books, peer-reviewed journals, nature magazines, and websites geared toward the average-intelligent reader. Given the ubiquitous presence of crows and ravens around the world, and given their uncanny abilities were readily observable, one can see that the ancient Romans, Celts, and Norse, the Indigenous peoples of North America, and modern-day Pagans are right to claim that crows and ravens are messengers who bridge humanity and the natural world in unique, even magical ways.

CORVIDS TALK!

Ginzberg's rabbinic tales of the raven verbally sparring with Noah bring up a second magical attribute of corvids that gained traction in the ancient world: these birds possess human speech!

Pliny, writing in the first century CE, is quite the opposite of the irascible Noah; he writes admiringly of a raven that "became accustomed to Man's Speech" and daily "would salute Tiberius, and after him Germanicus and Drusus, the Caesars, by their Names; and presently the People of Rome that passed by"—and did so for several years "to the Wonder of all."[71]

Armstrong mentions that spirits summoned by Siberian shamans speak their own language "unless it is a wolf, fox, or raven, which have human speech."[72]

Once again, modern science has confirmed—OK, not that corvids can carry on casual conversations with people, but that there may be more than mere mimicry involved in all those anecdotes and tales about talking crows and ravens.

Nobel Prize–winning Austrian ethologist Konrad Lorenz refers fondly to his tame raven, Roah, as "a close friend of mine." Whenever the corvid sensed the two of them were heading toward a place the bird had come to see as a dangerous environment, Roah would swoop down close to Lorenz, say his own human-given name "with human intonation," then fly away—hoping to lead the two of them to safer location. "The old raven must, then, have possessed a sort of insight that 'Roah' was my call-note!" Lorenz writes. "Solomon was not the only man who could speak to animals, but Roah is, so far as I know, the

---

71 Pliny, *Pliny's Natural History in Thirty-Seven Books*, 232.

72 Armstrong, *The Folklore of Birds*, 78.

only animal that has everspoken a human word to a man, in its right context— even if it was only a very ordinary call-note."[73]

THE RISE OF CORVID DEATH LORE

Ginzberg's rabbinic tales of Noah and the raven point to a third supernatural attribute of corvids that was suspected in the ancient world: crows and ravens are closely aligned with death.

Recall that in Ginzberg's *Legends of the Jews*, he relates that telling passage about the raven departing the ark to search for land, but the bird "saw the body of a dead man" and "set to work to devour it."[74]

That is, the raven's gluttony for carrion, even human corpses, was so powerful that the corvid couldn't resist it.

In the Old Testament, Proverbs 30:17 relates a bogeyman-will-get-you warning tale to children, with ravens as the bogeymen: "The eye that mocketh at his father, And despiseth to obey his mother, The ravens of the valley shall pick it out, And the young eagles shall eat it."

Again, such tales have a real-world counterpoint. Very, very few humans have chanced to witness, say, a wolf pack take down a bison in the wild—much less prey on a human. Yet many historical accounts relate that people through the ages have observed crows and ravens pecking at the eyes and otherwise feeding on corpses strewn on battlefields or gorging on dead humans in whatever set of circumstances. So, we should not be surprised that ravens feasting on human eyeballs has haunted humankind from the time of the ancient Hebrews to Alfred Hitchcock's 1963 avians-go-ape-shit horror movie *The Birds*.

Fleeting references to ravens—as agents or significators of either dark and disturbing divine vengeance or, sometimes, divine beneficence—are scattered elsewhere throughout the King James Version of the Old Testament, with one reference in the New Testament.

Leviticus 11 includes a lengthy list of dietary guidelines, including animals that are deemed "unclean to you" and an "abomination unto you" and shall therefore not be eaten by humankind. The many "fowls" cited include the eagle, vulture, owl, nighthawk, cuckow, swan, stork, heron, bat, "every raven after his kind," and many others.

---

73 Lorenz, *King Solomon's Ring*, 90–91.

74 Ginzberg, *The Legends of the Jews*, 163–64.

In Isaiah 34, ravens figure in the vengeance of the Hebrew god, along with owls, vultures, unicorns, and dragons:

> For the indignation of the Lord is upon all nations, and his fury upon all their armies: he hath utterly destroyed them, he hath delivered them to the slaughter. Their slain also shall be cast out, and their stink shall come up out of their carcasses, and the mountains shall be melted with their blood. ... And the unicorns shall come down with them, and the bullocks with the bulls; and their land shall be soaked with blood, and their dust made fat with fatness. ... the owl also and the raven shall dwell in it: and he shall stretch out upon it the line of confusion, and the stones of emptiness. ... it shall be an habitation of dragons, and a court for owls.

The tale of the prophet Elijah is puzzling, given he was befriended by ravens when he went into hiding to escape the wrath of Ahab. In 1 Kings 17: 4–7, the Hebrew god tells Elijah: "I have commanded the ravens to feed thee there. ... And the ravens brought him bread and flesh in the morning, and bread and flesh in the evening; and he drank of the brook."

Ernest Ingersoll points out the curious nature of this passage, given that here ravens act as benevolent agents of the Hebrew god even though ancient Jews considered the birds "unclean" because they eat carrion. The tale of Elijah is so incongruous and "so unnatural that commentators have done their best to explain it away."[75]

The Qur'an tells the story of how Allah sent a raven to show Cain how to bury Abel.

> Then Allah sent a crow scratching the ground to show him how to cover the dead body of his brother. He [Cain] said: Woe is me! Am I not able to be as this crow and cover the dead body of my brother? So he became of those who regret.[76]

---

75 Ingersoll, *Birds in Legend, Fable, and Folklore*, 158.

76 "Compared Translations of the Meaning of the Quran – 5:31."

Jewish rabbinic lore includes a similar tale, as Ginzberg notes. This very same story also reflects the ancient Jews'—and the Hebrew god's—ambiguous, love-hate relationship with the raven. Adam and Eve are mourning and unsure what to do with the corpse of Abel until they "observed how a raven scratched the earth away in one spot, and then hid a dead bird of his own kind in the ground. Adam, following the example of the raven, buried the body of Abel, and the raven was rewarded by God," who protects their young and "grants their petition when the ravens pray for rain."[77]

In the New Testament's only mention of ravens, Jesus says in Luke 12:24: "Consider the ravens: for they neither sow nor reap; which neither have store-house nor barn; and God feedeth them: how much more are ye better than the fowls?"

To which a corvid-phile or a practitioner of Crow-Raven Magic would reply: "None at all."

---

77 Ginzberg, *Legends of the Jews*, 113.

Chapter 10

LORE: MARCUS VALERIUS CORVUS AND THE BATTLE CROW

The supernatural reputation of corvids was amped up considerably when the Roman historian Titus Livius, also known as Livy (64 or 59 BCE–12 CE), wrote his epic *Ab Urbe Condita Libri* (Books from the Foundation of the City), commonly known in the modern era as *The History of Rome*. Livy's work chronicles the tale of Romulus and Remus, the Rape of the Sabine Women, and other early legends of Rome; the founding of the Roman Republic circa 500 BCE by Lucius Junius Brutus; numerous wars; and other events through the reign of Augustus in Livy's lifetime.

In one of those war chronicles, Livy relates the story of the real-life Roman military commander and statesman Marcus Valerius Corvus Calenus (circa 370–circa 270 BCE), who was part of a Roman force going to war against the Gauls of northern Italy. Yes, that "Corvus" is the Latin word for "corvid," the name given to the crow and raven family of birds. "Corvus" became part of the soldier and future consul's name following his astonishing battlefield encounter with a gigantic Gallic warrior who, prior to a battle between the two armies, challenged any Roman to single man-to-man combat. Well, there is that matter of the corvid, variously identified as a crow or raven, that made the fight a two-versus-one affair.

As Livy writes, in an 1823 English translation by George Baker:

> Just as the Roman began the combat, a crow pitched suddenly on his helmet, looking towards his antagonist, which, as an augury sent from heaven, the tribune at first received with joy, and then

87

prayed that "whatever god or goddess had sent him, the auspicious bird would be favourable and propitious to him." What is wonderful to be told, the bird not only kept the seat where it had once pitched, but as often as the encounter was renewed, raising itself on its wings, attacked the face and eyes of his antagonist, the Gaul, with its beak and talons, who became so much terrified by the sight of such a prodigy, that he was slain by Valerius. The crow then flew up on high towards the east, until it was out of sight.[78]

Livy's chronicle goes on to relate that "the Roman soldiers exulted at the victory of the tribune, and likewise at such attention and favour shown them by the gods," and "both gods and men contributed their aid to insure ... a complete and acknowledged victory was obtained" over the full contingent of Gauls. For his valorous efforts, Marcus Valerius was awarded ten oxen, a golden crown, and as Livy notes, a new nom de guerre: "Marcus Valerius Corvus, for that surname was given him from thenceforth; he was then only twenty-three years old."[79]

Modern-day scholars and lay readers, of course, ponder the reliability of Livy's accounts: How much is historical fact, and how much of his text is littered with myths and legends? Whether fact or fancy, the tale of Marcus Valerius Corvus has survived to modern times and provides a remarkable chapter in the history of Crow-Raven Magic.

Several aspects of the legend are worth noting. For one, the Roman battalion readily and naturally perceives, without question, that the crow's appearance is a sign of divine intervention. The corvid is an emissary of the gods and goddesses. The lifespan of Valerius was reputed to be 370–270 BCE, thus helping us moderns see that by the time of his era, the connection between corvids and divine entities was firmly established, at least in the Mediterranean world.

Yet this Roman tale is quite unlike the ancient Hebrew accounts. In rabbinic texts, corvids possess human speech and a sassy attitude, but they have no special connection to godhead. In biblical tales, yes, the raven is an agent of the Hebrew god or the divine master plan. Yet, when the raven leaves Noah's Ark to search for land, or when the ravens feed the exiled prophet Elijah, they are

---

78 Livy, *The History of Rome*, 121–22.

79 Livy, *The History of Rome*, 123.

acting in a perfunctory manner and are mere bit players in the cosmic scheme of the ancient Hebrews' world.

However, in the tale of Valerius Corvus, that fighting crow, proceeding at the behest of the gods and goddesses, shifts the tide of history for the ancient Romans. Crow Magic of the highest order, indeed.

A second aspect of the Marcus Valerius legend is more subtle yet quite telling. Livy writes that the Roman warrior initially sees the crow "as an augury sent from heaven" and he receives its appearance "with joy." But then caution and prudence quickly overcome the soldier, and he "then prayed that 'whatever god or goddess had sent him, the auspicious bird would be favourable and propitious to him.'"[80]

AMBIVALENCE TOWARD CORVIDS, THEN AND NOW

It is easy to see in this two-millennia-old tale the ambivalence with which humans behold corvids—whether that unease stems from the possibly dire, momentous auguries the birds portend for a nation-state, as in this legend, or whether someone's seemingly everyday encounter spurs thoughts of personal apocalypse. As we shall see in Norse and Celtic-Irish myths, warriors who see crows or ravens on the battlefield have reason to tremble—in such instances the birds are usually an omen of impending doom. But not always, as Marcus Valerius Corvus can attest.

This ambivalence survives into modern times. As mentioned earlier, whenever my friends or acquaintances have discovered I am writing a book about crows and ravens, reactions are divided to the extreme. Some people express their fascination with the birds and gleefully deliver an impromptu anecdote about their encounters with corvids. But just as many people shudder and relate their disdain of crows and ravens, their voices peppered by hints of anxiety and fear.

Pursue Crow-Raven Magic and you will encounter such divergent expressions from both muggles and magicians. The uneasiness expressed by many people may make you wonder if Jung's collective unconscious is at play—that the uneasiness of these modern-day humans is spurred by distant, subconscious memories of a Celtic warrior or a Viking raider who suspected they or

---

80 Livy, *The History of Rome*, 121.

their comrades were undone by some supernaturally conniving, malevolent crow or raven.

This ambivalence, this dread that many humans have for corvid kind, and the impact it may have on practicing Crow-Raven Magic, especially divination, will be discussed in chapter 22, "The Shadowy Side of Corvids."

Chapter 11

GRIMOIRE: A CROW-RAVEN TALISMAN AND AMULET

An amulet or talisman is a magically charged or consecrated object, often fashioned to a necklace chain or cord and worn around one's neck, or fashioned into a ring or earring. However, an amulet or talisman need not be wearable, and alternately the object can be placed upon one's altar or even a bookshelf or nightstand.

Its purpose is to bring a physical, palpable symbol of one's magical path into one's daily personal space, thus establishing a channel, whether actively or passively acknowledged, of sympathetic magic between you, the object, and what the object represents—in this case, Crow or Raven. I will share one amulet and one talisman project. You can do one of these or both. Or you can adapt the ideas, methods, and techniques for your own unique amulet or talisman.

AMULET VERSUS TALISMAN

Reflecting common usage, a number of dictionaries and other sources, especially those outside of magical and occult realms, make no distinction between amulets and talismans.

However, as noted by the renowned and revered Witch Doreen Valiente, C. Nelson Stewart, and other occult and magical-leaning sources, an amulet traditionally is a magically charged or consecrated object, whether worn, carried, or placed about one's home, which is meant to be protective and prevent misfortune. A talisman is a similarly charged or consecrated object whose purpose is to attract good fortune or good luck.[81] Stewart compares an amulet to a shield and a talisman to a sword.[82]

Put even more simply, perhaps overly so: amulets repel bad, talismans attract good.

The entry "Amuletum" by James Yates in the 1859 work *A Dictionary of Greek and Roman Antiquities*, edited by William Smith, reads:

> AMULETUM, an amulet. This word in Arabic (Hamalet) means *that which is suspended.* It was probably brought by Arabian merchants, together with the articles to which it was applied, when they were imported into Europe from the East. It first occurs in the Natural History of Pliny.
>
> An amulet was any object—a stone, a plant, an artificial production, or a piece of writing—which was suspended from the neck, or tied to any part of the body, for the purpose of counteracting poison, curing or preventing disease, warding off the evil eye, aiding women in childbirth, or obviating calamities and securing advantages of any kind.
>
> Faith in the virtues of amulets was almost universal in the ancient world.[83]

According to *Merriam-Webster,* talisman can be traced back to the ancient Greek word *telein,* meaning "to initiate into the mysteries," which in turn made its way into Arabic as *tilsam,* a charm, which in turn passed into the Romance languages.[84]

Will You Make an Amulet or Talisman?

To create an amulet or talisman, you must first set your intention. Ultimately, for your practice, you decide which one based on how you intuit the relationships you have with corvids. Given my personal experience with crows, I can

---

81 Valiente, *An ABC of Witchcraft,* 5–6.

82 Stewart, "Talismans," 2772.

83 Yates, "Amuletum," 91.

84 "Talisman," *Merriam-Webster,* accessed June 30, 2019, https://www.merriam-webster.com/dictionary/talisman.

say that Crow Magic particularly lends itself to the protective powers of an amulet.

Anytime I hear the piercing "Kee! Kee!" call of the red-shouldered hawk coming from the woods behind my home, I knew a crow ruckus will soon follow. Though I am unable to see them deep in the thick woods, a multitude of crows will begin cawing and squawking at their intruder in the hope of protecting their nests, their eggs, and their young from their fellow winged predator.

On one occasion during Beltane, I looked out of my living room window and past the Maypole to see a solitary crow perched on the bottom horizontal limb of the loblolly bay tree. Suddenly, the crow bolted straight up from its perch. It shot up like a rocket and flew away quickly. I'd never seen a crow move that quickly. Ten minutes later I looked up from my laptop to see a seven-foot alligator literally sniffing the base of my Maypole.

All of these observations are reminders that crows are alert, cautious, and protective when need be, aggressive when called for, and prudent in picking their battles—and all are attributes that your amulet, or even your talisman, will help you channel.

WHAT YOU WILL NEED

For the wand:
- A small branch or stick
- A stone or crystal selected for its magical properties
- Epoxy glue
- Crafting items such as black permanent markers, acrylic paint and a means of application, or a wood-burning tool
- Small knife or similar tool for carving
- Varnish and brush (optional)

For the talisman:
- A piece of pine bark
- Black permanent marker

For other amulets or talismans:
- You can use any other natural objects, such as tree bark, stones, and so on, and decorate according to your intuition and interest.

An Important Word of Caution

While a found crow or raven feather or skeleton may seem to be a natural fit for an amulet or talisman, the US Fish & Wildlife Service notes that the possession of feathers and other parts of native North American birds without a permit is prohibited by the Migratory Bird Treaty Act, first passed in 1918 as an agreement with Canada. It has since been broadened to include Mexico, Japan, and Russia. The MBTA was amended in 1962 to allow Native American tribes to collect feathers from protected birds for religious ceremonies. Over the years additional species have come under the treaty's protection, including eagles, hawks, and other birds.[85]

The act "protects wild birds by preventing their killing by collectors and the commercial trade in their feathers, and extends to all feathers, regardless of how they were obtained. There is no exemption for molted feathers or those taken from road- or window-killed birds."[86]

Despite the "migratory" part of the law's name, it does indeed apply to crows and ravens, and people are prohibited from possessing their carcasses and bones as well as feathers.

BACKGROUND

With people prohibited from possessing corvid feathers and bones, even those coincidently found in nature, how does one craft a true Crow or Raven amulet or talisman?

You may yet discover a gift from corvids. One day I was in my backyard photographing crows and was startled to hear a bustle high in a slash pine, and a nanosecond later I witnessed a nearly four-foot-long branch crash to the ground and break in two. I gazed back up at the lofty reaches of the pine and spotted a crow among the needles.

Had the crow perched on that branch and its weight caused it to break? Must have been an unhealthy branch. Or did Crow Magic send the branch tumbling to earth as an offering to me?

Even at that moment I knew how Crow Magic would manifest in the two portions of the slash pine: I would leave the twenty-six-inch piece intact, the better to preserve its natural Gaian splendor. On the seventeen-inch portion

---

85 National Audubon Society, "The Migratory Bird Treaty Act, Explained."
86 "Feathers and the Law."

I would apply my neophyte whittling and wood-carving skills to strip off the bark, then channel the Lascaux Cave artist to inscribe and paint Crow images and sigils on the wood to create a wand.

Sympathetic Magic

As for the mechanics of physical amulets and talismans, there is no more concise and insightful explanation than that of Scottish anthropologist Sir James George Frazer in his magnum opus, *The Golden Bough: A Study in Comparative Religion*, later retitled *The Golden Bough: A Study in Magic and Religion*. First published in a two-volume set in 1890, the tome was expanded by Frazer to twelve volumes that were published over a decade in the early 1900s, and several different one-volume abridgments also were released.

In the chapter "Sympathetic Magic" in the 1922 edition, Frazer defined the two "Principles of Magic." The first, the law of similarity, states that "like produces like, or that an effect resembles its cause." Thus, "the magician infers that he can produce any effect he desires merely by imitating it." Charms based on this law are considered a form of "imitative magic."[87]

The second principle, the law of contact or contagion, holds "that things which have once been in contact with each other continue to act on each other at a distance after the physical contact has been severed." Thus, the magician "infers that whatever he does to a material object will affect equally the person with whom the object was once in contact, whether it formed part of his body or not." Charms based on this law are considered a form of "contagious magic."[88]

A Brief Note on Wands

Below are instructions on how to craft what I call an amuletic wand. That's my term for an amulet in the physical shape of a wand, and therefore it can assume some of the many and varied attributes of a wand—but its primary purpose is to serve as an amulet.

Wands and variants, such as scepters, can be traced back to the ancient Egyptians, Greeks, and other cultures, when they served either practical functions (as emblems of kingship) or magical ones. Wands are "a sign of power

---

87 Frazer, *The Golden Bough*, 11.

88 Frazer, *The Golden Bough*, 11.

and virility, supernatural and physical. ... In its supernatural context, the wand is an agent of transformation, a well-known example being the fairy wand, which is supposed to draw its power from the sun, represented by the star at its tip."[89] Wands also have been used for divination and communication with spirits, as a test for chastity, and for healing and shape-shifting.[90]

Doreen Valiente writes that the wand, which she calls a "magical weapon," "is the expression of the magician's will and is used for invocations."[91] Scholar Sian Lee Reid notes that, unlike the magical tools the athame (dagger) and the sword, "the wand does not have the appearance of a weapon, and because the wood was once alive, the wand is the tool used to summon other forms of life energy, under the principle that 'life calls to life.'"[92]

It is in the latter sense that your Crow-Raven amuletic wand will function—as a summoner of the life energy and spirit of Crow and Raven kind.

PREPARATION

Certainly, no one can deny the mojo of coming upon a fallen branch or other natural object that one has just witnessed in proximity to a crow or raven perched in a tree or strutting about the ground. Any such occurrence would be a case of potent contagious magic that Crow or Raven has suddenly, unexpectedly bequeathed you for use as a talisman or amulet.

Alternately, you may procure a fallen branch, piece of bark, or stone from underneath your Crow-Raven Spirit Tree. If you choose to do so, ask permission from both Crow Spirit and Tree Spirit to take the object: "Crow Spirit, Tree Spirit—I seek a gift from you." If you intuit the answer is affirmative, then proceed. If you sense otherwise, thank the spirits and say you may return another day. Do not break off a branch from a living tree. Any patch of woods will have accumulations of fallen tree limbs and so will many tree-littered urban parks, although be sure to discern whether it is OK to remove a small branch or stick. Along with avoiding the desecration of a living tree, "re-purposing" a fallen branch carries the added mojo of bringing new life—and a *magical* new life at that—to a piece of Gaia.

---

89 Maple, "Wands," 2985.

90 Maple, "Wands," 2985–87.

91 Valiente, *Witchcraft for Tomorrow*, 80.

92 Reid, "Tools of the Art," 274.

When choosing a stone or crystal to mount on the tip of your wand, do your homework and know the magical, spiritual, and healing properties of crystals and stones before intuiting which one(s) to use.

If you don't live near nature-scapes that may lend bark, small branches, stones, or other pieces of Gaia suitable for crafting a talisman or amulet, what should one do? Head to the store.

Do not diminish or disparage the creation of one's own amulet or talisman from materials "sourced" from a metaphysical shop or even a chain craft store. Gifts directly from Gaia possess a potent contagious magic. But, as most any veteran spellcaster, ritualist, magician, shaman, or magical craftsman will know, and as any neophyte will quickly learn, it is the intention behind magical operations that is key—combined, of course, with one's focus and some degree of knowledge. Someone might find an unusual stone or plant blossom in a park, and she has a pretty adornment to place on her dresser. A Witch finds a stone or blossom on a nature trail and, knowing some of the attributes of crystals, stones, plants, trees, forest elementals, and the like, as well as the abilities and behaviors of corvids that may frequent the area, she will have the seed of a spell or amulet or an altar object with a special mojo.

Intention, intention, intention!

Don't underestimate the power of buying a piece of balsa wood at a craft store and drawing or using acrylic paints or a wood-burning tool to craft a raven image upon it. To do so is to place yourself in direct descent of that Lascaux Cave artist from 19 millennia ago.

Don't disparage the efficacy of buying a crow or raven figure at a metaphysical shop or even at some chain store and then subsequently consecrating it. Years ago, I bought a half-size crow figurine at a Halloween shop prior to Samhain. It had faux feathers, a curious tilt to its head, and an oddly attentive glint in its eye. I did not consecrate the Halloween crow figure in any direct way, but still, I should not have been surprised when I placed it in my library and it began to take on a magical, talismanic aura. Anytime I engage it, whether through a passing glance or deeper contemplation, I feel a surge of power, of Crow Spirit.

Again, don't despair if circumstances preclude you from scouting and collecting talismanic items from Gaia's breast in some field or forest. Create or consecrate with intention—or sometimes even with subliminal intent—and your amulet or talisman will become a potent part of your Crow or Raven Magic.

ACTIONS: WAND

To make an amuletic crow wand, use a branch or stick you have procured, one that is anywhere from one to three feet long and one or two inches thick. Don't fret if your branch doesn't fall within those parameters.

If you are skittish about any aspect of woodworking or your skills are, like mine, rudimentary, there are a gazillion how-to videos on the internet.

If you use a pine or sycamore branch, the bark will be flaky and easy to strip or even peel off. Use the smallest blade of a pocketknife, some carving tools or, if you are not experienced with knives, a dull-edged putty knife to pry off the bark. If you use a branch from a smooth-barked tree, such as a beech, birch, or aspen, you may decide not to peel or strip off the bark and so create your wand with it intact.

Varnish will protect your wood and give it a sheen, but it's optional. I rarely use varnish on the talismans, wands, and ritual objects I craft from wood. The tri-pronged wand I fashioned thirty years ago from a sturdy, shrub-like tree I no longer can identify has survived just fine on my altar without any coating.

If you varnish your wand, apply a coat by brush (outdoors) and let it dry for an hour before applying a second coat, then let your wood dry for twenty-four hours.

Next, create simple corvid silhouette images using a black permanent marker, acrylic paint, or a wood-burning tool. Don't fret about your artistic skills or lack thereof; if the Lascaux artist can do it, you can too.

Carefully use a pocketknife or a small wood rasp to create a notch in your wood as a place for your crystal to sit, if needed. Then, attach your chosen crystal to the tip of your wand with glue. Be careful to follow the instructions if you will use epoxy that comes in double tubes. It's simple to use, but you must follow the precise instructions. Allow the epoxied crystal to dry for twenty-four hours.

For my crow amuletic wand, I used a clear quartz crystal to amplify energy and activate the crown chakra. The crystal fit perfectly into a natural notch at the end of the branch—as if the two gifts of Gaia were designed and destined to come together.

Consecrate Your Wand

Consecrate your wand with sun energy by putting it outside at sunrise. The suit of wands in most tarots decks is associated with fire, and in many cultures and mythologies, the sun is seen as emanating guardianship and protection. Precisely at sunrise one day, place your wand at the base of your Crow-Raven Spirit Tree or, if known, at the base of the very tree from which the branch originally grew.

Be sure that your wand and especially its crystal will receive some amount of direct sunlight.

Alternately, you may also place your wand in a wooded or natural area, even your backyard, where crows frequent. That is the one simple aspect that should be a part of any consecration you conduct: your amulet or talisman should be magically charged in a location that is frequented by crows or ravens, even if they visit such a place only fleetingly.

Say or chant a simple invocation at the beginning of the consecration. You can adapt or alter the following to suit your needs. Remember, an invocation is more powerful if it's created by you.

> *Crow Mother, Crow Father, Crow Spirit*
> *One who walks and flies between worlds*
> *One who has shape-shifted the goddess*
> *One who has whispered to the gods*
> *One who has witnessed the eros of the Divine.*
> *Come speak your sweet arcana*
> *To this time*
> *To this place*
> *To this crow holy relic*
> *Where Crow Spirit*
> *Will reside forevermore.*

Pick up your wand precisely at sunset.

When I consecrated my wand beneath the pine tree that produced the branch, my heart leaped up to see several crows land and caw in the tree at various times during that daylight period.

ACTIONS: PINE BARK TALISMAN

To create this talisman, which attracts good fortune and the positive energy of Crow Spirit, set your intention with a basic visualization. Prepare by finding a pine tree from which you will harvest a small piece of bark, preferably one where you have witnessed corvids. If your Crow Spirit Tree is a pine tree, source the bark from it. Pine is suggested because it is prevalent and is a very giving and forgiving medium.

As mentioned in chapter 1, crows and ravens sometimes give gifts, literally, to their benefactors.[93] The following exercise will tap into that corvid behavior. With one palm held against the tree's trunk, follow this visualization:

> *Close your eyes and visualize a crow flying toward you from some distance away. As the crow draws closer and you hear the gentle whoosh of its flapping wings, you realize the corvid is carrying something in its black beak. You hold out your other arm. The crow alights on your wrist and drops an object into your outstretched hand. What is it? Crow will guide your intuition and let you know. Whether it's something playful and ridiculous or sublime, know that it is a gift from Crow Spirit.*

Open your eyes and ask the tree for permission to harvest a part of it. Say:

> *I come seeking a gift from Gaia—from Tree Spirit and Crow Spirit; I seek your blessings.*

Remove a roughly three-inch-square piece of bark by using your fingers or a putty knife to peel it from the trunk. This is one instance where you want to procure your Gaian gift from a living entity so that your talisman will be more infused by its life force. This can be done only because the tree will not be harmed and will continue living—just be sure not to pry too deeply into the pine's bark.

Again, don't dismiss the idea of buying wood pieces pre-shaped into geometric forms or polished stones or crystals at a craft store or metaphysical shop.

Go "Lascaux" on your bark piece or other object by drawing a very simple, stylized crow using a permanent black marker.

Consecrate Your Talisman

You may choose to consecrate your talisman with sun energy as detailed in the wand section. However, a talisman, given that it is intended to attract good

---

93 Marzluff and Angell, *Gifts of the Crow*, 108–113.

fortune rather than propel ill, is conducive to being consecrated by moonlight, which will channel any number of the magical, occult, or supernatural properties associated with the moon: goddess / feminine energy, the power of dreams, an affinity with Witchcraft, the province of hidden occult knowledge.[94] "Those who would work magic of any kind, observed the moon; and particularly Witches, skilled in the works of both the waxing and the waning moon," wrote Doreen Valiente.[95]

To moon-bathe your talisman, first determine the precise time of the next full moon *for your location*. Many people are surprised to discover that astronomical charts, such as those found at timeanddate.com, list the precise minute when the moon is full during each of its cycles. And yes, the moon can turn full during daylight hours even though, of course, you can't see it at that moment.

Consecrate your talisman in the evening during a *waxing* moon, right before and up to the moment it becomes full. Place your talisman at the base of your Crow Spirit Tree, at the tree from which you harvested the bark, or beneath a tree frequented by corvids at the precise moment of moonrise on the night of a full moon. Retrieve your talisman at the precise minute the moon becomes full. Or retrieve it at midnight if the moon is due to become full after midnight or any time before the next day's sunset.

This is how even an object crafted from human-made materials can metamorphose into a truly magical implement.

GOING FORWARD

Place your talisman or amuletic wand on your altar or on a bookshelf, a windowsill, or any place in your home that you intuit. A case can be made that your magical object should be placed somewhere other than your altar, the theory being that your altar will naturally radiate its potent energy, while other places in your home could benefit from an infusion of magical power.

Regardless, the contagious magic of your Crow or Raven amulet or talisman will seep into your everyday life, and it will surge when you handle them or employ them in ritual. They are gifts of the corvids—and Crow-Raven Spirit.

---

94 Walker, "Moon," 1876–82; Kramer-Rolls, "Moon," 160–61; MacRae, "Why You're More Likely to Have Weird and Wonderful Dreams When There's a Full Moon."

95 Valiente, *An ABC of Witchcraft*, 244.

Chapter 12

LORE: THOUGHT, MEMORY, AND RAVEN-FEEDERS

The connection "between Odin and the raven is old and deep," writes scholar E. O. G. Turville-Petre. "Many have wondered what is the foundation of Odin's relationship with the raven. No single answer can be given."[96]

The exploits of Odin, Thor, Loki, and other ancient Norse gods—and the "hungry ravens"[97] who are satiated by the "Raven-Feeder"[98] (that is, a warrior who has slayed his foes in battle)—survive in modern times through two major ancient Scandinavian texts as well as various works by skalds, or court poets.

All of the surviving works were written down after the coming of Christianity to Scandinavia in the eleventh century, although scholars note that historical evidence indicates many of the sources stem from the pre-Christian Viking Age—approximately 800 to 1100 CE.

The *Poetic Edda*, also called the *Elder Edda*, is the modern name for a collection of anonymous poems written down in the Old Norse language circa 1270 CE. Those writings were discovered in 1643 in a medieval Icelandic manuscript known as the Codex Regius. Scholars note it is difficult to determine when these poems were actually composed.[99]

96 Turville-Petre, *Myth and Religion of the North*, 58.
97 Sturluson, *The Prose Edda*, 188.
98 Sturluson, *The Prose Edda*, 149.
99 Jackson, *Norse Myths*, 15.

American historian and mythologist Hélène Adeline Guerber, writing in 1909, laments the influence of the usurping Christian religion and its effect on Scandinavian literature:

> [Christianity] brought with it the influence of the Classical races, and this eventually supplanted the native genius. ... The religious beliefs of the North are not mirrored with any exactitude in the *Elder Edda*. Indeed only a travesty of the faith of our ancestors has been preserved in Norse literature. ... We are told nothing as to sacrificial and religious rites, and all else is omitted which does not provide material for artistic treatment.

Northern mythology was treated "as the beginning of Northern poetry, rather than as a representation of the religious beliefs of the Scandinavians," but still "it is possible to reconstruct in part a plan of the ancient Norse beliefs."[100]

The *Prose Edda*, also known as the *Younger Edda* or *Snorri's Edda*, was written down (or perhaps *compiled* is a better word) by Icelandic scholar and historian Snorri Sturluson circa 1220 CE. Scholars also debate how much Snorri's confirmed Christian faith colored his tales of the Vikings' gods and heroes.

Arthur Gilchrist Brodeur, writing in the introduction to his 1916 translation of the *Prose Edda*, gushes over Snorri's work, proclaiming it contains "traces of genuine nobility of spirit" as he sought to

> enshrine his love for his people's glorious past, for the myths of their ancient gods, half grotesque and half sublime. ... Indefatigable in research, with an artist's eye for the picturesque, a poet's feeling for the dramatic and the human, he created the most vivid, vital histories that have yet been penned. Accurate beyond the manner of his age, gifted with genius for expression, divining the human personalities, the comic or tragic interplay of ambitions, passions, and destinies behind the mere chronicled events, he had almost ideal qualities as an historian.[101]

Other scholars disagree.

---

100 Guerber, *Myths of the Norsemen from the Eddas and Sagas*, xii–xiv.
101 Sturluson, *The Prose Edda*, xii–xiii.

The book *Norse Myths* notes that Snorri often quotes from the *Poetic Edda*, that his renderings are "tainted" by his Christian beliefs, and that he fails to connect the myths to the Vikings' actual, real-world theological views and worship practices.[102] In other words, Snorri tells a good story but fails to provide context that reveals the weltanschauung of the Norse.

As for the works of the court poets, or skalds, who created their tales from the ninth century to the thirteenth century, they too were written down after the coming of Christianity and are a hodgepodge of myths from the height of the Viking Age mixed with events contemporaneous to the poets themselves.[103]

Regardless of any bastardization of ancient Scandinavian sources by Christian historians, any survey of the *Eddas* and skaldic verses will reveal the Vikings' fascination with ravens: Brodeur's *Prose Edda* contains thirty-nine references to the corvids. Henry Adams Bellows's 1923 translation of *The Poetic Edda* cites ravens thirty-one times in various forms.

One of the most famous, or perhaps *the* most renown reference to ravens in Norse lore occurs in the *Grímnismál*, which is titled "The Words of Odin in Disguise" by Jackson Crawford, Instructor of Nordic Studies and Coordinator of the Nordic Program at the University of Colorado Boulder, in his 2015 translation of the *Poetic Edda*.

In the *Grímnismál*, we learn about Odin's ravens, Hugin and Munin, whose names are traditionally translated, respectively, as Thought and Memory. Hugin and Munin leave their perch on Odin's shoulder each daybreak and fly around the world, then return to the god in the evening and dutifully report what they have seen. Thus, we see that, akin to the Romans' Apollo, ravens once again serve as messengers to a god.

Crawford notes that "the war-god Odin's mental powers are literally embodied in his ravens Thought and Memory," and he adds that the famous passage sounds "like the poignant reflection of an elderly man worried about what he might forget in his old age."

Crawford's translation reads:

Thought and Memory,
my ravens, fly every day

---

102 Jackson, *Norse Myths*, 16.
103 Jackson, *Norse Myths*, 16–17.

the whole world over.

Each day I fear

that Thought might not return,

but I fear more for Memory.[104]

Crawford does not use the names Hugin and Munin in his main text, pre-ferring instead to directly translate the ravens' names there as Thought and Memory. However, numerous translations of the *Poetic Edda* and Snorri Sturlu-son's *Prose Edda* keep the source names and footnote their meanings in English.

Moreover, while many scholars translate *Hugin* as "Thought" and *Munin* as "Memory," a few give slightly variant, more nuanced interpretations of the meaning of Hugin. For example, the raven's name is translated as "Reflection" by Rasmus B. Anderson.[105]

In the chapter titled "The Beguiling of Gylfi" in the *Prose Edda*, Snorri reveals a bit more about Odin's relationship with his birds:

> The ravens sit on his shoulders and say into his ear all the tid-ings which they see or hear; they are called thus: Huginn and Muninn.[106] He sends them at day-break to fly about all the world, and they come back at undern-meal; thus he is acquainted with many tidings. Therefore men call him Raven-God, as is said:
>
>> Huginn and Muninn hover each day
>> The wide earth over;
>> I fear for Huginn lest he fare not back,
>> Yet watch I more for Muninn.[107]

---

104 Crawford, *The Poetic Edda*, xvi.

105 Anderson, *Norse Mythology*, 219.

106 The ravens' names are variously rendered with one or two of the letter *n* at the end.

107 Sturluson, *The Prose Edda*, 51.

KENNINGS

The "All-Wise Raven-Ruler"[108] and "Raven-God" are just two of the many kennings for Odin scattered throughout the ancient Norse tales. A kenning is a type of metaphorical naming that usually consists of two hyphenated words and was a linguistic device common in Old Norse, Icelandic, and Old English poetry. In the *Grímnismál,* Odin himself brags that "Of all the gods is Odin the greatest" before proceeding to cite many of what he confesses are self-given names: Father of Victory, Father of the Slain, the Shifty-Eyed, the Many-Shaped, Swift in Deceit, the Truthful, Helmet-Bearer, the Flaming-Eyed, Wide in Wisdom.[109]

Turville-Petre notes that kennings were not conceived randomly, that they were inspired by the contents of the myths and in turn "may present a myth in miniature."[110]

Danish scholar Karl Mortensen, writing in 1898, cites many of Odin's more than two hundred names, noting that

> most of them signify one or another characteristic of the god: All-father, the Blustering, the Changeable, the Stormer, the Wanderer, the Traveler, the Grav-bearded, the Bushy-browed, the Helmet-bearer, the Great Hat, Father of the Slain, Father of Armies, King of Victory, King of Spears, the Terrifier, God of Burdens, Fimbultyr ('Mighty God'), God of the Hanged, and Lord of Spirits (i.e., ghosts). From these examples alone it will appear that Norwegian-Icelandic poetry represents Odin as the world's chief divinity. But the clearest picture of him is that of God of Wisdom and the Art of Poetry, and in theories about Valhalla, as God of War.[111]

Ravens, and especially Hugin himself, also spawned a number of kennings scattered among the ancient Norse tales. Along with Snorri's citation of "Raven-God" as an epithet for Odin, other kennings stemming from the Odin-raven connection include "Raven-Tempter"[112] and "priest of raven sacrifice."[113]

---

108 Sturluson, *The Prose Edda,* 101.

109 Bellows, *The Poetic Edda,* 102–4.

110 Turville-Petre, *Myth and Religion of the North,* 16.

111 Mortensen, *A Handbook of Norse Mythology,* 63.

112 Turville-Petre, *Myth and Religion of the North,* 58.

113 Abram, *Myths of the Pagan North,* 177–78.

The previously cited "Raven-Feeder"—a warrior—and many other raven kennings, like those of Odin, concern battles and bloodshed. In an 1893 translation of *Egil's Saga*, a warrior "starved not the ravens' maw."[114] Blood spilled in battle was referred to as the "raven's drink" or "Hugin's sea."

In the introduction to his *Poetic Edda* translation, Crawford relates a grim but darkly humorous conversation between two ravens in the poem "Helga-kvitha Hundingsbana I"—the birds are giddy as they anticipate a feast following an upcoming battle. In the ancient sagas, warriors followed by scavenger predators, such as ravens or wolves, would take the animals' presence as an omen of success in an upcoming clash. Meanwhile, the Viking raiders—who ventured into the world to opportunistically "feed" on the weak—would identify with those beasts, Crawford notes.[115]

Turville-Petre bluntly states that the raven is "the bird of death, for he feeds on corpses," and that the raven also is "the bird of battle" because of its predilection for haunting battlefields, eager to feast.[116]

"SONG OF THE RAVEN"

Thorbjörn Hornklofi, a ninth-century Norwegian skald and one of the court poets of King Harald Fairhair, is commonly cited as the composer of the remarkable "Hrafnsmál"—Old Norse for "raven song" and variously titled in translations as "Words of the Raven" or "Song of the Raven." The work presents a conversation between a Valkyrie, also rendered as Valkyr, and a raven. Lee M. Hollander, an American scholar of Norse literature and mythology, includes his translation of "Hrafnsmál" in his 1936 book *Old Norse Poems: The Most Important Non-Skaldic Verse Not Included in the Poetic Edda*. He notes that "Hrafnsmál" is part of a larger Hornklofi work, *The Lay of Harold*, named after that historical king of Norway who lived circa 860 to 933 CE.

Hollander says that the "Song of the Raven" as known today was pieced together from untitled fragments found in the *Fagrskinna*, a work written around 1220 CE that includes a chronicle of Norwegian kings from the ninth to twelfth centuries, plus a collection of skaldic verse.[117]

---

114 Green, *Egil's Saga*.

115 Crawford, *The Poetic Edda*, xv–xvi.

116 Turville-Petre, *Myth and Religion of the North*, 58–59.

117 Hollander, *Old Norse Poems*, 56.

Scholars variously describe the Valkyrs—the battle maidens whose name is Old Norse for "chooser of the slain"—as having a supernatural or human essence or some combination. Crawford says that a Valkyrie is "an occupation" that human women can assume.[118]

Guerber provides an overview of the Valkyrs' role in the battle-riddled cosmology of the Norse people:

> The ancient Northern nations, who deemed warfare the most honourable of occupations, and considered courage the greatest virtue, worshipped Odin principally as god of battle and victory. They believed that whenever a fight was impending he sent out his special attendants, the shield-, battle-, or wish-maidens, called Valkyrs (choosers of the slain).[119]

After the chosen warriors "received the Valkyrs' kiss of death,"[120] "one-half" of the slain would be taken by the battle maidens "on their fleet steeds over the quivering rainbow bridge, Bifrost, into Valhalla. Welcomed by Odin's sons, Hermod and Bragi, the heroes were conducted to the foot of Odin's throne, where they received the praise due to their valour."[121] Such warriors were deemed "worthy to taste the joys of Valhalla, and brave enough to lend aid to the gods when the great battle should be fought"[122]—the end-of-the-cosmos battle known as Ragnarok.

A Norseman who died in battle was not automatically shuttled to Valhalla, and the method of selecting the favored dead is unclear. Various ancient texts cite Odin, the goddess Freya, the einherjar (the dead warriors who already dwell in Valhalla), and/or the Valkyries themselves as having dominion over selecting the dead for the honor.[123]

The title of the ancient Norse poem "Darraðarljóð" seems to refer to its narrator, translated as Daurrud or Dorroth, but it is also variously rendered as "The Valkyries' Song of the Spear" by Crawford, "The Song of the Valkyries"

---

118 Crawford, *The Poetic Edda*, 366.

119 Guerber, *Myths of the Norsemen from the Eddas and Sagas*, 19.

120 Guerber, *Myths of the Norsemen from the Eddas and Sagas*, 173.

121 Guerber, *Myths of the Norsemen from the Eddas and Sagas*, 19.

122 Ellis, *The Road to Hel*, 67.

123 Ellis, *The Road to Hel*, 67.

by Hollander, or "The Battle Song of the Valkyries" by Orkney Islands resident, journalist, and historian Sigurd Towrie on his website orkneyjar.com. Hollander says that the poem is "darkly prophetic" of the outcome of the epic Battle of Clontarf in 1014 CE, which pitted an alliance of Vikings and Irish against Irish King Brian Boru near Dublin.[124]

As for "Hrafnsmál," the poem—with its "grim Viking humor"[125]—relates the conversation of a Valkyrie who questions a raven about King Harold's prowess in war. British scholar Alison Finlay, a member of the Viking Society for Northern Research, provides a more contemporary rendering in her 2004 work *Fagrskinna, a Catalogue of the Kings of Norway: A Translation with Introduction and Notes.*

Consisting of only some two dozen, mostly four-lined stanzas, "Song of the Raven" opens with the curious Valkyrie questioning multiple ravens about their blood-stained beaks, the corpse flesh in their claws, and the stench of carrion that reeks from their bodies. Significantly, the Valkyrie states that the ravens "knew" where the corpses were strewn—that it was no mere accident that the corvids came upon a battlefield.

A raven replies that he and his kind have followed King Harold since they were hatched, then the bird proceeds to praise the generous king, who rewards his valorous warriors with gold and concubines. The raven also proclaims the bravery of the warriors, who are "happy" (in Hollander's translation) and "eager" (Finlay's translation) whenever a battle looms.

The Valkyrie notes that the ravens thrive on corpses, then presses the raven on the skills of Harold's warriors. The raven replies that the warriors eschew the protection of chain mail and instead wear wolfskins when charging into battle, where their shields and spear points will be covered by the blood of foes.[126]

But corpse-feasting ravens were more than just a readily observable fact of life for warring Vikings. Just as the Roman tribune Marcus Valerius Corvus quickly came to believe that the crow that landed on his helmet was a sign that the gods favored him in his impending battle, so too believed the ancient Norse. Various scholars note that several ancient texts state it was a good omen for a Viking warrior heading into battle to be followed by a raven.

---

124 Hollander, *Old Norse Poems*, 72.

125 Hollander, *Old Norse Poems*, 56.

126 Hollander, *Old Norse Poems*, 56. Also Finlay, *Fagrskinna*, 43–46.

No thought, apparently, was given to the possibility that maybe the corpse-lusting raven doesn't give a damn whether it's the warrior's foe or the warrior it is following who becomes the bird's "feeder."

FLIGHT OF THE RAVEN BANNERS

The ancient Norse were compelled to go beyond the mere telling of raven tales, beyond casting the birds in a large supporting role in their literature, and beyond passively taking note of raven omens. They also practiced Raven Magic, with an unknowing nod back to the Lascaux Cave artist-shaman and their depiction of that crow-man.

Looking for an edge in battle, the Vikings turned to augury—divination by signs or omens, particularly those involving the flight of birds. Well, sort of. In order to tap into the birds' preternatural nature and work practical magic, the Norsemen created visual representations of the corvids on raven banners that would fly on their longships and above their raiding forces as they advanced on land. The physical movements of the banners, or lack thereof, would portend what would befall the Norsemen in the coming battle.

The Welsh monk Asser, who served in the court of King Alfred the Great of England, wrote a biography of the monarch in 893 CE. The text includes an account of how Alfred and his army captured a raven banner from the invading Danes during a battle in 878 CE.

Joseph Stevenson (1806–1895), an English Catholic priest and translator of historical texts, includes the tale in his 1854 work titled *The Church Historians of England*, in the section "Asser's Annals of the Exploits of Alfred." The Danes laid siege to Alfred's stronghold, "but it did not turn out as they expected." Alfred's Christian army "rushed out upon the Pagans suddenly in the morning, and from the first cut down the greatest part of their enemies, with their king, allowing but few to escape to their ships. And there they obtained no small amount of booty, and among it a standard which they call Reafan."[127]

Asser writes that the banner was crafted by "daughters of Lodebroch,"[128] a Viking king whose exploits are chronicled in various medieval texts, although

---

127 Stevenson, *The Church Historians of England*, 458–59.
　　Reafan, or *Raven*, is likely a rendering from the Old Norse word *Hrafn*, which in Old English was rendered as Hræfn.

128 Lodebroch, which was also rendered as Lodbrok or Lothbrok, is a reference to Ragnar Lodebroch.

some historians doubt his actual existence. Others maintain if he did exist, the accounts of his exploits are legend rather than fact.

Asser continues, writing that the Danes "say that in every battle in which that flag was carried in front, if they were to obtain the victory, there appeared in the middle of it the figure of a live raven as it flies; but if they were doomed to suffer defeat, it would hang down without the slightest motion; and facts often proved the truth of this assertion."[129]

Scholar N. Lukman provides a more adamant—and intriguing—assessment of the power of the Lodbrok (Lodebroch) raven banner. Lukman quotes William Henry Stevenson's translation of the *Annals of St. Neots*, an ancient history of Britain up to the early tenth century, that states the raven banner's augury *"always proved true."*[130]

Any cursory first gleaning of this text reveals an obvious contradiction at play. If the ancient Norsemen believed in the efficacy and accuracy of their raven banners' prophetic power, why would they proceed into battle if the augury—a droop-winged raven—is portending doom? This seeming contradiction will be explored shortly.

The *Encomium Emmae Reginae*, the "Praise of Queen Emma," was written circa 1042 by a French-based monk in honor of the Normandy monarch. The text includes an account of a Danish force under Thorkell the Tall, also known as Thorkell the High, who invaded England in the early eleventh century while brandishing a peculiar raven banner. Thorkell's battle standard is detailed in a 1949 translation of the *Encomium* by British scholar Alistair Campbell (1907–1974).

The original chronicler begins by asserting the tale is true and that he will therefore include it in his history. Thorkell's "wonderfully strange" banner, we learn, is made of plain white silk and sports no image whatsoever—except in times of war, when a raven would appear "as if embroidered on it." If the Danes were near triumph in battle, the raven would appear with wings flapping and beak open. If defeat were imminent, the raven would appear to be subdued and slumping. Thorkell exhorts his soldiers into battle at Ashingdon in England, assuring them that the banner's restless raven is prophesying victory over the Anglo-Saxons and their leader Eadric. The raven's omen proves

---

129 Stevenson, *The Church Historians of England*, 458–59.

130 Lukman, "The Raven Banner and the Changing Ravens," 141; emphasis added.

true when Eadric, the *Encomium* relates, urges his men to flee at the height of the battle and "snatch our lives from imminent death."[131]

Thorkell's raven banner evidently served him much better than the carriers of the Lodebroch battle standard. Thorkell, who like Lodebroch was a historical figure whose exploits were subject to mythologizing, was a member of the Jomsvikings, an order of mercenaries.

Thorkell's further exploits are recounted in ancient texts, which sometimes contradict each other, until he disappears from the historical record in 1023. The last years of his life remain a mystery. Except for the *Encomium Emmae Reginae*, I could find no mention of Thorkell's miraculous white battle banner with the prophetic, reappearing-disappearing raven. Historians refer to Thorkell as "shrewd." We are left to ponder how much of his battle savvy he may have obtained by heeding the augury of his raven banner.

Turville-Petre cites another raven banner, although the exact interpretation of its name, Ravenlandeye, has been muddied within the historical record. Turville-Petre writes that Ravenlandeye is glossed as *"corvus terrae terror"* and that a thirteenth-century text relates that a mysterious old man gave the banner to Siward of Northumbria, who lived in the eleventh century, as he was about to fight a dragon.[132]

However, the translation of *Ravenlandeye* into Old English as "corvus terrae terror" (Raven, terror of the land) is in dispute. Both Lukman and William Henry Stevenson, in his 1904 translation of *Asser's Life of King Alfred, Together with the Annals of Saint Neots Erroneously Ascribed to Asser*,[133] trace that raven interpretation to a medieval English monk named William, who lived at the appropriately named Crowland Abbey, also known as Croyland Abbey.[134] But I could not ascertain whether Lukman and Stevenson are referring to William of Ramsey (fl. 1219) or William of Crowland, Abbot of Ramsey and later of Cluny, who died in 1179. And neither Lukman nor Stevenson comment upon the accuracy of the "Raven, terror of the land" translation.

However, a 1908–09 publication by the Society for Northern Research directly addresses the issue: The translation of Ravenlandeye as "corvus terrae

131 Campbell, *Encomium Emmae Reginae*, 25–27.

132 Turville-Petre, *Myth and Religion of the North*, 59–60.

133 Stevenson, William Henry, ed. *Asser's Life of King Alfred*, 267.

134 Lukman, "The Raven Banner and the Changing Ravens," 148.

terror" is a misunderstanding, likely a confusion with Norwegian King Harald Harthrathe's banner known as Landeytha, meaning "that which lays waste the land."[135]

Still, the fact that some medieval English monk named William would mis-translate *Ravenlandeye* as "corvus terrae terror" speaks volumes. Accounts of the marauding Vikings and their eerie connection to ravens and their supernat-ural powers, as evidenced in those raven banners, had obviously infiltrated that monk's mind and heart—and filled him with dread.

Another famous raven banner, borne by the fighting men of the Norse-man Sigurd of Orkney, was imbued with its own grim peculiarity—it would bring death to whoever carried it but victory in battle to the warrior behind the standard. Such was the case, over and over, at the historically documented Battle of Clontarf in 1014 near Dublin, in which an army of some 7,000 war-riors led by Brian Boru, High King of Ireland, defeated an alliance of Irish and Norse forces, estimated between 6,500 and 7,000 strong, led by Sigtrygg (also rendered as Sitric) Silkbeard, King of Dublin; Máel Mórda mac Murchada, King of Leinster; and the Vikings Sigurd of Orkney and Brodir of Mann.

---

135 Society for Northern Research, *Saga-Book of the Viking Club*, 233.

Chapter 13

LESSONS: THE WELTANSCHAUUNG OF THE NORSE

The Viking chronicles are inundated with blood, battle, doom, death, and carrion-lusting ravens. Warriors march into battle even though their Raven Magic—their drooping raven banners—may have prophesied their own blood will be shed. What is going on with these gore-obsessed ancient Norsemen and these equally grisly ravens?

Scholars note the chroniclers of the Vikings' exploits were merely reflecting the brutal realities of the age, much as twenty-first-century media—not just newscasts but also contemporary literature, film, and television—reflect modern society. Yes, those ancient bards poetically hyped their accounts with references to "Hugin's sea" and "raven-feeders," and yes, there was more to Scandinavian life back then than warfare and raiding. But, in their unflinching portrayal of grim subject matter, the *Eddas*, skaldic poetry, and other writings are not so different from the motto heard, for better and for worse, in modern newspaper and broadcast newsrooms: "If it bleeds, it leads." That motto, by extension, bleeds into Hollywood studio office suites, where corpse-strewn, bullet-and-bomb-riddled films—little more than mayhem fests—are greenlighted ad nauseam … and always seem to find an audience.

But there is a deeper and—at first glance—more disturbing dynamic at play in the ancient Norse texts than the mere recording and "reporting," however poetically rendered, of life as it was lived in those times.

In "Song of the Raven," after the corvid states King Harold will reward his valiant warriors with wealth, gold, swords, and the company of females, he follows with a proclamation that may be quite stunning to contemporary readers—even those who are familiar with Norse mythology. Quoth the raven in "Hrafnsmál": "Most happy are they [Viking warriors] when there is hope for battle."[136]

Happy, of course, because receiving the Valkyrs' kiss of death in battle may be a ticket straight to Valhalla, where the chosen dead warriors are resurrected to carouse and feast with Odin—at least until that nasty business of Ragnarok arrives.

Lest we moderns tend to romanticize such scenarios, ask any World War II or Vietnam veteran if they were "happy" to head into battle.

Furthermore, does the religious/cosmological-derived mindset of the Vikings, as portrayed in the ancient texts, sound familiar? The headlines from late twentieth-century and early twenty-first-century life say yes. We live in a time when religious fanatics readily spill blood and commit heart-numbing, terrorist atrocities because their worldview tells them it will please their god and provide them with a ticket to paradise.

How does the cosmology of the blood-lusting ancient Norse differ? The answer, of course, is found in an examination of historical forces that resist superficial comparisons between different eras.

From around 800 to 1100 CE, the Vikings ventured forth from their native Scandinavia to raid and pillage throughout western Europe. Their bards immortalized their exploits, their gods, and their mortal heroes—and those tales would be written down centuries later by their Christianized descendants.

Sir George Webbe Dasent describes the Viking weltanschauung, or worldview, in the introduction to his 1861 work *The Story of Burnt Njal*, his translation of the thirteenth-century Icelandic tale also known as *Njal's Saga*, which relates events between 960 and 1020 CE:

> ...as the creed of the race was one that adored the Great Father as the God of Battles...any appeal to arms was looked upon as an appeal to God. Victory was indeed the sign of a rightful cause...but he that lost it, if he fell bravely and like a man...went by the very manner of his death to a better place. The Father of the Slain wanted him, and he was welcomed by the Valkyries, by Odin's

---

136 Hollander, *Old Norse Poems*, 56.

corse-choosers [corpse-choosers], to the festive board in Valhalla. In every point of view, therefore, war and battle were a holy thing.[137]

Crawford also delves into the ancient Norse weltanschauung. Given the scarcity of natural resources and farmland at hand, the Vikings' raids on other lands, for food and treasure, "must have seemed no more ethically problematic than the killing of an animal for its flesh and hide." Thus did bellicose aggression, which helped assure survival, became a virtue in both the Norse and their gods. But the Vikings were not amoral. Rather, honor was paramount, and honor was gained through courage in battle and through a work ethic that ensured the protection and survival of one's family and clan—even if achieved through aggression and violence.[138]

Guerber notes, in her introduction to *Myths of the Norsemen from the Eddas and Sagas*, that the "most distinctive traits of this [Northern] mythology are a peculiar grim humour, to be found in the religion of no other race, and a dark thread of tragedy which runs throughout the whole woof.[139]

The belief that the chosen dead would receive a ride to Valhalla from a beautiful Valkyr may have been the only soul succor Viking warriors had to buttress themselves against the brutalities of their everyday lives.

But how and why did ravens come to play such a prominent role in the lives, legends, and mythology of the ancient Norse? How did ravens become so inexorably entwined in accounts of the brutality and bloodshed—and yes, the triumphs and heroism too—of the Viking Age? Yes, the Scandinavians readily observed, as did other cultures, that corvids are carrion feeders—ones that made no bother to distinguish between the corpses of humans, canines, other birds, or other creatures.

But the Norse-raven symbiosis goes deeper. The answer can be found in the Norse people's keenly perspicacious naming of Odin's ravens: Hugin (Thought) and Munin (Memory). The ancient Scandinavians' intuited belief that ravens possessed some sort of supernatural connection to their gods was no haphazard happenstance. As we saw in the chapter "Canny Corvids," it is now documented that crows and ravens indeed possess a kind of thought and memory

---

137 Dasent, *The Story of Burnt Njal*, xxvii–xxviii.

138 Crawford, *The Poetic Edda*, ix–x.

139 Guerber, *Myths of the Norsemen from the Eddas and Sagas*, xii.

far beyond that of most animals. The ancient Norse didn't have to be necessarily astute amateur naturalists, although they obviously were, in order to see that, yes, these birds *think*. They possess a cleverness and intelligence and behave accordingly. They also possess memory—to the point of recognizing human faces again and again. As John Marzluff's astonishing real-world experiments with crows demonstrated, crows remember and put their memory to practical use, to the point of communicating their assessments of "good human" or "bad human" to their fellow crows that did not have a direct encounter with the actions of any one person.

To grasp how astonishing this realization must have been for the ancient Scandinavians, recall the first time you witnessed a wild animal performing amazing feats on, say, the TV show *Wild Kingdom* back in the 1960s, or more recently in the BBC's extraordinary *Planet Earth* series, or in any number of National Geographic specials. Or perhaps you have been fortunate enough to witness such mind-blowing animal activity directly in the wild. That said, remember that the corvids, along with the apes and dolphins, possess capacities far beyond most creatures.

It bears repeating here: Corvids thrive on every continent except Antarctica. Their ubiquity means they are the most intelligent creature that the vast majority of humans will encounter, whether in the wild or in an urban setting.

As I wrote this sitting on the back patio of my new woods-side hermitage in east-central Florida, the new crow couple I named Boga and Baca perched patiently in a slash pine at the edge of my yard, eyeing the crackers I spread on my lawn for them. In less than a week since their first appearance, they learned to return almost every morning for a brunch snack at my home. Meanwhile, Carolina wrens and a male and female cardinal flitted mindlessly about my backyard—no doubt their instincts were guiding them as they forage for food, but they made no play for the crackers that were readily within their grasp. A new squirrel visitor I named Acro (for his acrobatic leaps among the slash pines of the woods behind my home) boldly ventured deep into my yard and snatched a cracker while Boga and Baca looked on. Like the other squirrels, Acro seemed clueless to the fact that the human in his midst—me—could pose a threat to his life.

But the crow couple suspected otherwise. They proceeded with caution and continue to do so each day whenever I am nearby. When I venture into my yard with my camera to photograph them, they will retreat to the higher branches in the slash pines, all the while cawing communiqués to crows elsewhere in my neighborhood or the deep woods behind me. When I retreat inside my home, Boga and Baca will finally make their play for their brunch, alighting on my lawn and snatching up a cracker or two. "You must earn our trust," they seem to be telling me.

Corvids are clever. They exhibit agency. They possess thought. They possess memory. The ancient Norse, along with other cultures down through the millennia, witnessed and were aware of this. Some long-ago Norse person spied a raven or two eyeing the human in their midst, and that person was struck by these birds' remarkable, extraordinary behaviors. Thus this observant human felt/intuited/believed/knew that these ravens must be supernaturally endowed creatures to possess such capabilities that far exceed most animals in this mundane earthly realm, in this abode of humankind that the Norse called Midgard: "Look how these birds move about! Look how they behave! They have hugin (thought)! They have munin (memory)! These birds must have an exalted place beside Odin, our All-Father. They are Hugin. They are Munin."

This is the lesson of Raven from the weltanschauung of the ancient Norse. Since the Industrial Revolution, if not before, the vast majority of humans have come to see the earth and her creatures, climates, and landscapes as the adversary—as forces to be subdued, tamed, harnessed, and held dominion over in the name of "progress."

But the ancient Scandinavians, even as they battled the harsh elements of their homelands and raided neighboring cultures to pillage their resources, also realized that, in their struggles to survive, the earth—Midgard—is populated with nonhuman allies. Those allies will aid humans who are aware, dedicated, savvy, and respectful enough to align themselves with their energies.

Ravens are creatures who not only perched on the shoulders of Odin the All-Father, the Raven God, and aided him. Akin to some sort of avian Prometheus, ravens also bequeath their special gifts to humankind.

Lesson: Gaia provides allies!

Chapter 14

GRIMOIRE: YOUR RAVEN BANNER

"Why should I create a raven banner?" you say. "I'm not about to board a Viking longship to raid and pillage a foreign land!"

Even if your Pagan path is not that of Heathenism or Asatru, if you create a hands-on raven banner, you will be palpably channeling the spirit of that long-ago Norse-raven connection.

Also, once again, you will have a magical tool that is more spirit-filled and potent for having forged it yourself.

And consider this: Symbol-rich banners, heraldic standards, pennons, and gonfalons, with their lions rampant and fleur-de-lys, have been used in quasi-magical ways for centuries. The Hermetic Order of the Golden Dawn, that magical society founded in London in 1887, used colorful, geometric-emblazoned banners in a specific, ritualistic manner. Yet, despite that rich history, creating a raven banner will give you a magical object that is uncommon among today's magicians, Witches, and Pagans.

Use your raven banner as a heraldic standard. Displayed outside near your front door, in your home, on your back patio, in your backyard, or on your Crow-Raven Spirit Tree, your banner will proclaim "Raven (or Crow) Spirit resides here."

Also, akin to the ancient Vikings, your banner can serve as a tool of divination—what I call incidental augury (discussed elsewhere in this chapter).

WHAT YOU WILL NEED

- Small piece (two-foot square or so) of a coarse earth-toned or white fabric, such as natural cotton duck canvas, jarfar burlap, or aida cloth (traditionally used for cross-stitch embroidery)—available at craft stores. Alternately, you may use a less-stiff fabric, which will be more sensitive to wind currents and make for a livelier banner.
- Two black, soft-tipped (felt-tipped) permanent markers—one with a broad point and one with a narrow-to-medium point—plus a soft-lead pencil
- A sheet of poster board (to create a template) and typing paper (to practice your drawing skills, but only if you feel so compelled)
- A wooden dowel rod, 24–36 inches long and ¼ inch or ½ inch in diameter—available at craft and home supply stores
- Twine, sisal rope, or any sort of cord, decorative or not, about ⅛-inch to ¼-inch thick
- Scissors

BACKGROUND

History tells us that the Norsemen's raven banners were an instrument of war—a magic-infused instrument that they—well, that Ragnar Lothbrok's daughters and Sigurd of Orkney's mother, Audna—created to prophecy the Vikings' success in upcoming battles and to inspire them as they unsheathed their swords and marched toward their foes. Though not specifically conceived as an amulet-like object, their raven banners, whenever the wings of the corvid appeared to be flapping, insured success in battle, and therefore the Vikings, in some manner, felt favored at such times by wyrd—fate—and likely they felt protected by Odin and their other gods.

Create a raven banner, and of course, it need not be an instrument of war or aggression. Neither must it actually be a raven banner. Craft a crow banner, and it will be an instrument of magic and yet another way to invoke and channel Crow Spirit, a way to time-trip you back to the deep, distant past to that Lascaux Cave artist who felt compelled to paint the world's first depiction of Crow Magic.

Just like words, visual art is magic, too. Throughout my thirty years as a newspaper arts and entertainment writer, I was privileged to interview many creators, including painters, sculptors, and multimedia artists, both Pagan and not, and so I have ventured inside their psyches and have been spellbound by their creations. And I have felt a ritualistic energy arise each and every time I have created one of my Mr. Crow artworks via my process that combines photography and digital art.

I am no traditional pen-brush-paper artist, but I still possess and marvel at the first Cernunnos drawing I ever created. I was emerging upon my Pagan path back in the early 1990s, and working at the newspaper in Daytona Beach, Florida. At my desk I took a scratch pad and a red pen, and I sketched a stick figure drawing of the antlered god of the ancient Celts. Yes, it is a crude depiction, yet all these decades later I am still amazed by the spirit and kinetic energy it exudes. Though I was only vaguely aware of it at the time, I was channeling Cernunnos at that very moment.

Art Is Magic

My many artist friends—some Pagan, some not, some otherwise metaphysically inclined, some not—have all conjured works that are veritable portals to higher consciousness and/or divinity.

As artist and Modern Traditional Witch Laura Tempest Zakroff notes:

> I use the term *visual alchemy* to succinctly describe where art and magic meet. One way to define visual alchemy is that it is the magic of what we can see combined with the powers of what we can do. But what is sight? Sight is more than what we perceive with our eyes; it's what our brain chooses to relate to us, the signals of a multitude of senses sharing information, and the capacity for imagination.... Alchemy at its core is the study and application of the magical processes of transformation and creation, imbued with spirit.... Visual alchemy is the process of transforming thought (conscious or unconscious) into a more tangible experience.[140]

---

140 Zakroff, *Visual Alchemy*, 10.

"Creative flow is its own transcendent state," says artist and Pagan Paul B. Rucker, who, with Helga Hedgewalker, a Gardnerian high priestess and Witch, founded the Third Offering Art Gallery, an art show presented in conjunction with the annual Paganicon conference held in the Minneapolis area.[141]

"Making art can be a form of deep meditation," says Rucker, who uses the term *visionary artist* to describe himself.

> Sometimes the art-making trance becomes like lucid dreaming while awake. Mircea Eliade, the scholar of religions, described the shaman's journey as a "round." The shaman goes from "here," the ordinary world, to "there," the Spirit World or the Other World, in order to receive a teaching, a vision, have a profound experience of a heightened reality. To complete the round, the shaman must return with a medicine, a teaching, or something that will benefit the community. This requires a technique "of ecstasy" as he called it. It's not so hard to go to the Other World—people can take drugs or have altered consciousness in a number of ways. What's much harder is bringing something back that can be shared.[142]

His need to make art, Rucker says, is "my method of acquiring a 'technique of ecstasy' so that the bits of sacred fire from the visionary plane could be held in something that others could engage with here, in this world."[143]

For Hedgewalker, who attended art school at the renowned Pratt Institute in Brooklyn and earned a BFA in visual communications, "the art I do outside of my day job is absolutely a magical act for me.... Usually I do my best work in a trance-state, and when I can achieve that flow, I believe the Gods make themselves known and I am merely a channel for them."[144]

As for visionary art becoming a magical act for viewers—"Good Gods, I hope so!" says Hedgewalker, whose paintings were featured in Llewellyn's 1997 Astrological Calendar. "I have several paintings in my house where deities in-dwell in them," she says. "Their eyes follow me as I walk through the room.

---

141 de Yampert, "Pagan Artists Present Third Offering at Paganicon."

142 de Yampert, "Pagan Artists Present Third Offering at Paganicon."

143 de Yampert, "Pagan Artists Present Third Offering at Paganicon."

144 de Yampert, "Pagan Artists Present Third Offering at Paganicon."

The art becomes gateways to their spiritual realm if the viewer is open to the experience."[145]

Rucker mentions his interpretation of Melek Ta'us, the Peacock Angel, "a tutelary divinity of primary importance for the Yezidi of Syria, and for the Feri culture / current of witchcraft." His image went viral on the Internet, and responses to the painting led him to believe that people see it as "a true and authentic portal to the Peacock Angel."[146]

Rucker says that "one essential purpose of Pagan art" is to "bring the wild magic of the Otherworld into this one," to "properly prepare the ground for a God or Goddess to be *really* present."[147]

Crafting a corvid banner will likewise summon the "wild magic" of Crow-Raven Spirit into this world.

PREPARATION

To create a raven-crow banner, first determine your focus—the phrase "set your intention" is too constricting to apply here. Whether you desire your banner to primarily be an instrument of incidental augury or a heraldic flag is a practical matter as well as a magical-metaphysical one, and it will determine the type of material you use. A coarse, stiff material, such as natural cotton, duck canvas, or aida cloth, will display boldly and steadily when hung from a horizontal wooden pole and will be less susceptible to breezes, thus making your raven or crow emanate strength and dominion. A lighter, fluffier material akin to a bedsheet will lead your raven or crow to flutter and flap its wings more readily in the wind, making for a livelier, kinetic presence. If you desire to go "full Viking" and employ your banner for divination (even if you do not plan to charge into battle anytime soon!), choose a lighter fabric. (See the "Using Your Banner for Augury" section later in this chapter.)

However, know that you are not making an either-or choice between heraldic banner and augury instrument—your banner inevitably will function as both. Rather, your choice of material is a reminder that the mundane and the magical are inevitably intertwined. If you practice candle magic, your

---

145 de Yampert, "Pagan Artists Present Third Offering at Paganicon."
146 de Yampert, "Pagan Artists Present Third Offering at Paganicon."
147 de Yampert, "Pagan Artists Present Third Offering at Paganicon."

choice of candle will affect your process. If you read tarot cards, the artwork and overall aesthetics of the deck you use will come into play, however technically expert its magical imagery may have been rendered.

Choose two felt-tipped, black permanent markers, one with a broad point and one with a narrow-to-medium point, which are available at any craft store. If your banner will be outdoors, be sure to choose a weatherproof-waterproof ink.

Unleash Your Muse

There is one tip and one tip only for tapping into the magic of visual art: just do it!

You certainly were an artist in kindergarten and throughout your childhood, and there is no reason to believe an inner artist no longer resides within you. Anthropologists are quite certain the Lascaux Cave artist had no formal lessons.

Silence your inner critic and your inner naysayer, take up a pen or paint brush, invoke your goddess or god if you choose, and allow your muse—yes, you have one—to frolic upon paper.

You are not trying to be the next van Gogh, Picasso, or Georgia O'Keeffe. You are seeking, once again, to open the portal between the mundane realms and the Other Realms and see what-who walks through. Do not throw away your first attempts, no matter how much they may seem crude or childish—adhere them to the pages of your magical journal. I am grateful I kept my first rustic stick figure Cernunnos that I sketched all those years ago. Only much later did I realize that it was—and still is—a significant marker of my then-nascent Pagan path, and its magical mojo has increased significantly over time.

ACTIONS

Before you take up your marker, speak aloud a simple and spontaneous—not composed—invocation of your muse to awaken her, respect her, and request her inspiration. Create your own invocation, but it may resemble this:

> Crow Spirit, come dance with my muse—a pas de deux of flesh, feathers, blood, spirit, and bone made manifest at this moment, this place upon Gaia's breast. Blessed be.

A Note about Process

You may desire to be spontaneous in your creation of your crow or raven image or, like me, you may choose to be more deliberate, or you may elect to strike some balance between the two approaches. Keep in mind that spontaneous creation possesses its own potent and peculiar magic. While the rational-pragmatic part of your brain (science no longer sees brain function as a right-left divide) is great at taking math tests, it tends to overanalyze and drain the lifeblood out of creative processes. The mystical-intuitive part of your brain, which is your gateway to Spirit, the Dream-time, the Other Realms, and non-ordinary realities, will bypass your naysaying, mundane-oriented brain and allow you to conjure, say, a two-headed purple raven.

Many rock music artists have confessed in interviews that, after recording numerous takes of a song in the studio, they revisited the very first take and realized it possessed a special, potent magic and so that track was the one that went onto the album. Your very first crow or raven may be your most magical creation.

Get the Ink Flowing

If you desire to rehearse, use the pages of your magical diary (revisit the chapter "Keep a Magical Journal") to sketch ideas, thus spicing its contents until it more resembles a Book of Shadows. Again, see my website mistercrowart.com for inspiration. The images of all of my crows—with heads titled this way or that, wings aflutter, and so on—are how my camera captured them in nature. I never digitally alter the shapes of the crows themselves.

After entering drawings into your Book of Shadows, sketch raven or crow images on typing paper, the better to get acclimated to drawing bigger images. Or alternately, if you are confident, proceed straight to drawing an outline of your crow or raven on your poster board. This will serve as a template for working on your cloth, so make your poster-board image the size you want your corvid to be on your finished banner.

Cut out your poster-board image, then find a suitable workstation (your dining table, perhaps) where you will begin applying ink to your cloth. Be aware that, depending on your choice of cloth, ink will likely stain through, so use some sort of drop cloth beneath your banner material. Also, be aware that while an ink marker may give you more control, even its ink may bleed when applied to cloth, and it may do so on some fabrics more than others. That is, your graceful, disciplined, black-line drawing of a raven's shoulder may seep into and across your fabric so that it looks like a Rorschach ink blot.

For my banner, I used a 15-by-18-inch piece of sandy beige fabric known as aida cloth, which is normally used for cross-stitch. It looks rustic, as if it could have been cut from a potato sack used by Vikings a millennium ago.

Cut your cloth to the size you desire, place your template upon it, and use a soft-lead pencil to faintly trace the outline of your corvid image. Use the permanent marker with a narrow-to-medium point to trace over the penciled image. Then use the broad-tipped marker to flesh out the lines. In all cases, don't feel that you have to use one continuous stroke.

After I added a small curved mark to indicate the eye on my crow's profile, I was so enamored by the way my sketch's minimalist nature resembled those Zen drawings that I declared it complete. In the realm of unintended consequences, I discovered that my marker's ink had seeped through the cloth just enough so that I serendipitously had a pleasing mirror image on the backside—one that required only a bit of tracing so that I had a two-sided banner.

Preparing Your Banner for Hanging

After your image has dried, fold your cloth down 1½ inches from its top, then carefully use the joint of your open scissors to cut a ¼-inch slit that's an inch away from each side of your banner. Unfold your banner and you will now have a ½-inch slit near each top corner.

Using a dowel that's just a few inches longer than the width of your banner, cut a piece of twine or sisal rope (or any type of rope or somewhat thick cord) so that's it's approximately 18 inches longer than the dowel. Thread one end of the twine through one corner of your banner and tie the twine to the dowel, then do so with the other end.

Your raven-crow banner is now ready to hang.

Raven Banner

GOING FORWARD

Place your banner around your home where energy is palpably present and/or in motion, whether it's the energy of Gaia, the energy of the elements, or even the energy and auras of people.

You may choose to post your banner in your backyard or any place near where crows or ravens visit. Thus will the energies of Gaia—sun, breeze, the comings and goings of corvids and squirrels and insects—be reciprocal with the energies of your crow-raven banner. They will nurture and charge each other as well as the surrounding spaces. That's good mojo.

Hanging your banner from a shepherd's crook plant hanger, available at home and garden stores, is fine but upon your Crow-Raven Spirit Tree, or any living tree, is better.

If you place your banner near a specific spot where corvids routinely congregate, they *will notice*—and they may be cautious or even skittish about approaching too close to your flag. This happened when I drooped my crow banner for a time over a branch in my Crow Spirit Tree. My goal was to have my crows "consecrate" it by landing on it. That happened, but only after several hours of wary behavior.

If you notice your corvids acting skittish around your banner, simply move it to another place. Mine currently hangs in an ornamental tree about twenty feet from my Crow Spirit Tree.

Remember, placing your banner outdoors, exposed to rain, sunlight, and animal behaviors, will weather it. That's Gaia's way, after all. You can always refresh it.

Another optimal place is near your front door—the portal to your hermitage, whether you hang it on or above the door on the outside or upon some sort of post or vertical column within or beside your entryway. A magical banner—or talisman or amulet—by your front door has the added advantage of wind or air currents carrying their mojo into your home each and every time the door-portal is opened.

You also may desire to place your banner wherever else Gaian energy manifests in your home: near a window where the breeze infuses your house with fresh air or the rising sun infuses your house with light and warmth or near potted plants on your porch or balcony—any place where something flourishes and grows, whether it is light, warmth, or greenery.

Using Your Banner for Augury

As an instrument of augury / divination, your banner will channel Crow-Raven Spirit as you interpret its movements much like the ancient Norse did—only, one hopes, you won't have a call to hoist your banner as you head into some battle, at least not a literal one.

Naturally, for augury your banner will need to be hoisted in an open-air environment where crows or ravens and the winds are prone to frolic. That is, where Gaia and corvids can either actively or passively interact with—and activate—the Crow-Raven Magic you have set about manifesting.

Simple Augury Method

Your raven-crow banner can be used for a basic augury technique. Face your raven-crow banner and posit a yes-or-no question: Should I start a new work project before I finish my current one? Should I attempt to hike that difficult deep-woods trail this weekend?

Then, over some span of time you have chosen, you can wait to interpret some sort of movement, or perhaps there will be no movement at all. As with the marauding Vikings, a vigorously flapping raven or crow upon your banner is a favorable sign. Conversely, a drooping bird is a sign to proceed with caution or to begin a more thorough examination of the ramifications of the decision or crossroads you face.

Keep in mind that prophetic signs, auguries, omens, and divinatory readings rarely manifest with black-and-white clarity. Only rarely are you likely to encounter a sign so potent that it seems like a cosmic grand conjunction and the gods and goddesses are pimp-slapping you and yelling, "Pay attention! This is the way it's going to be!" However, an inert banner is not necessarily an omen of ill will—rather, it likely is a message of "Slow down. Deliberate upon this matter. Search for other perspectives." Most often, any divination you reap will *tend* toward one outcome or another, and the more you practice the divinatory arts, the more your experiences—both your reading of the signs and your observations of how they subsequently may have manifested in your life—will hone your craft and intuition. Yes, divination is an art, not a science.

Do not undertake any divination flippantly, not even a simple, quick, non-taxing method, such as checking how vigorously the wind blows your crow-raven banner's wings. By resorting to any divinatory art, you are telling yourself that the matter at hand is important to you and deserves deeper examination and contemplation, even if it's not seismically life changing. Save your prophecy work for matters that matter.

Banner divination works best with what I call incidental augury, or augury that operates just like any sign or omen one may encounter unexpectedly in the wild—or the not-so-wild natural world of, say, a local park or your backyard. This applies whether the omen arrives via aeromancy (interpreting the shapes of clouds or assessing atmospheric phenomena), dendromancy (discerning signs in plants, especially oak trees and mistletoe), or interpreting the appearance and behaviors of snakes, frogs, or other animals including, of course, corvids.

You come across an anomalous matter in nature—a wild animal skull perched beneath a peculiarly shaped oak tree branch, perhaps—and you wonder, "Is this a sign?" Likewise, you look in your backyard one day to see your banner flapping insanely and you wonder, "Is my raven trying to tell me something?"

With incidental augury, you notice a sign—in this case your banner is flying or fluttering robustly—and you back-engineer your thinking in order to relate the sign to what has been recently occupying your consciousness or subconscious; perform an inventory of any pivotal matter you have contemplated in the past few hours or so, but certainly search no further back than that same day. Crow-Raven Spirit, as manifested in that sudden, vigorous flapping of your banner, may be giving you an affirmation or a sign to proceed.

Perhaps you are facing no crossroads. Perhaps you have not contemplated any truly pivotal matters recently. Your experiences with your crow-raven banner will mirror your encounters with other omens, or potential omens, from Gaia. To return to that animal skull spotted beneath a tree that is sacred to Druids, perhaps its possible import will tap dance into your mind and heart immediately, and you will experience that delicious ecstasy that tells you the veil has been parted and Spirit is communicating and communing with you. Or perhaps you may shrug and think, "What am I to make of this?" Again, divination and reading omens is an art, not a science. No need to force an augury or divinatory encounter into being.

But don't be surprised if your raven-crow banner comes alive with sudden, synchronistic flapping at the very moment you are contemplating some crossroad in your life.

Chapter 15

LORE: ANCIENT CELTIC BATTLE CROWS AND RAVEN HELMETS

As I gazed at the statue of the dead Cuchulainn, the ancient, mythic Irish warrior, in the General Post Office in Dublin during my first visit to Ireland in June 1995, I was in the nascent days of my Pagan path. Drawn to the Emerald Isle by my love of the poet William Butler Yeats, Irish "trad" folk music, and the rock band U2, I was only subconsciously aware that I was on a quest to connect to my Irish heritage.

I was only faintly cognizant of the legends of Cuchulainn—the Hound of Culann whose battle frenzy would warp his face and body into fearsome contortions that terrified his foes almost as much as his sword and spear. That I considered Cuchulainn to be more or less an Irish version of Conan the Barbarian reveals my ignorance of Irish mythology at that time. (However, I was comforted somewhat to later discover that archaeologist and Celticist Miranda Green calls Cuchulainn "the arch-destroyer, a fighting machine equivalent to the 'Terminator' of modern film."[148])

But I was intrigued just as much by the statue's spread-winged crow, perched triumphantly on Cuchulainn's shoulder. The eye-catching corvid, which different reliable sources identify as a crow or a raven, forms the highest point of the statute. The crow's majestic prominence, amped considerably by its aggressive, defiant pose, is apparent to any onlooker.

I had seen plenty of crows back home in the States—the birds were part of the mundane background fabric of daily life even though I lived in the heart of Daytona Beach, Florida, at the time.

---

148 Green, *Celtic Goddesses*, 45.

It didn't take a genius or deep intuition to realize this bronze crow in the heart of Dublin was different. Unbeknownst to me at the time, I had encountered the Morrigan—the shape-shifting Irish-Celtic battle goddess. For the first time in my life, I had palpably encountered Crow Magic face-to-face.

The ancient Norse had their ravens who talked to Valkyries; ravens who haunted their battlefields; ravens who graced their magical, combat-tested war banners; and their ravens Hugin and Munin, who perched on the shoulders of their raven god, Odin. Native Americans have long told tales of Raven, a shape-shifting trickster who can steal the sun and stars and make his poop and piss talk, along with his multitude of other supernatural shenanigans (see chapter 20, "Raven's Trickery"). Yet Raven nevertheless is not seen as a god by North America's Indigenous peoples.

The myths of the ancient Irish Celts, however—their tales of their goddesses, gods, and fighting men and women—are even more infested by the presence of ravens and crows. Unlike the Norse and Native Americans, the ancient Celts had war goddesses that would shape-shift into a crow or raven, leading British archaeologist and Celticist Anne Ross to label them as "the Celtic raven-goddesses." These raven-goddesses frequently exerted "sinister, oblique influence" upon the warring Celtic tribes.[149]

Those Celtic tribes consisted of an early Indo-European people who, from the second millennium BCE to the first century BCE, spread over much of Europe. These groups eventually settled in the British Isles (including Ireland) and northern Spain and ranged as far east as the Black Sea. "Linguistically they survive in the modern Celtic speakers of Ireland, Highland Scotland, the Isle of Man, Wales and Brittany."[150]

Many Celtophiles and scholars note these raven-goddesses—Badb, Macha, and the Morrigan—may be aspects of a triple goddess who most often are referred to collectively as the Morrigan. However, Ross, the prolific British archaeologist and Celticist Miranda Green, and other scholars note that Celtic mythology actually boasts four of the supernatural entities variously known as war goddesses, battle goddesses, or battle furies (Green uses all three of these latter terms in the space of two sentences in her *Celtic Goddesses*.)[151] This fear-

---

149 Ross, *Pagan Celtic Britain*, 313.

150 Editors of Encyclopaedia Britannica, "Celt."

151 Green, *Celtic Goddesses*, 41.

some foursome includes Nemain as well as the aforementioned trio of Badb, Macha, and the Morrigan.

Irish mythology, of course, sprang from an oral tradition, while surviving manuscript sources for the most significant tales date from the late eleventh century to the early fifteenth century and were mostly written down by—you guessed it—Christian monks. By the tenth century, the language of the land had evolved from what linguistic scholars call Old Irish to Middle Irish. Early Modern Irish, also called Classical Irish, was spoken and written from the thirteen to the eighteenth centuries, which is when the language transmuted into Modern Irish.

Thus the names of goddesses, gods, kings, queens, warriors, places, supernatural beings, such as the fairy folk (the *aos sidhe*), and concepts such as the otherworld (Tír na nÓg, the Land of Youth) vary in spelling when transliterated by scholars from Old Irish and Classical Irish into English. That said, modern readers can usually understand that, say, the Morrigan, Morrígu, and even the Modern Irish rendering of Mór-Ríoghain all refer to the same war goddess who had a love-hate relationship with the warrior Cuchulainn. I will use a single preferred spelling for each being, place, concept, or tale discussed—one that seems to be the most common usage among sources I have consulted. The exception is that I retain the spelling used by any one scholar in direct quotes from their writings.

More to the subject at hand—crows and ravens—the ancient Irish tales vacillate between the two corvids when referring to the same story or incident within a saga, depending on the source text and the translator. So it is that Green, when discussing "Cu Chulainn's death,"[152] cites both corvids: "the Morrigan … or the Badbh perched on his shoulder in the form of a crow or raven."[153] Ross, in at least one mention, calls the Morrigan a "crow-raven goddess."[154] Both corvids appear in the ancient, pre-Christian Irish-Celtic myths, including the variant tales of the Tuatha Dé Danann, "the people of the goddess Anu or Danu, a mother goddess and mother of the gods."[155]

---

152 Green's spelling of the warrior's name is a common variant.

153 Green, *Celtic Goddesses*, 45.

154 Ross, *Pagan Celtic Britain*, 314.

155 Smyth, *A Guide to Irish Mythology*, 175.

I will defer to the corvid species employed by whatever scholar is being consulted at hand—thus that may be a crow or a raven that lit upon the dead Cuchulainn.

Battle Goddesses

In discussing Badb, Macha, Nemain, and the Morrigan, Ross notes that *Morrigan* is seemingly an amorphous term that could refer to any of those entities.[156] Scholars note that *Badb* is Irish for "crow," and in the *Tochmarc Emire* (The Wooing of Emer), one of the stories in the Ulster Cycle of Irish mythology, the Morrigan is described as "an badb catha," the "battle-crow." The *Sanas Cormaic*—Irish for "Cormac's Narrative" or "Cormac's Glossary"—is a tenth-century encyclopedic dictionary of more than 1,400 Irish words, including the entry that *Macha* means "crow." Cormac also mentions that Macha possesses a mast composed of—yikes!—slaughtered heads, the inference being the heads came from warriors slain in battle.

Nemain is commonly translated as "frenzy," meaning the frenzied chaos and terror of war, while *Morrigan* has been translated as "great queen," "phantom queen," or even, Ross says, "queen of demons."[157]

However, Irish scholar W. M. Hennessy (1829–1889) sees *Badb*, not *Morrigu*, as the collective term for the entities that lord over battle. He interprets Neman, Macha, and Morrigu as separate, distinct entities, while referring to them as the "so-called sisters of the Badb." He compares Neman to Eros, given that she "confounded her victims with madness." Macha "reveled" amidst the carnage of battle. Morrigu "incited" warriors "to deeds of valour, or planned strife and battle."[158]

In a combination of etymology, biology, and mythology rare among nineteenth-century Celticists—especially that biology part of the equation—Hennessy also addresses the battle furies in "The Ancient Irish Goddess of War," a lecture he gave to the Royal Irish Academy in January 1869. That talk is an expanded and variant version of Hennessy's essay "On the Goddess of War of the Ancient Irish."

Hennessy says:

---

156 Ross, *Pagan Celtic Britain*, 313.

157 Ross, *Pagan Celtic Britain*, 313.

158 Hennessy, "On the Goddess of War of the Ancient Irish," 423.

bodb or *badb* (pron. *bov* or *bav*) [is a term] originally signifying rage, fury, or violence and ultimately implying a witch, fairy, or goddess, represented by the bird known as the scare-crow, scald-crow, or royston-crow, not the raven as M. Pictet seems to think.... The ancient tracts, romances, and battle pieces preserved in our Irish MSS. teem with details respecting this *Badb-catha* and her so-called sisters, *Neman, Macha,* and *Morrigan* or *Morrigu* (for the name is written in a double form), who are generally depicted as furies, witches, or sorceresses, able to confound whole armies, even in the assumed form of a bird.[159]

In the early 1900s, American anthropologist W. Y. Evans-Wentz conducted ethnographic fieldwork to collect fairy folklore from people living in Ireland, Scotland, Wales, Cornwall, Brittany, and the Isle of Man. That fieldwork and his studies of mythology led to his 1911 book *The Fairy-Faith in Celtic Countries*, which notes the sinister, peculiar abilities of the Celtic war goddesses, and the manner in which their identities are conflated, in the chapter "The Sidhe as War-Goddesses or the Badb." The Sidhe, pronounced SHEE, is the name of the fairy folk of Ireland who were descended from the Tuatha Dé Danann when that race of gods and goddesses were driven underground—figuratively and literally—by the invading humans known as Milesians (and who, myth says, are the ancestors of the modern-day Irish people). The word *sidhe* is Irish for "hill," or "mound," and denotes the places where the aos sidhe, the "people of the mounds," lived. The term *aos sidhe* was truncated to *sidhe* to indicate the fairy folk themselves.

Along with citing the Irish epic the *Táin Bó Cuailnge*, in which Cuchulainn comes under the influence and machinations of the war goddesses, Evans-Wentz also cites one of "our witnesses"—that is, one of the contemporary Irish citizens he interviewed:

It is in the form of birds that certain of the Tuatha Dé Danann appear as war-goddesses and directors of battle, and we learn from

---

159 Hennessy, "The Ancient Irish Goddess of War."

one of our witnesses that the "gentry" or modern Sidhe-folk take sides even now in a great war, like that between Japan and Russia.[160]

But it is the Morrigan, Green writes, who is the most prominent and fully realized of the Irish battle goddesses, both in the Ulster Cycle and in the Mythological Cycle, which are two of the four main cycles of Irish mythology that also include the Fenian Cycle and the Historical Cycle. She translates the Morrigan's name as "Phantom Queen."[161]

THE WORLDVIEW OF THE ANCIENT CELTS

While corvids play a more prominent and varied role in Celtic myths, the birds also exerted a considerably different influence upon ancient Celtic cultures than they did upon the Norse or Native Americans.

The moral code of the Norse was based on possessing honor, which was chiefly earned through a strong work ethic and courage in battle. Recall Sir George Webbe Dasent's reflections on the Norse weltanschauung:

> In every point of view … war and battle were a holy thing…. It was good to live, if one fought bravely, but it was also good to die, if one fell bravely. To live bravely and to die bravely, trusting in the God of Battles, was the warrior's comfortable creed.[162]

Also note the insight of British historian and Germanic mythology scholar H. A. Guerber:

> The most distinctive traits of this [Northern] mythology are a peculiar grim humour, to be found in the religion of no other race, and a dark thread of tragedy which runs throughout the whole woof.[163]

As noted, the Viking warriors portrayed in the ancient Norse sagas boasted of being raven-feeders, and they were uncowed and undeterred, even if their

---

160 Evans-Wentz, *The Fairy-Faith in Celtic Countries*, 303.

161 Green, *Celtic Goddesses*, 43.

162 Dasent, *Burnt Njal*, xxviii.

163 Guerber, *Myths of the Norsemen*, xii.

raven banners produced an ill omen. Death for a Viking could mean a ticket to Valhalla in the arms of a beautiful Valkyr, a seat beside Odin, and plenty of mead.

In Native American myths, Raven is a great trickster—sometimes cruel, sometimes inept, sometimes impish, sometimes stirring up adversity for both humans and his fellow creatures. But Raven is always too self-serving and plagued by very humanlike foibles to qualify as distinctly malevolent. Besides, his gluttony and lust often end up benefiting humankind as much as satiating his own wanton desires.

But the corvids of Celtic myth are a different matter, even though flashes of Guerber's "grim humour" surface occasionally, while feats of valor and derring-do on battlefields rival the Norse tales.

As for that sardonic humor, Irish cultural studies scholar Daragh Smyth notes that Cuchulainn rebuffs the amorous advances of the Morrigan by remind-ing her "he is fighting a battle and does not have time for 'women's behinds.'"[164] Alas, Smyth does not provide a source for the "women's behinds" translation. Scholar Eleanor Hull renders the warrior's reply as:

> The season is not opportune in which thou hast come to us; my bloom is wasted with hardship nor, so long as in this strife I shall be engaged, is it easy for me to hold intercourse with a woman.[165]

As for Cuchulainn's valor in combat, the Ulster warrior exhibits as much courage as any Viking while knowing that he is virtually invincible as long as he adheres to the *geas* (an Old Irish term meaning a taboo) placed upon him to never taste dog flesh—a prohibition that came about when, as a boy, he slayed the canine of Culann the smith in self-defense and thereafter vowed to be Cuchulainn, or the "Hound of Culann."

However, while the ravens of Norse lore are esteemed, or at least begrudg-ingly respected, by the Scandinavians, the corvids of the Celts can be quite adversarial and even malevolent toward humans and their affairs. That's true even though Smyth notes that "unlike the Valkyries, the Morrigna (which he

---

164 Smyth, *A Guide to Irish Mythology*, 126.

165 Hull, *The Cuchullin Saga in Irish Literature*, 164.

says is a collective term for the Morrigan, Badb, and Macha) are never the direct cause of the hero's death."[166]

But the malevolent effect of the battle goddesses upon the warring Irish factions is not always indirect. Cuchulainn, with his flippant remark about "women's behinds," makes an enemy of the Morrigan, and the war goddess attempts, unsuccessfully, to thwart him in battle and bring about his death by shape-shifting and attacking him in the form of a red-eared cow, an eel, and "a rough, grey-red bitch-wolf."[167]

Ross also cites Cuchulainn's antagonistic clashes with "evil otherworld ravens," including his ritualistic beheading of one of them, followed by washing his hands in the corvid's blood.[168] Cuchulainn does not enter into any of his battles with the hope of dying gloriously and being shuttled to an afterlife of drinking and feasting with his Otherworld father, the god Lugh. In the *Táin* and most other ancient Irish texts, Cuchulainn is silent on any sort of afterlife—he seems to realize his corpse will be, so to speak, a feeder of ravens and crows and little more.

The many intrusions of "an badb catha," the "battle-crow," in the wars of the ancient Irish, the Morrigan's strange love-hate relationship with Cuchulainn, and the confluence of Irish and Norse corvid legends at the supernaturally infested Battle of Clontarf in 1014 CE are amply documented, both by myth and history. Along with this book's explorations of Celts and crows, see the bibliography for more accounts by both storytellers and scholars.

BATTLE CROWS RUN RAMPANT

History tells us that Fergal mac Máele Dúin, High King of Ireland from 710 to 722 CE, lost his head—literally—at the Battle of Allen in modern-day County Kildare against a force of Leinstermen.

A tenth-century chronicle of that actual battle provides a horrifying account of what else happened that day, as summarized by Daithi Ó hÓgáin, a professor of Irish folklore at University College Dublin: "… the war-goddess … called 'the

---

166 Smyth, *A Guide to Irish Mythology*, 127.

167 Dunn, *The Ancient Irish Epic Tale Táin Bó Cúalnge*, 168–72.

168 Ross, *Pagan Celtic Britain*, 325.

red-mouthed and sharp-faced Badhbh' is said to have raised an exultant shriek over the decapitated head of Fergal."[169]

The Irish battle goddesses lorded over the fields of war of the ancient Emerald Isle, so much so that seemingly any prominent Irish myth or war chronicle finds a havoc-wreaking, blood-thirsty, treacherous, goddess-corvid entwined with the fates of men—lurking, harping, shape-shifting between human form and that of a corvid and/or other animals, waiting to feast on the carrion of human folly.

Green writes that these war goddesses "combined destruction, sexuality and prophecy."[170]

Indeed, the Morrigan was the mate (Ó hÓgáin says the "wife") of the Dagda, who scholars note was the chief father-figure deity in the Irish pantheon. A well-known tale relates how the Morrigan is standing astride a river in County Sligo, fulfilling her role as a death omen by appearing as the Washer at the Ford (see chapter 16, "The Washer at the Ford"), when the Dagda comes upon her and copulates with her. As cited earlier, another famous story details how the Morrigan attempts to seduce the warrior Cuchulainn.

Meanwhile, instances of corvid-inspired prophecy are scattered throughout this text—specifically in the sections on augury and death.

As for the destruction part of Green's triad: The corvids who populated the world of the ancient Celts certainly did not have a monopoly on warfare mayhem—any glance at the Vikings' exploits in the old Scandinavian sagas will prove that. Yet the shape-shifting battle goddesses of the Irish seem more active, even predatory, than comparable supernatural entities—corvid-affiliated or otherwise—in other cultures.

Scholar Eleanor Hull writes that the three goddesses of war—the Morrigan, Badb, and Macha—"appear frequently either before or during the course of a battle" and "show their partiality or dislike to the warriors by fighting for or against them." Irish sagas cite the historically documented Battle of Moira as "the fold of Badb," while at the Battle of Magh Lena "the blue-mouthed, loud-croaking Badb rejoiced at the extent of the banquet she found on the dead men." (Recall the previous description of the Badb as "red-mouthed," a more expected appearance given her association with the blood-soaked carnage of

---

169 Ó hÓgáin, *Myth, Legend & Romance*, 309.

170 Green, *Celtic Goddesses*, 42.

battle.) Hull further notes that "these three fierce terrific goddesses were capable of changing themselves into blackbirds or scall-crows [sic]. They may possibly be cognate with the Norse Valkyre maidens."[171]

The Irish war goddesses typically did not physically engage in combat. Rather, their modus operandi was psychological and magical. They instigated war. Their allegiance to one side or the other was capricious and unpredictable—like warfare itself. Their presence might show favor to an army—or portend doom. Their mere appearance or bone-rattling shrieks could cause warriors to tremble or even die of fright. Each of the Irish battle furies further terrorized warriors by shape-shifting into crows or ravens. In such instances, Green pointedly characterizes the corvids as "sinister black carrion birds of death."[172]

But Ó hÓgáin indeed cites accounts in which the war goddesses actively joined the fray of combat. During the mythic First Battle of Moytirra, also rendered as Moytura or Magh Tuiredh, the Tuatha Dé Danann fight their enemy the Fir Bolg. The Tuatha are aided by the trio of battle furies—Badb, Macha, and the Morrigan—who "stand on the Hill of Tara and fling magical showers and masses of fire and blood" onto the Fir Bolg army.[173]

During the Second Battle of Moytirra, another mythic clash chronicled by ancient Irish texts, the Tuatha Dé Danann fight the Fomorians, also rendered as Fomhoire, who are variously described as a "monstrous" or "demonic" and malevolent supernatural race inimical to both gods and humans. The Morrigan aid the Irish god the Dagha, says scholar Proinsias Mac Cana, "by depriving the leader of the Fomhoire of 'the blood of his heart and the kidneys of his courage.'"[174] The Morrigan also has the Dagda summon the poets of Ireland, and she commands them to "sing spells" against their enemy.

Such accounts reveal that the Morrigan is a complex goddess of fertility, sexuality, death, destruction, war, and sovereignty and a protectress of her people.[175]

---

171 Hull, "Observations of Classical Writers on the Habits of the Celtic Nations, as Illustrated from Irish Records," 152.

172 Green, *Celtic Goddesses*, 42–43. See also Mac Cana, *Celtic Mythology*, 86–90.

173 Ó hÓgáin, *Myth, Legend & Romance*, 307.

174 Mac Cana. *Celtic Mythology*, 86.

175 Ó hÓgáin, *Myth, Legend & Romance*, 307. Also Green, *Celtic Goddesses*, 43, 45.

Green, whose works sometimes reflect that she is quite in tune with both ancient and modern-day Pagan practice, notes that the Morrigan announced an end-of-the-world prophecy after the Second Battle of Moytirra and that the battle and prophecy occurred at Samhain, the fire-harvest festival of October 31 and November 1, "a liminal, dangerous occasion when time and space were suspended, and the barriers between the supernatural and earthly worlds were temporarily dissolved, so that the spirits could interfere with human affairs and mortals could enter the realms of the dead."[176]

As seen in the 1891 translation of "The Second Battle of Moytura" by Irish-born Celtic scholar Whitley Stokes, the prophecy of the Morrigan, which also is attributed to Badb, is dire and disturbing, making the visions of Nostradamus seem like a chat with Mr. Rogers.

Scholars emphasize, however, that the Morrigan's most prominent role was not as a fertility or sovereignty goddess but as a war goddess. A warrior who encountered her as the Washer at the Ford would know he had witnessed an omen of his own death. In the din of battle, an ancient text states, warriors would hear her laughter and be reduced to shuddering.

Ó hÓgáin argues that Badb, not the Morrigan, is the battle goddess who appears most often in the ancient Irish texts, and he goes on to note her name is the common word for a scald crow and reflects the real-world occurrence of such "ugly carrion-birds haunting the battlefield." The Babh, he adds, revels in "slaughter for its own sake."[177]

The Badb haunts the doomed King Conaire in *The Destruction of Dá Derga's Hostel*, a myth from the Ulster Cycle found in various ancient manuscripts. The oldest dates to 1100 CE, although scholars say the tale originated several centuries earlier.

In Whitley Stokes's 1901 translation, the Badb—"her lips...on one side of her head" and "casting the evil eye on the king and the youths who surrounded him in the hostel"—confronts and confounds Conaire. The hag then reels off thirty-one names, including three of the Irish battle goddesses—Badb, Némai (Nemain), and Mache (Macha). She also baits Conaire into violating his taboo that he shall not "receive the company of one woman after sunset," thus

176 Green, *Celtic Goddesses*, 44.

177 Ó hÓgáin, *Myth, Legend & Romance*, 308.

instigating his doom. "Great loathing they felt after that from the woman's converse, and ill-foreboding; but they knew not the cause thereof."[178]

Nemain, whose name means "frenzy," is the least-frequently cited battle goddess in the Irish myths and historical accounts. True to her name, her magical modus operandi was to incite fear and panic among warriors, thus spurring them to commit mindless, wanton slaughter.

Cuchulainn receives a considerable supernatural assist from Nemain as he is about to face warriors from Ireland's other four provinces, as recounted by Hennessy's translation of the *Táin* from the *Book of Leinster*:

> The Neman, i.e. the Badb, confused the army; and the four provinces of Eriu dashed themselves against the points of their own spears and weapons, so that one hundred warriors died of fear and trembling in the middle of the fort and encampment that night.[179]

Cuchulainn is not the only warrior in the *Táin* to be plagued by the battle goddesses. MacRoth, the chief messenger of Queen Maeve of Connaught, and Fergus, an Ulster king who has exiled himself in Connacht and allied himself with Maeve and her forces, are visited by a terrifying sight: "Three red-mouthed, crow-shaped demons of battle sped around them as swift as hares, circling the three wheeled towers."[180]

A short time later, the fickle Morrigan herself delivers a dire, grisly prophecy designed to stir up dread on both sides of the conflict:

> It was on that night that the Morrigan, a daughter of Ernmas, came, and she was engaged in fomenting strife and sowing dissension between the two camps on either side, and she spoke these words in the twilight between the two encampments:

> "Ravens shall pick
> The necks of men!
> Blood shall gush

---

178 Stokes, "The Destruction of Dá Derga's Hostel," 59.

179 Hennessy, "Ancient Irish Goddess."

180 Dunn, *The Ancient Irish Epic Tale Táin Bó Cúalnge*, 340.

In combat wild!
Skins shall be hacked;
Crazed with spoils!
Men's sides pierced
In battle brave."[181]

In the 1800s, the term *the fog of war* was coined to express the angst, uncertainty, confusion, and dread experienced by armies in the fray of battle. For the ancient Irish, such fog came in the shape of a crow or raven.

Battle Flap—The Ciumesti Raven Helmet

Foes of a Celtic army circa 200 BCE were confronted by a bizarre, frightening sight. They not only faced the spear point of the Celts' battle-frenzied chieftain, but also the pointed beak of their enemy's raven—perched atop the chief's head!

Historical records do not provide an account of what the Celts' adversaries thought of this battle raven. Did they take it to be an actual flesh-feather-and-bone bird or some sort of supernatural creature? Or, in the heat and fog of war in what is present-day Romania, were they able to perceive the reality of the matter: that this raven—even its flappable wings—was fashioned from bronze along with the other parts of the Celtic warrior's helmet.

History has provided us with the actual artifact, which was discovered in 1961 in Ciumesti, Romania, at what scholar Paul MacKendrick calls a "Celtic necropolis." The burial site also included chainmail, bronze greaves, and an iron spear point, but there were no bones and no evidence of cremation. Scholars concluded the place likely was the cenotaph of a "prince" who was slain in battle.[182]

The metallic bird, which is thirteen inches long with a nine-inch wingspan, could be a raven, eagle, or falcon, but it "is obviously a totem" in any case, MacKendrick says, noting that a warrior with a bird-crested helmet also appears on the Gundestrup cauldron, the Celtic/Thracian artifact from the first century BCE.[183]

---

181 Dunn, *The Ancient Irish Epic Tale Táin Bó Cúalnge*, 345.

182 MacKendrick, *The Dacian Stones Speak*, 51–52.

183 MacKendrick, *The Dacian Stones Speak*, 52.

However, Green adamantly proclaims the Ciumesti helmet is topped by a raven figure, and she notes that it was engineered with hinged wings that would flap "in a realistic and unnerving manner" when its wearer charged into battle.[184]

Excusing, for the moment, Green's accompanying comment that "these birds are cruel," her case that the Ciumesti bird is a corvid is well-founded—"the raven or crow was the bird of battle *par excellence*."[185] As noted previously, the collective psyche of the ancient Celts, like that of the ancient Norse, was permeated with conceptions of ravens and crows as birds of war and death—the result not of leaps of sheer imagination but of lived experience, of witnessing corvids haunting battlefields and feasting on the corpses of the slain.

While the Irish Celts' fascination with crows and ravens is amply revealed in their mythology, the Ciumesti helmet brings to mind another bit of crow lore that became part of the actual historical record: the account of how Roman military commander Marcus Valerius Corvus was aided by a rampaging crow as he defeated a Gallic warrior in hand-to-hand combat (see chapter 10, "Marcus Valerius Corvus and the Battle Crow").

We do not know whether the era and locale of Valerius Corvus, who lived circa 370 to 270 BCE, neatly aligns with the possessor of the Ciumesti helmet. Yet these two footnotes in corvid history, assuming one gives credence to the Roman historian Livy, parallel each other enough to make one wonder: was the Ciumesti Celtic warrior-chief inspired by the Roman and his battle crow?

---

184 Green, *Animals in Celtic Life and Myth*, 87–88.

185 Green, *Animals in Celtic Life and Myth*, 88.

Chapter 16

LESSONS: THE WASHER AT THE FORD

Three days after Samhain, I awake on a typically balmy, early November day in my home in east-central Florida. As the sleep-drunkenness of the hypnopompic state slowly oozes out of my brain software, I realize something is not "normal." My dream—a dream that had seemed very nondescript a nanosecond ago—is lingering and continuing to shape-shift, even as my Rat-Prag Brain (Rational-Pragmatic Brain) strives to make sense of it.

My mind replays last night's dreamscape cinema, but already the celluloid film has corroded and the images flicker and flutter like Edison's ancient Kinetoscope. Still, I realize ...

The Washer at the Ford! A death omen ... prominent in my Irish heritage.

The woman in my dream is clad in a blackish-gray robe and hood. She's shrouded in a heavy charcoal-gray mist, as if a rain-heavy cloud is engulfing her. I cannot see her face. She is standing at the edge of a stream, but the waters and the rocky bank and indeed the entire tableau around her are also awash in gray.

She is occupied by something in the stream, but she is not, as Washer myths dictate, washing bloodied clothes in the dark waters. Yet I know she is the Washer at the Ford. She tilts her head upward in my direction. Her face remains shadowed, yet I know she is looking at me.

I am familiar with Washer legends—that the entity is a sort of banshee-like creature, while in some accounts she is equated with the Morrigan. Either way, she is a death messenger. In my quest

147

to refresh my knowledge of the Washer and to find out more about my dream, I come across a passage by Celtic/Irish studies scholar James MacKillop:

> The Washer at the Ford is an English name for a familiar figure in Irish, Scottish Gaelic, Welsh, and perhaps Breton oral tradition, who may appear locally under different names. A death omen, she is sometimes beautiful and weeping or may be ugly and grimacing. She washes bloody garments at the ford of a river and turns to tell the beholder that they are his or hers. The persona of the washer may be derived from the Mórrígan, although Badb can take on this role. In Irish oral tradition the washer is nearly synonymous with the banshee, in Scottish Gaelic tradition is the bean nighe, in Welsh Modron, in Breton tunnerez noz.[186]

Though I am not a devotee of the Morrigan, I realize it is her I have encountered in my dream—something that never happened during my two trips to Ireland or any time after. Until now. And, though no bloody garments were discernible in my dream movie, my Mysti-Intu Brain (Mystical-Intuitive Brain) tells me it is in her Washer role that the Morrigan visited me.

I am not shaken by my dream. I don't know that I have ever feared death, but any subconscious dread certainly was banished after my wife, Cheryl, died in my arms at our home, struck down by the Breast Cancer Demon. While the Vulcans of *Star Trek* have their thing—"Live long and prosper"—Cheryl's death shape-shifted me into more of a Klingon: "May you die well." I believe all any of us can hope for is to "die well."

I will be fine whenever my time comes, I tell myself.

My curiosity leads me to hopscotch deeper into the Google-verse, and I am gobsmacked by a striking image I discover: the Washer at the Ford surrounded by swirling crows! The image accompanies a Samhain-Morrigan ritual by Candice Ruck, although the webpage leaves me uncertain whether this is her artwork.

This Washer artwork parallels my dream, but not exactly. The entire scene is rendered in black and shades of gray. The robed Washer stands on the shore

---

186 MacKillop, "Washer at the Ford."

of a lake or ocean, her face in shadow, her arms upraised and unleashing a swarm of crows or ravens that swirl upward into the cloudy gray sky.

Stunning, I whisper to myself.

This unexpected melding of my Washer dream with crows leaves me fascinated but not fearful, even though I realize that myth and folklore say crows and ravens, with or apart from the Morrigan and Washer legends, can be omens of death.

Seven days later, I travel to Deltona, Florida, thirty miles away to officiate the wedding of two friends. Before the ceremony, to be held at the home of a third friend in a wooded neighborhood, I take a walk along a woodsy path and arrive at the shore of Sidney Lake—and I witness the largest flock of crows I have ever seen!

A hundred or more of the birds are swirling and circling and swarming in the overcast sky. I have never witnessed anything close to that many crows at once—maybe a flock of fifteen or eighteen at most.

I am spellbound. I watch the birds pirouette and dance and frolic in the sky above the lake. Time melts. My heart leaps up. I am sky-dancing with these crows, and with Lord Valiant and Ms. Skitta and Mr. Piggy and Boga and Baca and every crow I have ever known.

Crow Magic!

My joy is not tempered by my sudden realization: *This—this circle of crows— is eerily similar to that Washer at the Ford image I saw online! No, the Washer is not here … yet she is here. Two Washer visitations in one week … a death messenger … and in the wake of Samhain, the great Celtic-Pagan festival of the dead.*

My dream of the Washer a week earlier had given me pause. But this vision spawned by Crow Magic has instantly tossed me into deeper, more intense thoughts on my own mortality.

Is my time really almost up?

I am discombobulated but not disturbed. Given my friendship and fascination with crows, I embrace this Washer. I am at once tantalized, mesmerized, seduced, and strangely comforted—much as I found comfort watching the crows in our backyard when Cheryl was battling the Breast Cancer Demon. Then, I had sensed/intuited/felt that the birds, rather than being harbingers of dread and death, were instead psychopomp companions come to accompany my Beloved and me, to escort and guide us, as she transitioned into the next world.

If you are a death messenger, so be it, I tell myself as the crows continue their sweet, ecstatic sky-dance above me. I am surprised by the serenity that has washed over me.

HARBINGERS OF DEATH

Scholars note the intertwining of myths and legends about the Morrigan, the Washer at the Ford, and the *bean si*, an ancient Irish term for a supernatural death messenger that has been anglicized as "banshee."

Anne Ross writes that the Morrigan is a "crow-raven goddess...who appears as the prophetic washer-at-the-ford, in which role she has survived into modern folk tradition."[187]

Ward Rutherford writes that the banshee, although beautiful, pale skinned, and long haired, "was an omen of disaster whose dirge" could be heard throughout Ireland and Scotland. She was "certainly a surviving aspect of the triple Macha (the Irish battle goddess) and it is significant that in Ireland she was often called the Babd (*sic*—yet another rendering of the name of this war goddess) and believed to be able to appear as a trio of death-presaging hooded crows."[188]

Ward goes on to note that the trio of battle crows were witnessed "reveling in the slaughter" at the Battle of Clontarf and that Macha appeared to Cuchulainn in the guise of the Washer at the Ford. Also, the historical figure known as Strongbow, whose exploits helped establish an Anglo-Norman presence in Ireland in the twelfth century, was warned he would lose an approaching battle when he encountered an apparition of a hag washing at a ford "till the red gore churned in her hands."[189]

Gertrude Schoepperle, a scholar of medieval Celtic, French, and German literature, cites two ancient Irish texts in her 1919 journal article "The Washer of the Ford." *The Destruction of Da Chocha's Hostel*, composed in its original form before the tenth century, tells the story of "the unfortunate Cormac Conlingas." He and his army are about to cross the Ford of Athlone on their way to a battle when they encounter the Badb, in the guise of the Washer, who is rinsing blood from a chariot. At Cromac's inquiry, the Badb says it is his chariot

---

187 Ross, *Pagan Celtic Britain*, 314.

188 Rutherford, *Celtic Lore*, 198; emphasis added.

189 Rutherford, *Celtic Lore*, 198.

she is tending. "Evil are the omens thou askest for us," says Cormac. "Grimly thou chantest to us."[190]

Schoepperle also writes that Cuchulainn, apart from his encounters with the Morrigan in the *Tain*, receives an omen before a battle in the tale *The Great Defeat on the Plain of Muirthemne*. The druid Cathbad tells the young Cuchulainn he has witnessed "Badb's daughter" washing the warrior's gear "with woe and mourning," foretelling his doom. But Cuchulainn is unfazed and defiantly replies: "What though the fairy woman wash my spoils?" His "consolation" is that Badb's daughter will also wash the spoils of his enemies.[191]

The conflation of myths concerning the Washer, the Morrigan/Badb, and banshees—and by extension, crows—is explored by Irish-born scholar and folklorist Patricia Lysaght. While accounts sometimes describe banshees as performing some sort of washing activity, such actions are attributed to the Badb or Morrigan in ancient Irish texts, Lysaght notes. However, in what she labels "folk tradition," the motif of washer banshees "is apparently first noted in Matthew Archdeacon's *Legends of Connaught* (1839)" with more references appearing in "folklore manuscripts" from the 1930s to the early 1970s. Lysaght concludes that the banshee's appearance as a washer woman was likely more prominent and widespread in earlier times than in contemporary times.[192]

Lysaght goes on to note an important distinction revealed by her field research as a folklorist, in the form of a "Banshee Questionnaire" given to residents of Ireland, and by her investigation of nineteenth- and twentieth-century Irish folklore traditions as revealed in archival texts: Such sources reveal that folk traditions in the 1800s and 1900s contain no solid evidence that banshees or death messengers under other names "ever appeared in the shape of a royston or scald-crow or any bird of the crow family." Beliefs that death messengers sometimes appear in the form of crows "has not existed within living memory and probably died out long before that," Lysaght concludes.[193]

---

190 Schoepperle, "The Washer of the Ford," 61.

191 Schoepperle, "The Washer of the Ford," 62.

192 Lysaght, *The Banshee*, 130, 133.

193 Lysaght, *The Banshee*, 106.

The Meaning of the Washer at the Ford

I am left pondering what Patricia Lysaght might think about my threefold death-messenger encounter: my Washer at the Ford dream, the spellbinding Washer-Morrigan-crow image I discovered online, and the awe-inspiring sight of a hundred-plus crows sky-dancing above me.

I do not feel that I have been visited by a banshee. I do feel that I have been visited by the Morrigan in her Washer incarnation. Yet, years later, I am alive and able to tell the tale. I recall that some devotees of the Morrigan believe her appearance may augur some sort of symbolic or nonphysical death.

If you encounter the Washer at the Ford, or the Morrigan or Badb in Washer-Crow guise, know that her visit need not be an augur of impending doom. Readers of tarot will be familiar with the dilemmas posed by the "shadow" cards: the Nine of Swords (Cruelty in Crowley's Thoth deck), the Ten of Swords (Ruin), the Tower, the Hanged Man, Death (although the Grim Reaper card has been almost universally ameliorated, and perhaps rightfully so, as transformation). Whenever these cards manifest in a reading, one's tendency is to flinch and then soften the blow of any dark portent. It's our human nature to seek the light when encountering darkness, and so, as we run to the light, we will be shunning any lessons that await us in the shadows.

Crow-Raven Magic may present similar dilemmas. As we have seen, the sagas of the ancient Norse and the ancient Irish are inundated with crow and raven mayhem, and the myths and folktales of other cultures sometimes associate corvids with death and misfortune at one extreme or annoying mischief at the other. The shadowy reputation of the birds survives even into modern times. Mention crows and ravens to someone and you may be greeted by a smile—or a shudder.

And so we are left with one lesson of the Washer at the Ford—or perhaps, more accurately, it is a lesson gleaned from the actions of Cuchulainn and Cormac: rather than flee the Washer/Badb/Badb's daughter, the mythic warriors bravely confront the grim fate that is being revealed to them.

For modern-day practitioners of Crow-Raven Magic—who likely are not carrying a sword or spear in their hand as they head into battle—what is the lesson if you encounter the Badb in her Washer guise?

As with all divinations and potential omens, whether pursued or visited upon you, try to discern connections and synchronicities with what is happening in your life. However, don't force those connections. If they are not there, then shrug and tell yourself that your encounter, however intriguing, must remain a mystery until more synchronicities have been revealed—if ever.

Sometimes the veil between this world and the Otherworld will open only partially, revealing a tantalizing but inconclusive glimpse. Sometimes the broadcasts from what psychonaut and dolphin researcher John Lilly calls "Cosmic Coincidence Control Center" arrive jumbled in our bio-computer processor—our brain—after being filtered through our fallible, limited, and easily deceived senses. Why should we be surprised that otherworldly, supernatural communications may leave us discombobulated when everyday person-to-person human communications sometimes falter and lead to confusion and misunderstandings?

But yes, an encounter with the Morrigan-Badb-Washer can be startling and unnerving. Whether you intuit such a vision as an omen of some possible symbolic or literal death, heed this lesson: it is certainly a sign to contemplate the "big picture" of your current station in your life's journey—to assess the goals and dreams you still hope to achieve and the "death" of dreams you have abandoned and why you did so.

It is a sign, as the English poet Andrew Marvell wrote in his mid-seventeenth-century poem "To His Coy Mistress," to recognize that at our backs we "always hear Time's wingèd chariot hurrying near; and yonder all before us lie deserts of vast eternity."[194] It is a time to realize that the Wiccan Wheel of the Year applies not just to 365 days but to the arch of one's lifetime. It is a time to embrace our Jungian shadows and to join with Shiva Nataraja in his eternal, cosmic dance of birth, death, and rebirth.

Lesson: heed "Time's wingèd chariot."

---

194 Marvell, "To His Coy Mistress."

Chapter 17

LORE: CORVID AUGURY

The ancients—whether Celt, Turtle Island inhabitant, Norse, Greek, Roman, or other culture—took note of the expansive vocabulary of corvids. Given that the ancients also witnessed the extraordinary, seemingly supernatural intelligence of crows and ravens—they used tools, they followed in the wake of wolves and warring humans to scavenge upon their kills, they exhibited both "thought" and "memory"—it is not surprising that our ancestors saw these birds as oracles. That is, given that these uncanny birds were of this world but their behaviors somehow transcended this mundane world, the ancients intuited corvids' sounds and actions just may be freighted with the wisdom and will of the goddesses and gods—if only we humans could interpret them.

The ancient Greeks practiced ornithomancy—bird divination. In ancient Rome, the practice of interpreting omens from the sounds, flight patterns, and other behavior of birds was known as augury, although the interpreter, known as an augur or auspex—one who looks at birds—also would study thunder and lightning, other animals' behavior, and random events for signs from the gods. Thus the word *augury* eventually became synonymous with the interpretation of omens from any source.

The way of ancient corvid augury is preserved, sometimes in vivid detail, in the historical record.

The 1875 edition of *A Dictionary of Greek and Roman Antiquities*, edited by William Smith, notes that:

It was only a few birds which could give auguries among the Romans. They were divided into two classes: Oscines, those which gave auguries by singing, or their voice, and Alites, those which gave auguries by their flight. To the former class belonged the raven (corvus) and the crow (cornix), the first of these giving a favourable omen (auspicium ratum) when it appeared on the right, the latter, on the contrary, when it was seen on the left.[195]

In ancient Tibet, a traveler who witnessed a crow cawing and pulling human hair with its beak would shudder—such was "an omen that one will die at that time."

So says an elaborate, even byzantine corvid divination system detailed in a ninth-century text discovered in the Cave of the Thousand Buddhas in what is modern-day China. German-born anthropologist Berthold Laufer, who emigrated to the United States in 1898, explores this corvid augury, including its origins in India, in his article "Bird Divination among the Tibetans" in the 1914 issue of the journal T'oung Pao.

Both the Tibetan text and Laufer's commentary are silent on whether that death omen refers to a crow tugging a stray human hair or a lock that's still attached to a person.

Avian scholar Ernest Ingersoll gives a succinct overview of Laufer's work, which included categorizing crow vocalizations such as "the tone ka-ka... the tone da-da... the tone gha-gha" and so forth. Laufer also detailed the construction of a complex "mystic table" consisting of "ninety squares, each square holding an interpretation of one or another sound of a raven's or crow's voice," as well mentions of the time of day, direction of a corvid's call, etc.[196]

Those included such prophecies as:

You will obtain flowers and areca-nuts... there will be numerous off-spring... this is a prognostic of the king being replaced by another one... you will obtain the fulfillment of your wishes... a storm will

---

195 Smith, "Augur Augurium."

196 Ingersoll, Birds in Legend, Fable, and Folklore, 173–74.

rise in seven days…misery will befall you…a state of happiness will be attained.[197]

The ill omens of corvids could be avoided, the Tibetans believed—especially if someone had frog meat:

> When an omen causing fear is observed, a strewing oblation must be offered to the crow. As the flesh of a frog pleases the crow, no accidents will occur when frog-flesh is offered.[198]

Celtic scholar W. H. Hennessy, writing in the 1860s, notes:

> The croaking of the Badb (a crow, whether literally or in the shape-shifted form of the Irish war-goddess) was considered to be peculiarly unlucky much more so than the croaking of a raven. In fact, not many years ago, sturdy men who heard the scare-crow shriek in the morning would abandon important projects long fixed for the same day.[199]

Irish scholar R. I. Best translated what he called "two scraps of early Irish folklore…written by a late scribe into blank spaces left in the well-known codex H.3.17."[200]

One of those "scraps" from the sixteenth-century manuscript is *Fiachairecht*, translated as "Raven Lore." As for the original scribe who recorded this list of raven vocal omens, we must marvel at their ability, like that of the Tibetan chronicler with their "ka-ka," "gha-gha," and so on, to understand and render raven-speak into human tones—never mind the ability to intuit and interpret the prophetic meanings of the various calls.

As someone who has been listening to crow talk for decades, I can vouch that such vocalizations are easy to distinguish upon hearing them, but they are a bit more difficult to approximate in English language, whether written or

---

197 Laufer, "Bird Divination among the Tibetans," 12–18.

198 Laufer, "Bird Divination among the Tibetans," 19.

199 Hennessy, "On the Goddess of War of the Ancient Irish," 423.

200 Best, "Prognostications from the Raven and the Wren," 120.

spoken—especially if one human wants to convey their list of crow words to another human. A crow phrase that sounds like "gha-gha" to you may sound like "grua-grua" to me. (See the "Speech and Language" section in the chapter 3, "Watching the Watchers.") Translating crow speak is an inexact science.

So, we are left wondering as the ancient records fall silent: Is the "gha-gha" that the Tibetan scribe heard the same as or similar to the "grob-grob" perceived by the Irish scribe? And when we moderns hear a crow or raven, where would that particular sound be found among these ancient oracles?

Regarding *Fiachairecht*, Best warns that "in a tract so inconsequent it is difficult, without the support of a second manuscript, to feel at all sure of one's rendering, and some of these prognostications are decidedly ambiguous."[201] Best, one assumes, was speaking without irony when he notes that prognostications are "ambiguous"—and one can assume he likely had never read the arcane prophecies of Nostradamus or heard the Pythia of Delphi whisper her cryptic, visionary sweet nothings.

Regardless, among the revelations of *Fiachairecht* are that ravens call "gracc gracc" if "warrior guests or satirists" are coming, while a call from above the door means "satirists or guests from a king's retinue are coming." A call from the northeast end of the house is a sign that robbers are about to steal the horses. A raven calling from a pillow means the woman of the house is about to die. If a raven voices "err err," sickness will fall upon someone in the house or on some of the cattle. A raven calls "carna carna grob grob coin coin" if wolves are about to prey on the sheep.[202]

We moderns readily esteem the ancient epic sagas, from Gilgamesh to Cuchulainn, as examples of a Campbellian hero's journey, and the more superhuman and supernaturally infested the feats therein the better. However, such texts as the Tibetan corvid oracle and the Irish *Fiachairecht*—reflecting, as Best noted, "scraps … of folklore"—are easy for modern minds to dismiss as mere superstition. That's especially so when we realize that, say, a Cuchulainn tale, while perhaps being a cautionary story about the horrors of warfare or the unpredictable yet inexorable treachery of fate, also was an entertainment told by seanachies (storytellers) around campfires. Conversely, we can assume the beliefs revealed in the Tibetan "mystic table" and the "Raven Lore" text of the

201 Best, "Prognostications from the Raven and the Wren," 121.
202 Best, "Prognostications from the Raven and the Wren," 123–25.

Celts were held by the common folk and likely affected to some degree how people lived or approached their daily lives.

If a raven calls from the northeast end of the house, check your horse barn now for robbers! If a raven calls "from the pillow," the woman of the house is about to die. A crow's nest in the middle of a tree means "a great fright." Corvids may herald the arrival of kings!

Rarely, if ever, do such catalogs of omens reveal the history of, say, why the "gracc gracc" of a raven means the arrival of warriors or satirists.

And so we are left to intuit and speculate upon the history of these signs— and how the ancients judged their efficacy and accuracy. Once upon a time, did a raven call out just before some hapless farmer discovered his horses had been stolen? Or did three, four, or a host of farmers report a similar occurrence over some length of time, and so that specific augury passed into accepted lore?

Were the ancient scribes who cataloged corvid oracles seen as divinely inspired by the gods or by crows and ravens themselves? Was the *Fiachairecht* scribe haunted by the Morrigan or Badb? Or were these ancient chroniclers merely the Stephen King, Rod Serling, or the Amazing Criswell, that outrageous psychic, of their day—that is, fabulous fabulists?[203]

What did the ancients make of their augurs' wisdom that various omens, including thunder or the calls of crows and ravens, are favorable if perceived on one's left, while those occurring on the right portend misfortune?

That is, so said the oracles if you were alive in ancient Rome. However, as the skeptical Roman philosopher Marcus Tullius Cicero snidely observes in his work *De Divinatione* (Latin for "Concerning Divination"), written in 44 BCE, that left-is-good, right-is-bad paradigm was reversed by the civilization across the Ionian Sea—the ancient Greeks.[204]

One's Rat-Prag Brain (Rational-Pragmatic Brain) will want to know, akin to Cicero, the how and why behind any mode of augury that has come to be accepted as accurate—and therefore accepted as being perspicacious, utilitarian, and effective if one puts its portents into play. Even one's Mysti-Intu Brain (Mystical-Intuitive Brain) demands something to hang its excursions upon, whether something wholly tangible or something more tenuous—such as, say, a track record in which someone proclaims: "Seven times in the past month I

203 Criswell, *Criswell's Forbidden Predictions*, 121–23.

204 Cicero, *On Old Age. On Friendship. On Divination*, 463–65.

saw four crows in the loblolly bay tree in my yard, and each time within three days I was visited by a stranger knocking on my door!"

Standing in opposition to Cicero sixteen centuries later is, of course, Hamlet—Shakespeare's melancholy Dane. Yes, it's an old saw, one that skeptics always poo-poo as a facile response by New Agers, light workers, Pagans, quantum physicists, or anyone who trots out Hamlet's mantra to respond to criticism of the woo-woo arts, but that mantra bears repeating: "There are more things in heaven and earth, Horatio, than are dreamt of in your philosophy."

It should be noted, too, that—as Virginia Woolf wrote—"on or about December, 1910, human character changed."[205] Or maybe that happened when the Industrial Revolution arrived in the late 1700s or at some other juncture in history when humans woke up one day and didn't even realize that our slow, inexorable alienation from Gaia and her ways had begun—that we humans were both willfully and unknowingly distancing ourselves from the great Earth Mother, her creatures, her now-nurturing, now-harsh topographies, and her beautiful mysteries.

It's no secret: We humans are more alienated from Gaia, from nature, than at any time in our history. The carrots and tomatoes at the local corporate grocery seemingly come from a produce truck and a stock clerk, while the seed, dirt, water, and sunlight that created our food is forgotten. Each day the winds whip cumulus and cirrus clouds into yet another fresh, never-before-seen tapestry upon the azure sky, but few humans pause more than five seconds to notice. A silly crow snatches an errant French fry spilled onto the parking lot of a burger joint, and few human observers realize the ancestors of this magical, amply sentient creature were glamouring our human ancestors at least 19,000 years ago, as immortalized on the wall of a cave in Lascaux.

So, perhaps long ago, Gaia whispered some of her sweet mysteries, just as she always has and always will, and a Tibetan farmer and an Irish country dweller heard her say, "When a crow caws from the south . . ."

---

205 Woolf, *Mr. Bennett and Mrs. Brown,* 4.

Chapter 18

GRIMOIRE: A METHOD OF CROW AUGURY

Since the origin of tarot almost six hundred years ago, the cards have evolved from being a parlor game to being a divination tool—one that, up to modern times, has variously encompassed countless occult and esoteric systems, numerous card layouts, and an ever-increasing roster of symbolic images, ranging from European medieval life, Celtic lore, Witches, and Greek gods to cats, dragons, baseball, and yes, crows and ravens.

As chronicled in this book, corvids have played a role in the divination practices of the ancient Greeks and Romans, the Celts, the Norse, and other cultures, up to and including modern-day Witches and Pagans. The Crow-Meets-Tarot spread detailed in the following sections is a method to tap into and meld the divinatory legacies of both the cards and the corvids.

WHAT YOU WILL NEED

- A favorite tarot deck (It need not be a crow-themed one.)
- An intermediate level of knowledge and experience with tarot
- A familiarity with various decks, reading methods, and spreads will aid in your awareness and appreciation of the various mechanics of tarot reading, what they can do, and how they work in numerous ways; there is not one "right way."

BACKGROUND

The origin of tarot cards can be traced to Italy around 1430 CE, when the by-then common four-suited deck of playing cards was supplemented by twenty-two cards featuring allegorical drawings. These new cards were known as triumphs, or trumps, which reflected how they were used in card games. Such trumps as the Fool, the Mountebank, the Emperor, Love, the Wheel of Fortune, the Hanged Man, the Devil, and others were in existence by 1500.[206]

Circa 1780 in France, the cards—buoyed by the rich symbology of the trumps—began to take on occult associations and were increasingly used for fortune-telling.

While a number of occultists, occult/esoteric organizations, and societal factors contributed to the further development of the cards as a divination tool, that aspect was amped up considerably by the rise of the Hermetic Order of the Golden Dawn in 1890s London. After the Golden Dawn splintered circa 1903, tarot divination was solidified when former Golden Dawn members A. E. Waite and artist Pamela Colman Smith created what would become known as the Rider-Waite (later the Rider-Waite-Smith) deck, originally published by the Rider Company in 1909.

Tarot cards continue to proliferate even today, with dozens of new decks—featuring either traditional images and concepts reconfigured or radically novel ideas—being published each year.

Corvids form a natural symbiosis with tarot for one overarching, obvious reason: since antiquity, crows and ravens have been esteemed as messengers who are able to travel between the mundane world and the otherworldly realms. Odin's ravens, Hugin and Munin, are prime examples. In Tibetan mythology, a raven "is the messenger of the Supreme Being."[207] Ravens and crows were sacred to Apollo, and when Raven informed the Greek god that his lover Coronis had been unfaithful with a mortal, the enraged Apollo scorched the bird's feathers from white to black. This and other corvid tales are related in *Metamorphoses* by the Roman poet Ovid (43 BCE–17/18 CE).

The Mechanics of Tarot as Divination or Exploration of the Inner Self

However much those long-ago scribes of corvid prophecy may have been kissed by Gaia and privy to her semisecret lore, I have always eschewed oracular systems that rely heavily on a catalog of one-to-one correspondences, akin to those old-timey dream dictionary books: "If you see/hear/dream *this*, then it means

---

206 Giles, *The Tarot*, 9.

207 Armstrong, *The Folklore of Birds*, 78.

that." A dream about rabbits means sexuality or, conversely, timidity. A dream with a table indicates the dreamer has some hidden issue that their subconscious is yearning to "put on the table" and reveal. And it goes on as such.

Such systems, for me, are too inflexible and limited. As discussed in the chapter "Corvid Augury," that Tibetan oracle states that any and every time a crow caws a certain way "when in the north, a king will appear." In the Irish *Fiachairecht*, any and every time a raven calls "from above the door, satirists or guests from a king's retinue are coming."

Thanks to modern scholarship, the texts of both those systems are easily and readily available to twenty-first-century seekers, to be contemplated or employed as one sees fit—whether for divination, bemused contemplation, or simply to add to one's knowledge about the history of corvids, omens, and oracles.

I confess that I have not deployed either system as an oracle, but I have scoured their texts in an attempt to decipher if the Tibetan crows' "ka-ka" or "da-da" or the Irish ravens' "bacach" or "grob grob" is analogous to the calls I have heard from Lord Valiant, Ms. Skitta, Mr. Piggy, Baca, Boga, Bella, Bola, and others in my local crow clan. In the case of *Fiachairecht*, I'm assuming the very real possibility, as shown by the Celtic scholarship cited in this book, that the oracle's "Raven Lore" could just as well have been referencing "Crow Lore."

For me, a flippant response to support my apparent dismissal of these ancient oracles could be: "So, every time I hear a crow caw from the north, the king will be visiting me soon?" You see the dilemma here, even if *king* is substituted with *president, governor,* or *county commissioner.*

However, both the Tibetan and Irish oracles, whatever their efficacy, serve an invaluable and treasured function for anyone practicing Crow-Raven Magic. Their very existence is yet another reminder of the deep, mystical connection between corvids and humankind across the centuries.

In yearning to tap into that connection, and into the readily observable, otherworldly spirit and material-world abilities of corvids, I was inspired to create a Crow-Meets-Tarot reading technique. Succinctly stated, it is this: crows shuffle the deck.

Discussion of the following Crow-Meets-Tarot method assumes one knows the basics of tarot—the how and why behind any of these sets of seventy-eight cards of wisdom freighted with myth, archetypal imagery, and magical, astrological, and Kabbalistic correspondences. For anyone who is a tarot neophyte, there are ample resources available via books and websites.

The Crow-Meets-Tarot method makes extensive use of multiple relationships among seven cards in a single spread, requiring a reader to be attentive and intuitive far beyond the basic three-card past-present-future layout.

Here's a simple (and perhaps too-reductive) test to assess your tarot reading abilities: How do you react to the Devil, Death, or the Ten of Swords when they appear in a spread? If those cards unnerve you and you view them only as dark, dire, or even catastrophic, or conversely, if you tend to gloss over them and fail to weigh their shadow sides, then I suggest you return to the Crow-Meets-Tarot or any other complex spread only after you have acquired more experience on your tarot journey.

That said, I will state that, as with all of my approaches to tarot and oracle decks, the Crow-Meets-Tarot technique is meant to be as much of a path to explore one's inner self as a method of divination.

Consider this technique as a way to stimulate new ways of exploring your life's circumstances, your responses to those circumstances, your emotions, your decision-making processes, your relationships, your behavior ruts, your honesty with assessing yourself—in short, any matter that you spend time thinking or feeling about.

Tarot is an amazing tool not only to face and assess the brimming cauldron that is your consciousness, but also the even vaster realms of your subconscious. The latter is where thoughts and memories reside that are familiar once summoned, and it's also where bizarro thoughts and images lurk that may seem utterly alien, as if some *Star Trek* creature has wormed its way through your ear and deep into your mind and soul and is breeding strange visions. Remember that everything you've ever experienced, encountered, thought, read, witnessed, tasted, smelled, heard, touched, feared, loved, and loathed is in your gray matter somewhere.

Then consider that esoteric traditions and the weltanschauungs of some wisdom teachers say the byzantine byways of one's subconscious also contain hidden—"occult"—knowledge that one has acquired not by direct encounter but through other channels: Jung's collective unconscious, for example, or the

Akashic records of Theosophy, Rudolf Steiner's anthroposophy, or Colin Wilson's Faculty X.

And here is the not-so-secret secret: the cards *indeed* may serve a divinatory role, if one is so inclined to allow that, by suggesting possibilities of what lies ahead. Explore the deeper realms of your consciousness and the shadowy realms of your subconscious, and your discoveries will affect your mind, heart, and soul both overtly and subtly—and you may find yourself beginning to "prophesy" new, previously un-glimpsed avenues for your life ahead.

You will become your own oracle.

PREPARATION

Before setting your hands on your cards and proceeding to do your first Crow-Meets-Tarot reading, read the remainder of this chapter thoroughly and to the end. Then and only then should you return to this Preparation section and proceed from here.

Choosing Your Deck

Which deck to use? Crow Tarot by M. J. Cullinane is an enchanting deck that captures Crow Spirit, even as it utilizes the symbolism and structure of the Rider-Waite-Smith deck. I smiled the first time I encountered its Hanged Man and recalled that stunning moment when I witnessed a real-life crow dangling upside down in the loblolly bay tree in my backyard, imitating that card's imagery.

Murder of Crows Tarot by Italian comic book artist Corrado Roi is stunning and dark—physically and metaphysically. The standard version is rendered in black, white, and grays, while a deluxe limited edition adds subtle bloodred splashes to the medieval scenes, thus heightening the deck's gothic, macabre aura.

But I don't use these decks exclusively for Crow-Meets-Tarot readings. You can—and should—use any deck with which you feel a connection. For me these include the Morgan-Greer Tarot (whenever I intuit a need to utilize classic medieval British Isles imagery); Aleister Crowley's magisterial, deeply esoteric Thoth Tarot, painted by Lady Freida Harris; the Crowley-inspired Liber T: Tarot of Stars Eternal; and the rich, pan-cultural, medieval-leaning Tarot Illuminati, among others.

ACTIONS

Crow-raven augury came into being because the ancients noticed the uncanny behaviors of corvids and humans began to recognize and/or intuit correspondences between those behaviors and happenings in the real world.

For a Crow-Meets-Tarot reading, you will be doing the same. Rather, you will be utilizing the casual corvid observations you already are making on a typical day, but you will be watching, and listening, to them more keenly.

Numbers are of prime importance here, but you will not be referencing that eighteenth-century folk tale/nursery rhyme, or its gazillion variations, that say witnessing a specific number of crows, or more commonly magpies, at a specific time is prophetic of such-and-such happening. The sheer number of variations—is six crows a sign of gold or of hell?—refutes the rhyme's efficacy as augury and points to its nursery rhyme origins as a playful, if occasionally sinister, children's game.[208]

For a Crow-Meets-Tarot reading, you will first determine your "crow number," which you will utilize for that reading. Basically, this is making note of the number of crows you see or the number of caws you hear at any one time.

How long a time do you set for your count, and do you use sightings or caws? You, and your intuition, decide. If I decide early in the morning to consult the cards that day, I usually set noon as the end of my window for keeping count of my crow sightings, either in my backyard and/or during a trip to the grocery store, or wherever. Same if you decide to count caws. Or you may set your window for one hour—or from sunrise to sunset.

A serendipitous benefit of counting crows for a reading is that it will make you more aware of their everyday presence in your life—or perhaps the lack thereof, unfortunately.

You may choose a more spontaneous method to determine your crow number via your crow encounters. If a group of them—I loathe the term *murder* to describe a gathering of crows—arrives suddenly in your backyard, take note of their number. When I noticed six crows in a single tree in my backyard recently—a very rare occurrence at my place—I knew I had to do a reading with six as my crow number.

---

208 "One For Sorrow ... Magpie Nursery Rhyme"; "One for Sorrow (Nursery Rhyme) about Magpies."

Likewise, if a single crow shows up, I may note the number of caws in its first vocal outburst, which usually will be two to five caws. However, just as I was writing this, I heard a burst of seven caws from an unseen crow in the distant woods—it's a rarity to hear that many in a single cry!

Whatever your final tally of crows or caws may be—two, five, or twenty-five—becomes your crow number for that reading. If by happenstance you have no crow encounters during the time frame of your chosen method of tracking the birds, of course take that as a sign to abandon the reading for that day.

Formulate Your Question

You have decided to do a reading because you have some question about your life or some matter that you want to explore and contemplate. You are now a psychonaut—an explorer of your inner space and the mystic, unseen other-world—and the tarot is the tool you will use to excavate those realms in relation to the matter at hand.

Formulate your question or inquiry. Keep in mind that a vague question or stated subject—"What will my life be like over the next three months?" or "My near future"—will tend to evoke vague, ambiguous responses from the cards. Better is "What factors should I be aware of in my new job search?" or "My partner seems distant—what's going on?"

I have had great success framing my tarot inquiries as yes-or-no questions while—very important—never expecting the cards to reveal a yes-or-no answer. Rather, the cards will reveal only tendencies toward one side or the other—not a black-white yes-no dynamic but a Taoist-like yin-yang. This approach causes one to laser focus their intention for a reading. True confession: I typically use this approach when I am in the early stages of dating someone and at some juncture, I will be moved to consult the cards and ask: "Will Lady X and I become lovers?"

Pre-Reading Meditation

Whatever space you have chosen for your reading, put the cards to one side, close your eyes, and meditate on your question and on the sights and/or sounds of the crow encounters that preceded this session. Alternately, you may choose to meditate upon or even invoke Odin's Hugin and Munin, the Morrigan, or Turtle Island's Raven—if you commonly work with those divinities/entities or feel a special calling to do so now. The goal here is twofold: One is to focus your thoughts. The other goal is to begin to channel Crow Spirit—to open one's Third Eye, one's inner eye, one's intuition to tune in to the abilities and nature of these creatures that have visited you, which history, cultural anthropology, and mythology tell us thrive upon Gaia's breasts while also readily transcending this world.

Laying Out the Cards

Shuffle the cards of whatever deck you have chosen, make a final cut of the cards, then prepare to place them in your spread. Use my Crow-Meets-Tarot layout detailed in this chapter.

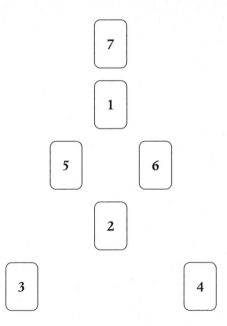

If your crow number is seven, deal the first six cards, sight unseen, into a discard file. Turn over the seventh card, which will now be at the top of your deck, and place this seventh card into the first card position of the layout.

Repeat this process. Deal the next six cards, sight unseen, onto the top of your discard pile, then turn over the seventh card, which, again, is now at the top of your deck, and place it in the second position of your layout, and so on. If you have a high crow number and you run through the entire seventy-eight cards before completing your layout, simply pick up the discard pile and resume your counting and dealing with it.

You thus are allowing the crows—the very crows you have encountered—to shuffle the deck. The intention here is twofold:

One, you are thus communing with Gaia/Earth Mother/the goddess through her creatures. Whatever may happen throughout the remainder of the reading, you have opened your inner realm and placed yourself in a special relationship with nature. As a follower of an earth-based religion—or perhaps not—you have already stepped outside mundane reality. Even though, at this stage of the reading, this stepping outside process (your crow counting) is likely undramatic, entering into that relationship with intention and openness is something that even fervently practicing Pagans may forget or take for granted.

Two, by allowing the crows to shuffle your deck, you have opened yourself and your ritual reading—yes, surprise, this is a ritual!—to the energy and synchronicity of the universe: your universe, right here, right now. At the same time, you once again are very much following in the long, storied footsteps of those ancient traditions—that of the Lascaux Cave artist, the Vikings marching under their raven banners, the seanachie spinning Cuchulainn tales, that Tibetan crow augur, the Irish prophetess pondering *Fiachairecht*. You are channeling the same otherworldly spirit-energy that they sensed in these beguiling creatures who, it seems, must be prophets from the unseen realms, who must be the messengers of the gods, who must be the goddesses themselves in shape-shifted form.

Interpretation with the Crow-Meets-Tarot Spread

Here is a detailed look at my Crow-Meets-Tarot spread—and yes, its layout is in imitation of a crow or raven ascending in flight. This layout makes multiple use of the relationships between adjacent cards, and some cards will serve double or triple duty depending on which subset of cards you are considering. Yes, that means a single card can and will serve more than one role in this reading—a concept that may rankle some traditional tarot practitioners. But what people, creatures, places, and things in this life—and the goddesses and gods themselves—do not serve multiple roles each and every day in this world?

The "main" thrust of this layout—the prime nature of the individual cards and their relationships—is discussed immediately below. The meanings of subsets of adjacent cards in the layout—columns and rows—is discussed afterward.

Card One Position

This card is you or a reflection of you in your current state—the essence at the heart of your question, situation, or the matter at hand. It may be an obvious reflection, making you think, "Yes, of course." If this card seems distant from the matter at hand, don't feel compelled to hammer its meaning into your situation. However, this is where tarot shines—as in shines a light upon your inner selves. However "off" or paradoxical this key card may seem, dare to explore its meanings and ponder its possible relation to your inquiry. Any tarot or oracle card reading should always be about more than what you already know or intuit.

Card Two Position

This card represents a foundation of your current self—it's a reflection of a *part* of your self-being, a *part* of your psyche, that you consider to be an aspect of the "natural" or "true" you. More subtly, it can represent a dominant aspect of your emotional or psychological state—especially before the subject of your inquiry came into play. That is, this is the "you before things changed." But it is not "the" foundation of yourself. We humans are complex beings—don't forget that—and regardless of whether this is a light or shadow card, it is only one aspect of you … but one that warrants your attention. As with most things foundational, we tend not to see them, we do not spend much time thinking about them, and we take them for granted—until something or someone rocks those foundations.

Cards Three and Four Positions

These cards represent the past, whether that be situations, events, or people that have affected the matter at hand. As William Faulkner famously wrote: "The past is never dead. It's not even past."[209]

Five and Six Positions

These cards represent the present, whether that be situations, events, or people who potentially may play a role as the subject of your inquiry plays out.

---

209 Faulkner, *Requiem for a Nun*, 85.

Card Seven Position

This card is the culmination or resolution of the matter at hand, the "prophecy card," the answer to the querent's question, the will-it-or-won't-it-happen card, the money shot. This is the card that would prompt comedian George Carlin to say "Either the thing 'flams' or it doesn't 'flam,'" (a reference to his routine wondering why there are three words—*flammable, nonflammable,* and *inflammable*—to express a dualistic concept).[210]

Destiny Is Not a Single Card

However—big caveat!—I am always hesitant to freight tarot with a strict divinatory/prophecy function. I *will* see possibilities or tendencies revealed in the cards, and I will consider how those may play into my circumstances. Indeed, that is the function of the cards, as I see them: tarot will lead us, sometimes kicking and screaming, into utterly startling new perspectives on the matter at hand, which we can then take under advisement as we move forward.

As for the "prophecy card" in the seven position: one card does not a reading make, however potent or confusing or bemusing this key card at the tip of the corvid's beak may be. While a daily draw of a single tarot or oracle card certainly has its place, there is a reason tarot is often read in spreads. Destiny cannot be contained in a single card—well, usually not! The possibilities of life's pageant are too rich and vast for our future to be confined to a rigid interpretation of a single card or even a set of cards. Most of us realize that even interpreting real-life events in hindsight—events that happened to us two years or two days ago—may be too complex for us to make ultimate sense of them.

Accordingly, that's why I designed the Crow-Meets-Tarot spread to unveil—OK, prophesy—two possible paths to the culmination of the querent's matter at hand (see the following section on the Three-Five-Seven and Four-Six-Seven vertical pillars). Yet be mindful that both of the revealed paths are merely tendencies or possibilities and that they, in turn, can influence the questioner to take actions that lead to a third—or fourth, fifth, or seventeenth—path. The future is mutable. Tarot is more art than science.

Deeper Interpretations

Below is a look at interpreting five subsets of cards within the Crow-Meets-Tarot spread. Here is where you arrive at more familiar tarot-reading territory: Think

---

210 Carlin, *On Location at USC.*

of these as, in essence, three-card spreads within the larger seven-card layout. As you read each subset as a group, the relationships between adjacent cards, whether they are "friendly" or "inimical" to each other, will come into play.

Cards Three, Two, and Four

The Two Card still represents a foundation of your current being—the "you" before the current situation began to affect and shape (and shape-shift) your life. Cards Three and Four are additional aspects of your core psyche in the immediate or perhaps distant past. As such, these are matters/conditions/behaviors/weltanschauungs that, regarding how they shaped the person you are today, are immutable and cannot be changed. However, of course, the past is prologue to the future, and one who is self-aware can take such knowledge and shape-shift one's present and future.

Cards Five, One, and Six

The One Card still represents you in your current state—the essence at the heart of your query, the situation, or the matter at hand. Cards Five and Six are additional aspects of your core psyche at the present time—reflections of your current thoughts and emotions, which may be readily recognizable by you, or perhaps they have been obscured from you—or by you. It's an old saw, but the essence of this set of three is contained in Socrates's mantra: "Know thyself."[211]

Cards Two, One, and Seven

Considered a pillar, this set of three represents the Axis Mundi or the World Tree, a motif common to many religions, spiritual paths, mythologies, and cultures. In typical World Tree symbology, the tree—just like the living, leafy ones of the real world—connects the underworld, the earthly plane, and the upperworld. The World Tree's roots extend deep into the earth and permeate the chthonic realms, the abode of the dead and the ancestors. The trunk is the pillar in the knowable, see-able world with its people, fauna, and flora. The tree's upper branches extend to the cosmos, the heavens—the symbolic realm of the gods and goddesses, divine wisdom, cosmic consciousness.

---

211 Barker, *The Political Thought of Plato and Aristotle*, 46.

When contemplating the World Tree aspect of the Crow-Meets-Tarot spread, the Two Card represents an aspect of ancestral knowledge, the wisdom of the ancestors speaking to you.

The One Card in this instance represents an aspect of worldly wisdom or mother wit, which has been reimagined in modern times as "life hacks." This is the common-sense knowledge we have acquired that helps us navigate not only the mundane, necessary chores of life, but also office politics, the complexities of personal relationships, the mysteries of the love thing. In short, it is the knowledge required to deal with most any matter that occupies our daily lives. As such, this card is a reminder of some aspect of your "life knowledge"—a clue to utilizing some part of your everyday intuition as opposed to the lofty concerns of your Third Eye, that gate to the higher realms.

The Seven Card reflects—yes, that Third Eye knowledge—the soul wisdom that one has glimpsed—obtained?—through entering into communion with the Divine, with cosmic consciousness, or however one may define these things. When contemplating the World Tree pillar, the attributes of this card may be elusive or aspirational—it is a reminder, in a glimpse, of how higher forces are at work and at play in our lives, and we may not be able to fully grasp their import. But they are there. Once again, what scientist, dolphin researcher, and psychonaut John Lilly impishly termed "Cosmic Coincidence Control Center" is afoot.

The Three-Five-Seven and Four-Six-Seven Vertical Pillars

Each of these pillars, read from bottom to top as past (the bottom card), present (middle card), and future (top card) represent a possible path into the future—a culmination or resolution of the reader's query. As such, these two columns can be read as advice or prophecy, but again, the reader is cautioned to contemplate each card in its relative position as pointing toward certain factors that *may* come into play, rather than being some sort of rigid, scripted play itself. Such factors, of course, can alter any script that has yet to be written.

The goal is to use tarot symbology to open the gate to the occulted higher consciousness that resides in your own inner space and in goddess/god, the "cosmic mind," the "cosmic soul," in what the Irish poet William Butler Yeats calls "Spiritus Mundi."[212]

---

212 Black Letter Press, "W. B. Yeats - Spiritus Mundi."

Note that each prophecy pillar culminates in the same future card at the crown of the corvid's beak. This does not mean that each path will lead to the same resolution. Recall that wands are inimical to cups, and swords are inimical to pentacles. So, that pinnacle Seven Card may be "ill-dignified," for better or worse, by the Five or Six Card on either side, or both.

Also note that the path of a journey affects what we find at the end of a journey, meaning the same final destination will be viewed quite differently by two travelers who have walked different paths to get there.

So, which of the two future-path pillars should one heed? The glib but honest answer is—who knows? However, it is very likely that one or the other will resonate more with the querent's circumstances, or intuition will lead a reader to embrace one path over the other. A wise soothsayer may even hold both paths as valid, akin to Schrodinger's cat in quasi-eternal stasis—even if, or perhaps especially if, the two future paths are contradictory. No doubt the cards in each path will unlock hidden aspects of one's psyche that will lead them to at least a bit of self-enlightenment.

Alternately, a reader may follow in the footsteps of that ancient Tibetan crow augur or the Irish scribe behind the raven prophecies of *Fiachairecht*. If, after completing your Crow-Meets-Tarot layout, you see or hear a crow or raven to the left, then heed the left-hand pillar. If a corvid appears or calls from the right, then must ye pay greater heed to the right-hand path.

Going Forward

All practitioners of tarot will benefit from using multiple decks and multiple layouts, with their intuition guiding them in their choices as each occasion to read the cards arises.

The Crow-Meets-Tarot method is admittedly a complex spread and one you should utilize only when a life situation begs for an in-depth examination—don't use it if you are trying to decide whether to have tacos or Chinese food for dinner.

However, the counting crows technique of using the behavior of corvids to guide you in shuffling your deck and laying out your cards can be easily adapted to any tarot spread, whether it's the three-card past-present-future reading or the Celtic cross method.

Chapter 19

LORE: NATIVE AMERICANS' NOT-TOTEM POLES

The term *totem* has come to have a broad usage, both mundane and magical, in modern society, but the word can be traced to the Ojibwe (also spelled *Ojibwa* or *Objibwe*) language of the mid-1700s, spoken by the Ojibwe (Chippewa) Native American people of present-day Canada and the United States. Their *doodem* is a stem word that means "clan," but it is paired with various prefixes to create such words as *indoodem*, meaning "my clan," according to the Ojibwe People's Dictionary, an online resource established by faculty and students in the Department of American Indian Studies at the University of Minnesota.[213]

Alternately, scholar Larry J. Zimmerman writes that *totem* is "a word that anthropologists derive from the Objibwe *odem*, which may be translated as 'village.'"[214]

Britannica says the term *totem* is derived from the Ojibwa word *ototeman*, which means "one's brother-sister kin" and "signifies a blood relationship." The essay also states:

> In English, the word totem was introduced in 1791 by a British merchant and translator who gave it a false meaning in the belief that it designated the guardian spirit of an individual, who

---

213 "Totem," Ojibwe People's Dictionary, accessed June 6, 2023, https://ojibwe.lib.umn.edu/main-entry/indoodem-nad.

214 Zimmerman, *The Sacred Wisdom of the Native Americans*, 91.

appeared in the form of an animal—an idea that the Ojibwa clans
did indeed portray by their wearing of animal skins.[215]

Yes, that incident may be seen by many Native Americans, and also non-Indigenous people, as an early example of cultural appropriation—or cultural misappropriation. However, the spurious origin of the English word *totem* did not prevent it from infiltrating the language and assuming a meaning much like that assigned to it by that British merchant. In colloquial terms, a totem is an animal or, less often, a plant or natural object whose nature or attributes have a spiritual, supernatural resonance with an individual, a group, a clan, a tribe, or a culture—even to the point in which the animal, plant, or object is regarded as embodying a tutelary (guardian) spirit. *Totem* can variously and simultaneously refer to this spirit entity, the animal, plant, or object itself, or some physical, symbolic representation of the animal, plant, or object.

Scottish social anthropologist and ethnologist John Ferguson McLennan, writing in his series "The Worship of Animals and Plants" in the *Fortnightly Review* in 1869 to 1870, argued that all of humankind engaged in totemism at some point in time across the ages.[216] However, McLennan's theory certainly had its detractors, and the French ethnologist Claude Lévi-Strauss went so far as to vehemently deny totemism had anything at all to do with religious practice, instead relegating it to a sort of tribal system of taxonomy.[217]

Need it be pointed out that, despite the fallacious entry of the word *totem* into the English language, the beliefs and practices grouped by ethnologists and anthropologists under totemism exist independently from whatever name, spurious or otherwise, one may give them. The ways of totemism existed in worldwide cultures before the word *totem*, and those ways persisted, and persist, after its errant coinage.

Meanwhile, it should be noted that the North American Indigenous peoples—especially the Tlingit, Haida, Chinook, and other Native American tribes of the Pacific Northwest of Canada and the United States—have long forged relationships with crows and ravens as totem animals, and those corvids have directly figured in their legends and totemic art and iconography.

---

215 Haekel, "Totemism."

216 "John Ferguson McLennan."

217 Lévi-Strauss, *Totemism*, 1–16.

Also, numerous Indigenous cultures around the world, such as the Walbiri, an Aboriginal people of Australia, and the Birhor of Jharkhand, India, hold a similar set of beliefs and practices that come under the somewhat large umbrella of totemism.

Zimmerman notes that animals play a major role in Native American mythology, and those myths say that in ancient times "people and animals were indistinguishable and could change appearance at will. Tricksters frequently appear in the form of animals to provide their human neighbors with valuable moral lessons," while numerous myths portray marriage between humans and beasts. He goes on to note that, while "only a few clans see themselves as the direct descendants of an animal spirit or totem ... most tribes believe that animals and people are closely related."[218] For example, a totem animal may have helped one's ancestors hunt or guided a lost human back home.

> Individuals who did not belong to a totem-based society or clan could develop their own relationship with a totem animal, which became their personal spirit guide. Clans and individuals were often thought to assume the characteristics of their spirit totem.[219]

TOTEM POLES VS. NOT-TOTEM POLES

Anthropologist Edward Malin, in his book *Totem Poles of the Pacific Northwest Coast*, relates the time when he was a member of the US Navy during World War II and he came across a magazine's photo of a totem pole village in a remote corner of Vancouver Island, Canada. As a University of Colorado student after the war, Malin went on a quest to see that village in person.

After bumming passage on freighter ships and salmon trawlers, he arrived in the village beside Alert Bay just before daybreak. There he discovered the totem poles, for some unknown reason, had been relocated from the village street, as depicted in that photo, to the graveyard. He heard the call of an eagle and "the raucous cries of restless ravens" as the faces of the poles slowly emerged in the gray dawn light: birds with big beaks and huge wings, mammals, sea monsters,

---

218 Zimmerman, *The Sacred Wisdom of the Native Americans*, 91–92.

219 Zimmerman, *The Sacred Wisdom of the Native Americans*, 91–92.

humans—each and every one a mystery to him. A spell had been cast. An "obses-sion" was born.[220]

In North America, authentic totem poles historically were found among some—just some—of the Native American peoples of the Pacific Northwest, who lived along what is now the southern panhandle of Alaska, and the coastal lands and islands of British Columbia and Washington state.

The main creators of totem poles were the Haida, the Tlingit, and the Tsimshian people, but Malin says that identifying them as single "tribes" is problematic, even inaccurate. The Haida, whose homeland was mostly the Queen Charlotte Islands off the coast of British Columbia, consisted of three distinct groups more or less determined by geographic location within that small area. *Tlingit* is the collective name given to a group of fourteen tribes bound by language more than culture, and *Tsimshian* is the collective name for twenty-six tribes.

Given that totem poles were thus confined to a relatively small geographic area, most Americans' familiarity with these astonishing works of functional art likely has come through documentaries, National Geographic articles, or some reference book—or as I remember from my childhood days, some Saturday morning cartoon occasionally would depict a grotesque caricature of a totem pole.

The pop-culture bastardization and debasement of Indigenous traditions, while unfortunately common and not limited to any one culture, is especially pointed and poignant given the accomplishment of the Northwest Native Americans. Malin notes that carved wooden poles have been created in cultures around the world for centuries, but he adds "the Northwest Coast Indian tribes were the supreme masters and users of carved poles." The poles' size, height, and girth, the intricacy of their artwork and the complexity of their symbolism "achieved an artistic significance without parallel in human experience. Totem poles were one of the culture's crowning accomplishments." Malin gives par-ticular high praise to the carving skills of the Haida people.[221]

For anyone outside of the Indigenous cultures of the Pacific Northwest, the iconic totem pole image that likely springs to mind—a bird creature with

220 Malin, *Totem Poles of the Pacific Northwest Coast*, 3–4.

221 Malin, *Totem Poles of the Pacific Northwest Coast*, 5, 12–13.

wings majestically spread—is most likely not a raven. Pole ravens typically are portrayed standing upright with wings held at their side. Another telltale clue is that a totem pole raven will have a straight beak that comes to a point. Those iconic totem birds with spread wings typically are an eagle, whose beak tip is sharply curved downward, or a thunderbird.

While authentic totem poles were confined geographically, so, too, is knowledge of their true nature limited: totem poles actually are not...well, *totem* poles. As cited previously, the rather broad umbrella of totemism can be loosely defined as a system of religious/supernatural beliefs in which humans forge a mystical relationship with a spirit entity in the form of an animal, plant, or natural object.

Malin says if he had written a book titled *Carved Columns of the Pacific Northwest Coast*, it would have generated "little interest." But, he adds, "totem poles—that is another story."[222]

Malin recalls a conversation with Viola Garfield, a fellow anthropologist who focused on the Tsimshian people of coastal British Columbia and southern Alaska and who was adopted into the tribe's Eagle Clan: Garfield stressed that, "anthropologically speaking," the poles created by the tribes of the Northwest Coast "were not totems at all."[223] (For more on totems, see chapter 11, "A Crow-Raven Talisman and Amulet.")

Zimmerman observes that totem poles are "basically *heraldic* emblems, representing status, wealth or ownership," but that they also served as memorial poles, mortuary poles (erected beside the graves of chiefs), and "portal poles" that represented a symbolic gateway to the supernatural world.[224] He also notes the Indigenous people of the Northwest Coast "honored the totem animals of their clans by incorporating them as family crests in almost all their carving, weaving or painting." However, the clans did not worship the creatures they portrayed, nor did they believe their artistic creations were imbued with a fetish-like supernatural power—rather, they portrayed a "family's history and powers" and provided a connection to their past.[225]

---

222 Malin, *Totem Poles of the Pacific Northwest Coast*, 6.

223 Malin, *Totem Poles of the Pacific Northwest Coast*, 6.

224 Zimmerman, *The Sacred Wisdom of the Native Americans*, 95; emphasis added.

225 Zimmerman, *The Sacred Wisdom of the Native Americans*, 94.

Along with ravens, poles also depicted the wolf, beaver, frog, grizzly bear, shark, sea lion, goat, and many other creatures—even dragonflies and mosquitoes! Images of the sun and moon were anthropomorphized with human faces. Humans, too, were carved on the poles, as were humans with animal or bird characteristics—that is, therianthropes. Conversely, animals and birds were sometimes depicted with distinctly human features including faces, arms, legs, fingers, or toes.

As previously noted, such shape-shifted and anthropomorphized creatures reflect Native myths in which both animals and humans share a kinship and possess supernatural abilities to transform themselves.

To put the heraldic nature of carved poles into sharper focus, Zimmerman notes that much of Native American ritual and art indeed are representations of their totem animals, and in those cases, such depictions are a way to tap into the abilities and characteristics of an animal spirit. For example, a hunter might emblazon his spear with images of a wolf in order to channel its predator prowess, or a warrior might adorn his arrows with images of rattlesnakes, the better to harness the sympathetic magic of the serpent's rapid-strike abilities.[226]

A raven carved as a totem is intended to evoke (bring to mind) or invoke (summon forth) some aspect of that animal's abilities or power, perhaps its cleverness or resourcefulness, and the totem is put into service that way, whether it is used in ritual, during some mundane activity, or even as a "mere" spur to contemplation or meditation—a "reminder" that the totem animal's abilities are accessible to the members of a clan.

A raven cast onto a "totem" pole is neither intended nor expected to serve such functions, although, as Malin notes, a creature represented on a carved pole—a creature that obviously played some part in a clan's history—might possess some measure of totemic meaning.

As discussed in the chapter on talismans and amulets, intention combined with focus and knowledge are key in any magical working, passive or active—whether that operation involves an animal image, herbal plants, chant, drumming, moon magic, or some other modality.

So, what are we to make of these totem poles that are not totem poles? What do we make of the poles' depictions of Raven?

---

226 Zimmerman, *The Sacred Wisdom of the Native Americans*, 92–94.

While scholars repeatedly note that totem poles were not objects of worship and were not used in rituals, the line between mere representational art and mythic art that evokes or invokes something more can get blurred.

Malin notes that a totem pole's depiction of Raven recalls not only a clan's history and lineage, but also "the culture hero of ancient mythology."[227] Thus, for anyone familiar with Raven tales, the poles reinvigorate Raven's role in bringing light into the world and indeed his bringing the Haida people themselves into the world. The poles may remind one of the comic tale of how Bear and Wolf, fed up with Raven's mischief, stole his beak or the time Raven supernaturally animated his feces. They may recall Raven's more ignoble, even cruel shenanigans, as Paul Radin details—along with Raven's beneficent works—in his book *The Trickster: A Study in American Indian Myth*. In one such incident, Raven invites bears to a feast, then coaxes a wren to tug out the entrails of one of them through its anus—and no, that bear does not magically revive.[228]

Once again we return to the power of image—to the 19,000-year-old Lascaux shaman crow-man painted on a wall deep in that cave in France—an image which, if it wasn't the first magical, totemic artwork to emerge in our world, certainly was among the first and is one of the longest enduring. Also recall that beside that prostrate bird-headed shaman is a pole with a bird perched at its top ... a totem pole?!

TRANSCULTURAL APPRECIATION OR CULTURAL APPROPRIATION?

While contemplating photos and drawings of the magnificent totem poles of the Pacific Northwest peoples, I am invariably led to contemplate the various statuary, fetishes, masks, and artworks around my home.

Whatever statuary, fetishes, masks, and/or metaphysical artworks reside on your altar or in your home, you are aware these artifacts possess varying degrees of power. Their power radiates not only through their readily apparent physical presence and their visual symbology, but also through their subliminal effects on the vibrations and feng shui of a room and through the myths they embody—myths that will swirl in our subconscious upon the slightest notice of an icon, fetish, or even a sacred image in a book or on a laptop screen.

227 Malin, *Totem Poles of the Pacific Northwest Coast*, 57.
228 Radin, *The Trickster*, 107.

These artifacts and images are the embodiment of the goddesses, gods, and the supernatural emissaries of the unseen realms we are talking about, after all. If Odin, Oshun, or Cernunnos can't fill a room, who can?

Images have power.

Perhaps because I grew up in northern New Mexico amid the very palpable presence of the Navajo, the Hopi, and the Pueblo people of Taos, I am uniquely attune to the cultural appropriation of Native American culture. The historically documented physical and cultural genocide perpetrated upon the Indigenous peoples of the Americas by mostly Western Europeans, as well as the inadvertent or callous decimation of Native populations through European-borne diseases and/or the westward expansion of Manifest Destiny, gives me pause—as it should anyone.

At the same time, mythic and spiritual art around the world has transcended time, borders, and cultures to touch people everywhere. So it has been with, say, the erotic stone sculptures of the sun temple at Konark in India; the ancient Buddhas of Bamiyan, Afghanistan, tragically and ruthlessly destroyed by the Taliban; and the stunning Paleolithic cave paintings of Lascaux in France.

In that spirit of deep appreciation, perhaps one can hope to marvel at the Pacific Northwest tribes' stunning carved-pole art that survives, both old and modern, and to respectfully connect to the totemic-talismanic power of the creatures there depicted. One can hope that, perhaps, this is something their creators will see as their gift to humankind.

Raven, Eagle, Thunderbird, and other pole creatures radiate a potent energy whenever I encounter them in photographs or documentaries—I can barely imagine the power they would exude in a face-to-face encounter.

Chapter 20

LESSONS: RAVEN'S TRICKERY

It is common knowledge that Native Americans forged (and still do) a close spiritual relationship to the natural world. Its creatures, the land and sky, and the forces and phenomena that play out upon the earth and in the cosmos—the change of seasons, the movements of sun and moon, the hunt and harvest—are infused with supernatural beings and/or powers.

According to the book *Keepers of the Totem*, which surveys the tribes of the Pacific Northwest, in ancient times "the paths of spirits and humans intersected often," and thus were the native peoples gifted with such skills as hunting and fishing. Also, the boundaries between the natural world and the spirit world were indistinct, and "people sometimes stumbled into a spirit village without warning," finding themselves in the midst of beings who appeared and talked like humans but who were "actually wolf or bear spirits." While spirit entities could shape-shift from animal to human form, people could shape-shift into animals "if they lingered overly long among the supernaturals."[229] (See chapter 25, "Be the Crow.")

Indeed, pick up almost any work on Native American cultures, and seemingly more so than the other cultures explored in this book, animals will feature prominently in its pages. *The Sacred Wisdom of the Native Americans* by Larry J. Zimmerman and *The Aquarian Guide to Native American Mythology* by Page Bryant are just two examples. Hamilton A. Tyler takes two entire books to explore the beliefs and practices of just the Pueblo peoples of the American Southwest in his works *Pueblo Animals and Myths* and *Pueblo Birds and Myths*.

---

229 Editors of Time-Life Books, *Keepers of the Totem*, 79–81.

As Zimmerman writes, in many Indigenous American origin myths, humans and animals were created as equals, even as companions who communed with one another.[230]

The traditions of the Haida people of the Pacific Northwest include the belief "that all animals possess human souls and can assume human form at will."[231]

The ancient Norse had their Hugin and Munin, hanging out on the shoulders of Odin the Raven God and then leaving their perch each day to fly around the world and spy for their master. But in the worlds of the Vikings and the ancient Celts, ravens and crows were never far from mayhem, battle, bloodshed, and dread.

Native Americans, however—particularly those tribes west of the Mississippi, and especially those of the Northwest Coast—noticed ravens windsurfing, hanging upside down on branches, teasing other animals or humans, and engaging in other impish behaviors, and they thought: "Raven is playful! Raven is clever! Raven is a trickster!"

And therein lies a tale ... well, many of them.

RAVEN TALES

The exploits of Raven and Crow feature in many Native American tales that serve as wisdom teachings or as stories that explain how the natural world came to be the way it is. Raven especially holds an exalted place in the cultures and myths of the Indigenous people in what today is coastal British Columbia, Washington state, and southeast Alaska.

Like Coyote, who figures in numerous tales of Native American cultures in the West and Southwest, Raven is almost always a trickster figure: a mischievous, conniving, sometimes bumbling, sometimes cruel, sometimes benevolent, often self-serving, supernatural being—not a god—who possesses human consciousness and speech and is almost always looking to satiate his lusts for power, control, food, and pleasure.

Sometimes Raven is beneficent, as in the tale of the Haida people of the Northwest Coast in which Raven coaxed the first humans out from hiding in a

---

230 Zimmerman, *The Sacred Wisdom of the Native Americans*, 150.

231 Editors of Time-Life Books, *Keepers of the Totem*, 80.

cockleshell and into the world—and yes, that tale does make Raven into a sort of creator-god figure.

But more often, Raven is looking out for himself. Fortunately for us humans, Raven's devious plotting and/or his often-inept trickery backfire, and his impish ways may, for example, bring light and fire into the world, thus inadvertently benefiting humankind.

One tale of how Raven captured fire and gave it to people portrays him as an unappreciated benefactor of humankind. After all, the smoke from the fiery stick he procured on his quest permanently turned his white feathers to black and hoarsened his voice to an unlovely "grawk" (very distinctive from a crow's "caw," remember). And so, humans do not recognize the true identity of their fire-bringer, and they shun him.

That story, like almost every Raven tale and, indeed, like folktales in many cultures, springs from an oral tradition and exists in numerous written-down versions in modern times. And so it's not surprising that in one version, "How Raven Brought Fire to the Indians," as presented on the World of Tales website, Raven is up to his impish, self-serving, lust-fulfilling trickery: After procuring fire and light and bringing them to the earth, he hoards fire and refuses to share any of his stash with humans. After learning how to make fire, he realizes he can use it as a bargaining chip with people. His motivation? He wants to trade fire to obtain "many wives," which he does.[232]

Following are two Raven tales that carry lessons for us humans from the canny corvid.

Raven Brings Light to the World

The Haida and Tlingit tribes of the Pacific Northwest tell similar tales about how Raven brought light into the world.

"There are dozens of Raven stories," said Miranda Belarde-Lewis, an assistant professor of North American Indigenous Knowledge at the University of Washington's Information School.[233] Belarde-Lewis is enrolled at Zuni Pueblo and is a member of the Takdeintáan Clan of the Tlingit Nation.

"Raven is a trickster, and regularly finds himself in trouble, or finds that the shortcuts used to benefit him almost always backfire," Belarde-Lewis said.

---

232 "How Raven Brought Fire to the Indians."

233 Belarde-Lewis, "There Are Many Versions of the Tlingit 'Raven' Story."

"Many times, the consequences of his actions have influenced the world as we now know it."

The story of "Raven and the Box of Daylight," which is told in numerous versions, "has captivated the imagination of Tlingit peoples for thousands of years, just as it has captured the imagination of non-Tlingit anthropologists since the late 1700s," she said. "Its appeal is multifaceted: It has drama, it helps explain the world, and it has many similarities to other iconic stories from other cultures and religions that are easily compared."[234]

Here is my summary of a Haida version of how Raven brought light to the world:

> The entire world was dark because an old man had hidden all the light in the universe in boxes within boxes. He was afraid his daughter might be ugly, and he couldn't bear to look at her. Raven was tired of bumping into things in the darkness and wanted the light for himself.
>
> So, Raven shape-shifted into a pine tree needle floating in a basket of drinking water, and the pine needle was swallowed by the daughter. Soon she gave birth to a raven/human child who, although a bit peculiar, was accepted by the old man. Raven soon began pestering the old man to open the boxes, one after another.
>
> When the old man gave in and finally opened the last box containing the light, Raven grabbed it and flew away. Eagle saw Raven and tried to steal the light, causing Raven to drop some of it, which became the moon and the stars. As Eagle continued the chase, Raven became exhausted and dropped his last piece of light, which became the sun. And so light came to the Earth and all its creatures, and the old man saw that his daughter was indeed beautiful after all.

Thus selfish Raven inadvertently releases the lights of the heavens—an amazing boon for humankind.

---

234 Belarde-Lewis, "There Are Many Versions of the Tlingit 'Raven' Story."

While this Native American trickster tale and others about Raven explain how the natural world came to be as it is, they also address the caprice of life and the natural world—its randomness and indifference.

But these are also spirit-lifting teaching tales—they provide a curious sense of hope. We all know that bad things happen to good people. But this Raven tale and others let us know that good things can happen to good people—even if the universe, the gods, and/or supernatural forces may not be looking out for us.

Raven steals light not because he wants to help humankind—he wants it for himself. But he bungles his heist and—boom—suddenly we humans have the sun, moon, and stars. That isn't some Pollyanna tale that everything is going to turn out for the best. Rather, despite its fantasy elements, this is a tale that realistically illustrates how the natural world works—the ebb and flow of forces and fortunes at play. As the antihero Meursault says near the very end of the Albert Camus novel *The Stranger*: "I laid my heart open to the benign indifference of the universe."[235] The key word there is *benign*. The harsh and harrowing challenges of nature can make us forget that the flesh, breath, and tears of Gaia—the land, the sky and winds, the oceans and rivers and rain—are benignly indifferent to us. Some of Raven's exploits remind us of that. Those dark clouds on the horizon may bring a frightening tornado or hurricane, but more often they are going to bring the rains that nourish our crops.

Any Pagan, Witch, Wiccan, or polytheist seeking to work Crow-Raven Magic—or any weekend naturalist who seeks a deeper connection to corvids, other creatures, and the land—would do well to embrace that lesson. While it's tempting to borrow that snarky pop culture phrase and say, "It's Gaia's world— we just live in it," the truer lesson is: "It's Gaia's world—but we can attune ourselves to it, both its gifts and caprices, and seek communion with it."

Raven Steals Berries

Unfortunately for us humans, Raven can make us wince as his greedy, selfish ways often hold up a mirror so that we see reflections of our own foibles and character flaws. Ultimately that is not so unfortunate for us two-legged, upright animals, who need to be confronted with the realities of our true, sometimes destructive nature so that we can be better citizens of Turtle Island (as some

---

235 Camus, *The Stranger*, 154.

Indigenous peoples of Northeast America refer to planet Earth). Indeed, teaching such self-knowledge is one of the aims of Raven tales.

Raven's greed and self-serving nature are in full bloom in a tale related by James Teit in his article "Traditions of the Lillooet Indians of British Columbia." However, there is more to this tale than a simple depiction of greed and gluttony. Here's my summary, supplemented with quotes from Teit's work:

> Four women—Xwitx', Bluejay, Crow, and Snail—decided to invite Raven to go with them on a canoe trip down river to deliver berries to a relative. "The women could not go alone, for they had no canoe, and, besides, they needed a man to accompany them."
>
> After they had been paddling two days, Raven announced he had to go ashore "to ease himself. Going downstream some distance, he defecated and urinated, and told his excrements to shout loudly, which they did."
>
> Raven returned to the canoe and told the women to hide because they were coming under attack by enemies. Hearing the ruckus, the women believed Raven and ran to the bushes. Raven began shouting and banging on the canoe with his paddle, tricking the women into thinking he was fighting the attackers. After the noise ceased, they thought he must be dead.
>
> Raven ate all the berries, then took the juice from the bottoms of the baskets and smeared it on his head and body to appeared bloodied. At last the women returned to the canoe, where they found Raven lying in the bottom. "We must return home with all speed," Raven said. "I am badly wounded, and our enemies may attack us again."
>
> When they returned home, a young man met their canoe, and the women related their story to him. "Raven lies," the young man said. "He is not wounded. He has eaten all your berries." And so Raven's trickery was exposed.[236]

Yes, we readily see that Raven is a greedy bastard who will serve himself and to hell with everyone else. Significantly, in this retelling—just to make

---

236 Teit, "Traditions of the Lillooet Indians of British Columbia," 287–371.

sure we human readers get the point—Raven is referred to as a "man," while the women, who have the names of three birds and a snail, are ambiguously human. This is a tale about the greed of humankind.

But, as often is the case with Native American folktales and myths, there are more dimensions at play in this story—dimensions with deep import for anyone practicing Crow-Raven Magic.

This Raven tale once again reflects a world in which humans and animals share language, thoughts, and behaviors. Even if one considers that to be mere metaphor, such sharing between humans and the natural world is at the heart of Crow-Raven Magic. It is the leitmotif that runs throughout this book—and, I would aver, it is the leitmotif that informs Pagan practice both ancient and modern.

Time and time again we have seen how the Paleolithic cave artists, the ancient Greeks and Romans, the Celts, the Norse, and Native Americans made simple observations of the natural world and consciously or intuitively attuned themselves to it, leading them to discern the truth of things both seen and unseen. Thus they were able to enrich their lives and those of all the inhabitants of Turtle Island—and intuit and connect to the realms of Spirit, the gods and goddesses.

Sometimes I wonder if the sum of Pagan practice is "Pay attention! Be aware!"—whether one is tossing popcorn to squirrels in an urban park, stepping over an ant bed in one's backyard, or going on walk-about upon the mountain Knocknarea in western Ireland, on the Appalachian Trail, in Sherwood Forest, in the Australian Outback, or in the Puebloan ruins of Tsankawi near Los Alamos, New Mexico.

It sounds so simple, this idea of communion with nature. Yet how often had I ignored communion with these intelligent creatures all around me, the corvids, until that fateful day in the post office in Dublin, Ireland, when I stared, transfigured, at the statue of Cuchulainn and the Raven—the shape-shifted Morrigan—on his shoulder?

Or are these Raven tales so fanciful? Encounter real-life crows and ravens and you will begin to suspect that the Native American storytellers were not making such huge leaps of the imagination after all and that communion with these creatures will teach us valuable lessons: that we humans do and must share this planet, that we must dispense with the foolish notion that we are the only truly intelligent beings upon Gaia, and that from the animals we can learn new ways, or revitalize old ways, to be and behave in this world—and discover new ways to connect to deity and the sacred in the process.

The Spirit that made Crow and Raven, and gave these creatures extraordinary gifts, also made us. Commune with the corvids and we commune with the goddess and gods.

Raven tales hold other lessons for anyone practicing Crow-Raven Magic.

Consider the supernatural abilities that Raven exhibits in the Lillooet tale above: He's able to give voice to his feces and urine. Really, Raven? *That's* your superpower? To give voice to your poop and piss?

No doubt Raven takes great pride in this ability because it enables him to smugly trick his fellow creatures (or so he believes) and satiate his lust for food. But what being—divine, supernatural, or otherwise—would be proud of such a feat of truly low magic?

One lesson of this tale is: "Your greed and self-servitude will always be discovered, so be mindful of such behaviors."

But a deeper, more subtle lesson can be found here. Although Raven is not a god, he is a creature with amazing supernatural abilities…or perhaps not so amazing. Talking poop and piss? Here is a lesson for anyone walking a path of magic, exploring the Mysteries, or seeking communion with the Divine: Shit and piss may be, can be, will be part of your journey. Yes, the path of high magic can be couched in lofty terms: "Your feet will be stuck in the mud while you reach for the stars!" Or: "Your journey to the metaphysical realms must proceed with a first step from the mundane world." Or that vintage chestnut: "As above, so below," which means its inversion also must be true—"As below, so above."

All such mantras expressing the link between the Divine/supernatural/ magical realms and the mundane world are true enough. But Raven is having none of that lofty eloquence or reverence for such matters: If magic sometimes requires poop and piss, so be it. Get on with it. Of course, Raven deploys such earthy magic in an unadmirable pursuit for personal gain at the expense of others. And need one be reminded that "for personal gain" is not necessarily a bad thing in and of itself, whether on the road to enlightenment or the road to work or the road to the grocery store. No one is totally altruistic—go to a bookstore and the Dalai Lama's words of wisdom are not free. It's how, why, and to what degree one pursues personal gain that is crucial—the phrase "enlightened self-interest" comes to mind, as does, of course, that ol' Wiccan mantra: "If it harms no one, do as you will."

Yet Raven graphically—and absurdly and comically!—reminds us that any magic we pursue must of necessity begin in the grit and grim of everyday life.

We readily, if not so easily, embrace the lofty pathways of the heart—its roads that beckon us to seek love and Spirit and to explore the mysteries of the soul. But the heart has its base, self-serving and myopic emotions, too. If you are walking a path to enlightenment, you will step in piles of shit and puddles of piss, placed there by Raven or some other trickster. The goal is not to avoid them—to do so requires time and effort and will likely force us to take our eyes off the horizon ahead or even divert our eyes from the beauty and lessons that beckon to us in our immediate place upon the path. Raven teaches this to us, even if he does so inadvertently.

Raven's Play

Raven and his exploits also teach us another valuable lesson, one that is big-picture wisdom outside of the teachings we can learn from his folly. That lesson is—play!

John Marzluff and Tony Angell, in their book *Gifts of the Crow: How Perception, Emotion, and Thought Allow Smart Birds to Behave Like Humans*, devote an entire chapter to corvid play, which they title simply "Frolic." While many birds exhibit a sense of play, they report, none do so as often or in such complex ways as corvids.[237] A quick tour of YouTube will turn up numerous videos of corvid silliness: Ravens and crows love to slide down snow-covered roofs and car windshields. They have a penchant for pestering cats by walking behind them, pecking at their tails then quickly hopping away. They will torment or frolic with dogs or mice. Corvids will swing upside down from the supple branches of elms and other trees.

You can picture Native Americans of the Pacific Northwest smiling and nodding in agreement at how modern science has confirmed what their myths and religion have long known.

How often in the world's spiritual traditions—whether Paganism, Buddhism, the monotheistic traditions, or any other tradition—do adherents get

---

237 Marzluff and Angell, *Gifts of the Crow*, 119.

caught up in doing "the work"? How often do we allow ourselves, in our pursuits of the Mysteries and magic, to become, if not downright dour, at least overly studious? How often does spellwork seem like a recipe for baking a cake?

Yes, the efficacy of magic may depend on precision and attention to detail. Certainly. Yet I have seen ballroom dancers who move with their feet and not their hearts—you can tell their brains are overly concerned about where to step next. I have heard guitarists in rock bands who are amazing musicians, yet their solos have an air of scientific studiousness, as if they were plotted out on graph paper. More amazing are those dancers and musicians who move and play with their heart—after all, as Alan Watts noted, we "play music" rather than "work music."[238] When I was a newspaper entertainment writer covering Woodstock '94 in upstate New York, I heard Carlos Santana perform, and then I attended his press conference in the press tent. "Playing here is a spiritual orgasm!" said Santana, who also performed at the original Woodstock in 1969. Yes, Santana truly *played*—frolicked!—at Woodstock.

Likewise, some of the most effective, beautiful, and transformative Pagan rituals I have participated in were those that sported an occasional sense of play—even if, a few times, that sense of play was introduced inadvertently when something went amiss, but the high priestess wisely was able to smile, laugh it off, and move on while acknowledging that Raven or Coyote or Loki or some other Trickster had dropped into the circle for a visit.

To add to the cake-baking and scientific-guitarists analogies, consider another metaphor: the road map. Yes, maps are a wonderful tool and allow us to get from point A to point B. Use a road map and you will find yourself, eventually, at point B—the exact place you intended to go. However, you will have missed any wonders, curiosities, or enlightenments that may have engaged you if and when you had wandered from the beaten path—or if you had deliberately chosen to put your road map aside and playfully taken a left turn into mystery, if only for a time.

Although the internet-fueled Pagan revival of the past twenty years is changing things much more rapidly than the Pagan revival of the 1960s and early '70s, there was a time not so long ago (within my lifetime) when growing up in Western society meant having little exposure to "alternative spiritualities." Coming of age in the 1960s far from Witch-friendly England, the Magical

---

238 Watts, *The Tao of Philosophy*, 76.

Childe bookshop in New York City, or the dizzying, occult-laden high weird-ness of Southern California (see Robert Anton Wilson's delightful book *Cosmic Trigger: Final Secret of the Illuminati*), I encountered "Pagan-witchy" ways (note the quote marks) only through *The Wizard of Oz*, Andre Norton's *Witch World* series, or the kids' television show *H.R. Pufnstuf* (remember Witchiepoo?). Oh, and there were occasional glimpses of the sort-of-scary Sybil Leek books on the paperback racks at the local drugstore, nestled beside even more alarming tomes such as *Flying Saucers—Serious Business*.

Concepts of Paganism, Wicca, Witchcraft, and magic began to infiltrate my mind and soul only when I took a wrong turn at the public library in Dothan, Alabama, when I was attending a community college there, and I came face-to-face with Colin Wilson's magisterial, insightful, historical-based study *The Occult*. Still, it took an equally, seemingly serendipitous encounter with Robert Anton Wilson's *Cosmic Trigger* a bit later in the mid-1980s to finally make me realize there are more things under heaven and earth than had been dreamt of in my previous philosophies.

At the precise moment I discovered each of these life-changing books, I was overcome with the sensation that John Lilly calls—here's that term again—"Cosmic Coincidence Control Center." This wasn't some ominous sense of foreboding, as if I suddenly had become a pawn of sinister forces. Neither did I feel I was being randomly, mindlessly shuffled into the path of some mysterious, automaton-like energy. Quite the opposite. I instead felt as if the Universe was not just expressing its agency but was joyously playing with me, as if it were saying, "New worlds are awaiting you! Here's your portal! Have an adventure!"

Yes, we all know how that Edgar Allan Poe guy quoted that surly, downer Raven: "Nevermore!"

But Raven has another saying that one should take to heart: "Play!"

Lesson: Quoth the Raven: Play!

Chapter 21

GRIMOIRE: RAVEN'S CRAZY WISDOM

Alter your consciousness so that you may "altar" your consciousness. That is one of the leitmotifs of this book, of practicing Crow-Raven Magic.

When you alter your consciousness using what religion scholar Georg Feuerstien calls the "shock tactics" of "crazy wisdom" teachers—and yes, Raven is one!—you tamp down your chattering "monkey mind" and wake yourself out of the "robot mind" that so often is at the wheel of our daily lives.[239] You thus open the door to "altar-ing" your consciousness and subconscious. You will see your reality (*realities*, actually) in a fresh way and place yourself in a liminal mindset that is conducive to entering non-ordinary realities—and there you will be opened to communion with the Other Realms and God-Goddess-Spirit.

The list of mind-altering "shock tactics" employed by the world's spiritual traditions is long and storied: meditation, shamanic drumming, yoga/breathwork, ritual, entheogens, tantric sex. The following are simple exercises for brief escapes from your monkey mind, until you are able to pursue deeper inner work (see the chapters "Candle Shadow Scrying" and "Be the Crow").

WHAT YOU WILL NEED
- Solitary ritual space
- Access to various everyday environments with trees, such as your backyard or a park
- Access to music on your favored device

---

239 Feuerstein, *Holy Madness*, 3.

BACKGROUND

Wes "Scoop" Nisker, in his delightful book *The Essential Crazy Wisdom*, reveals how crazy wisdom is not just the province of some kooky Zen master who asks a seeker, "What is the sound of one hand clapping?" and then slaps the poor bastard silly as he fumbles for the "correct" answer. Crazy wisdom also is:

> lurking beneath the unruly hair of Albert Einstein and between the bushy eyebrows of Groucho Marx, inside the howly voice of Allen Ginsberg and the crazy ranting of Lily Tomlin's bag lady ... whatever disguise it wears, crazy wisdom arises again and again to expose us to ourselves and to remind us of the strange impossible nature of our enterprise here on earth—life.[240]

What Feuerstein calls "holy madness or crazy wisdom" comes about when "crazy-wise teachers" use techniques "that are designed to startle or shock the conventional mind." Such adepts "use their eccentricity to communicate an alternative vision to that which governs ordinary life. They are masters of inversion, proficient breakers of taboos, and lovers of surprise, contradiction, and ambiguity. They share these skills and penchants with the traditional figures of the trickster and the clown."[241]

Nisker notes that the Trickster in all his many guises, including Raven, is a part of crazy wisdom traditions along with such archetypal figures as the Clown, the Jester, and the Fool.

And, ironically, there's that *T* word—tradition. How often, whether it's in ritual or other aspects of your spiritual practice (Pagan or otherwise) or in your daily, mundane life, do you do something only because "that's the way I've always done it"? Sure, we slap that lofty word *tradition* on our rituals and ritualized practices, and yes, traditions have their place. But *tradition* may be a term we unthinkingly substitute for a far more ignoble practice—habit.

If you are suffering from a spiritual repetitive motion disorder, a carpal tunnel syndrome of the soul, a too strident passion for order, an unexamined or subconscious notion that your belief systems are too rigid, look to Raven the Trickster. No, you don't have to devise a talking poop and piss ritual (hmmmm)

---

240 Nisker, *The Essential Crazy Wisdom*, 11.

241 Feuerstein, *Holy Madness*, 3.

or connive to steal someone's food. Rather, frolic! Do something back-asswards. Hang upside down with Crow and Raven. Prank someone (in a fun rather than cruel manner). Prank yourself. Embrace Chaos—or at the very least, do not run fraidy-cat from her each and every time she shows up unexpectedly. And she always shows up unexpectedly.

Here are four simple, Raven-inspired techniques (that hardly seems the right word) to help you play and frolic, to alter your perspective and alter your consciousness so that you can "altar" your consciousness.

ACTION: GODDESS-GOD ROCK

The Southern Delta Church of Wicca-ATC in Arkansas once used *Grease* as the theme of a new moon ritual. That's not a typo. The ritual theme centered on *Grease* the movie musical and not Greece the birthplace of Aphrodite, Persephone, Hekate, and all those classical goddesses and gods.

High priest Terry Riley says the church used the song "Greased Lightnin'" "to raise the cone of power" while ritual participants portrayed "all the characters from *Grease* and *Grease 2*."[242]

Using rock and pop music—the actual original recordings of well-known hits and not rock-oriented works written by Pagan artists—is not unheard of in Pagan rituals. Jason Mankey, a Witch and author who, with his wife, Ari, runs an eclectic Wiccan coven and a Gardnerian coven in Silicon Valley, California, has crafted rituals using the song "Green Man" by the English band XTC and the music of the Doors and Fairport Convention.[243]

For his Doors-oriented ritual, Mankey used "Break on Through" to cast the circle and call the quarters. He used "Hello, I Love You" to call the goddess. To call Dionysius, he deployed "Alabama Song," a 1920s Bertolt Brecht/Kurt Weill work rejuvenated by Mr. Mojo Risin' and company, that references whiskey and bars.[244]

Samhain festivals I have attended at the Florida Pagan Gathering have featured a recording of "Forever Autumn" by Justin Hayward of the Moody Blues and a solemn live performance by ritualists of Pink Floyd's "Wish You Were Here."

---

242 de Yampert, "Bang a Gong."

243 de Yampert, "Bang a Gong."

244 de Yampert, "Bang a Gong."

Such rock and pop classics are deployed just like any other music used in ritual: to set the mood and intentions, to evoke sacred space, to alter consciousness, and to commune with the gods and goddesses.

Taking a cue from these ritualists cited, design—or sketch—a ritual using the music of your favorite rock, pop, or hip-hop god or goddess. Or you can deify the music of multiple artists in a single ritual. Avoid the works of Pagan artists whose music readily fits your spiritual paradigm. Rather, this is a Raven-esque Trickster exercise, even if you decide to leave it as an entry on theoretical ritual in your Book of Shadows or magical journal rather than manifest it on the physical plane.

If you are a member of a traditional Wiccan coven or have experience participating in Wiccan rituals, choose a sabbat from the Wheel of the Year to celebrate: Yule (Winter Solstice), Imbolc, Ostara (Spring Equinox), Beltane, Litha (Summer Solstice), Lughnasadh (or Lammas), Mabon (Autumn Equinox), or Samhain. Also, you may choose a goddess and/or god to honor.

With those choices in mind, select a song to be the musical background for casting the circle and calling the spirits of the four directional quarters, another track to serve as the theme song (or songs) for the goddess and/or god, and a final song to release the quarters and close the circle.

Even if you deem your ritual to be a theoretical one, carefully consider the theme song(s) of the deity you will be invoking. Why that song? What characteristics or signature magical abilities of the deity (wisdom, strength, love, shape-shifting, fury, fecundity, beneficence, wildness, a trickster tendency) do the lyrics of the song express?

Theme Songs for a Goddess-God, the Moon, or the Elements

Rather than thinking in terms of a ritual, instead craft a list of rock, pop, or hip-hop songs that—for you—will invoke (using that term loosely) your deity, orisha, or a spirit entity you work with, be it Hekate, Cernunnos, the Morrigan, Oshun, Odin, Kokopelli, Rainbow Serpent, or Raven himself. Whoever makes the longest list wins! Devotees of the love goddess Aphrodite may have the advantage in this exercise.

Alternately, create a list of lunar-themed songs for a full moon meditation, or create lists of songs that invoke the four magical elements of earth, air, fire, and water.

Find a place of solitude, outdoors if possible, where you can take your favorite listening device and cue up one of your chosen songs as a soundscape for contemplation or meditation.

Yes, there are the obvious songs for this Raven game: Fleetwood Mac's "Rhiannon" or the Waterboys's "The Pan Within." But also consider, say, Al Stewart's wistful "Flying Sorcery" for east/air and the Ohio Players' lusty "Fire" for south/fire, a Beltane ritual, or a paean to the Hawaiian goddess Pele. You can use the sinewy soul of Al Green's "Take Me to the River" for west or a water goddess or the jacked-up country folk of Dar Williams's "Go to the Woods," with its talk of spooky shadows and an "angry woman" who may be lurking there and ready to eat you, for north/earth or a Hekate devotion. Beyoncé's "Mood for Eva" invokes Oshun, a Yoruba river deity.

Allow yourself to create a Vulcan mind-meld between your spiritual devotions and these songs or many, many others—the more "out there" the song, the better. Yes, by all means force the lyrics of, say, Led Zeppelin's "The Ocean" to fit into your spiritual weltanschauung's conception of Manannán mac Lir, Mami Wata, Namaka, or other water deities. Remember, this is not a test—this is play. Gerald Gardner will not be grading your final paper.

For inspiration along these lines, read Erik Davis's "Led Zeppelin IV," a masterly, book-length, trippy romp through the rock band's fourth album using an occult lens, in which Davis finds as much magical and esoteric meaning in "Going to California," "Black Dog," and "Misty Mountain Hop" as in "Stairway to Heaven."

ACTION: MOVE LIKE A CROW

Crows and ravens move through the physical world in weird and wonderful ways. Crows hang upside down on tree limbs!

Here is a lesson from Crow and Raven: change your physical stance, your physical movement in the world. We do this intuitively as children. Walk beside youngsters and invariably they will break into a skip or a faux game of hopscotch on an unmarked sidewalk. A children's playground is simply a veritable cornucopia of apparatuses and devices designed to enhance kids' natural predilection for seeking novel ways to move and contort one's body. Youngsters, akin to Crow and Raven, intuitively want to swing, twirl, slide, spin, tumble, and climb up high so they can get—ahem—a bird's-eye view of their world, a view that to them is new and astonishing.

As adults, we move about with … well, not with our heads in the clouds, but with our heads perpetually some five to six feet above the earth when standing or walking or three to four feet up when we are sitting at our jobs or at the dinner table. When we do go supine, it's usually in bed right before sleep, and we are staring at a darkened ceiling.

While many rituals and magical workings (spellcraft, scrying, tarot, trance meditation) focus on the mind aspect of the mind-body-spirit connection and the mind aspect of altering/altar-ing one's consciousness, we may tend to forget the physicality that can be involved in Mircea Eliade's "archaic techniques of ecstasy."[245] Yoga and its accompanying breathwork are the obvious example, but the physicality of drumming, chanting, sacred sex, and moving about in ritual are others.

Be like Crow and Raven. Try the following simple exercises I've labeled the Axis Mundi/World Tree Meditation and Climb a Tree (one can hardly label them "techniques") to alter your physical perspective and your physical relationship to Gaia. You may end up "altar-ing" your consciousness, perhaps not in any profound way but rather in a manner that will make you marvel anew at the world—a gift from Crow and Raven.

Action: Axis Mundi/World Tree Meditation

My flesh still tingles as if fairy sprites are frolicking upon it whenever I recall the first time I performed this "ritual" as a solitary many years ago at the Florida Pagan Gathering, and without anticipating any outcome at all.

In our daily lives, our eyes are almost perpetually focused four to ten feet in front of us. The simple act of going supine in nature can bring you into surprising communion with the earth below and the sky above. As the tactile sensations of soil, grasses, and tiny plants caress your backside, your new, sudden weltanschauung also will consist of blue sky and, perhaps, as was the case during my first supine "trip," a flotilla of fluffy cumulus clouds and, in my peripheral vision, a surrounding group of loblolly and slash pines.

To perform the meditation, lie supine outdoors. Do so sky-clad (unclothed) if desired and it's feasible, comfortable, and you have a private, secluded area.

---

245 Eliade, *Shamanism*.

Use a blanket if you must, but allowing the flesh of Gaia, her soil or grass, to caress you is much more preferable. I am amazed how often we adherents of the so-called earth-based religions—we Pagans, Wiccans, Witches, and others—are hesitant to play in the dirt. Some degree of solitude is also preferable, not necessarily a hermit's glade but at least a small clearing with little human noise. Your backyard may be not only doable but preferable in a way—you will come to see your immediate eco-space in a new manner.

Allow a few minutes, or perhaps many, for your "monkey mind" to chatter itself out. Do this by focusing on the clouds or the regal, friendly-sentinel stance of any nearby trees. When the "monkey" reappears, don't chide yourself—simply refocus on, say, the geometry of the tree leaves or pine needles within your peripheral vision or the rabbit or dragon you see hiding in the cloud shapes. Or you may be blessed to channel your attention on the caw of crows, the gronk of ravens, the coo of mourning doves, or the chirp-song of cardinals.

At some point (don't be in a hurry), allow your mind to drift into contemplation of the World Tree. An archetypal myth common to cultures around the globe, the World Tree is a spiritual representation or "map" of the cosmos. Typically, its roots extend down into the chthonic realms of the earth, the underworld, the abode that receives our ancestors' physical vessels—and ours too, one day—upon death. The World Tree's trunk springs up through the surface of the land and into life on the earthly plane—the abode of humans, fauna, flora, mountains, the oceans, and the sweet waters of rivers and lakes. The World Tree's branches extend skyward and into the heavens—the abode of the goddess, gods, Spirit, and spirits, a place where skilled shamans, soul travelers, mediums, and divine messengers, such as Crow and Raven, can visit and then return to the earthly realm with special knowledge.

The goal here is not to seek a deep trance state, although if that seems to be emerging, by all means allow it. Rather, the purpose is, once again, to find communion with nature, with Gaia, however brief and *seemingly* unspectacular that may be.

A simple supine trip will activate four of your five senses—sight, sound, touch, scent—so be sure to pay heed to each of them. The result will be that you are not merely meditating upon the World Tree (although that is a worthy goal in itself)—rather, you will be *experiencing* the World Tree. I have found that activating the fifth sense—taste—by bringing nuts or a piece of fruit into this ritual actually disrupts the trance journey, although that might change if I ever were to take a supine trip within arm's reach of a blackberry bush or wild spearmint plant.

ACTION: CLIMB A TREE!

When was the last time you climbed a tree? Of course, it's very likely that you were very young. And it's very likely that you, as an adult, see tree climbing as silly and childish or impractical at best. And yes, we humans over a certain age— say, eight or nine—are not well suited for tree climbing. When I was in middle school, a young boy in my neighborhood bet me that he could climb a pine tree. That's crazy, I thought—the lowest branches on the pine were about fifty feet above the ground. The youngster smiled and then, before my astonished eyes, bear-hugged his way up the tree's trunk.

But most of us, young or old, are not so agile. So, paradoxically, something as simple as climbing a tree may be one of the most difficult challenges in this book.

Find a tree to climb—a *climbable* tree, one with low, sturdy branches. Climb your Crow Spirit Tree if that is doable, or seek another tree where you have seen crows or ravens.

Keep in mind that the quest to climb a tree does not mean to scale one up to its lofty branches or to set yourself a physical endeavor that is reckless and dangerous. By all means, be safe and even cautious, and don't allow this to become a task. Don't fret if you can't find a climbable tree like the Chinese tallow, my Crow Spirit Tree at the edge of the woods behind my home.

The goal here is twofold and simple: One is to achieve a Crow's-eye or Raven's-eye view of our planet, even if you scurry only a few branches high up a tree. The second goal is to achieve a physical, tactile communion with Crow and Raven and, by extension, with Gaia. You will find that gripping a tree's branches and hoisting yourself skyward, in defiance of the gravity pulling at your own body, will create physical sensations quite different from caressing a tree's trunk with feet planted on the ground. Your childhood self knew this— now you are merely reminding yourself of it.

GOING FORWARD

The not-so-profound (but maybe it really is profound) message here: Allow, or even embrace, Raven's crazy wisdom and sense of play into your life—just a bit of it, at least. Chaos, disruption, silliness, occasional frolicking can-will spawn new ways of seeing life and new ways of seeing what lies beyond the veil that seemingly separates this world from the Other Realms.

Incorporate this chapter's exercises occasionally into your spiritual path, or devise your own crazy wisdom techniques. At the very least you will discover the simple joy that comes from surprising yourself.

Writer Kurt Vonnegut, in one of his most-famous commencement speeches, advises graduates to indulge in "skylarking," which he defines as an "intolerable lack of seriousness."[246] Perhaps that term should have been *raven-larking*.

---

246 Vonnegut, "Address to Graduating Class at Bennington College."

Chapter 22

LORE: THE SHADOWY SIDE OF CORVIDS

When it came to ravens, Lady Wilde—the mother of Irish writer Oscar Wilde—didn't mess around.

In an 1890 collection of Irish folklore, Lady Wilde gives a reassuring prescription for anyone unfortunate enough to encounter one of the corvids:

> When a raven is seen hovering round a cottage, evil is near, and a death may follow, or some great disaster; therefore to turn away ill luck, say at once: "May fire and water be in you, bird of evil, and may the curse of God be on your head for ever and ever."[247]

Lady Wilde has company, even more than one hundred years later.

When a friend, a well-read editor of a local news website that serves my county in Florida, found out I was writing a book about crows and ravens, he asked me: "Don't they have a sort of dark side, a fearful, superstition-leaden side? Are they maligned that way? And what about that unfathomable sound they make?"

He is not alone. While a few of my friends count themselves as corvid-philes like me, most are cautiously reserved around me if I happen to mention my latest crow adventure or post photos of Lord Valiant, Boga, or Baca on Facebook. For some it's the crows' cawing that is a turnoff—"I like birds that sing!" is a common response. One friend told me she witnessed a crow attack and kill a dove, and she now sees all crows as barbaric, malevolent predators—never mind that

---

247 Wilde, *Ancient Cures, Charms, and Usages of Ireland*, 61.

crows themselves, and especially their nests, are preyed upon in turn by owls and hawks. Other people are like my editor friend. They vaguely sense that crows and ravens are ominous creatures, even though they can't quite pinpoint their disdain for corvids.

Despite the prevalence of this crow-phobia that I have encountered, I was surprised to read that Lyanda Lynn Haupt experienced a quite similar response as she was writing her 2009 book, *Crow Planet: Essential Wisdom from the Urban Wilderness*. Many people, she writes, expressed

> a nuanced dis-ease, a shadowy sort of crow ambivalence that runs unusually deep.... Several women I have spoken with will not walk in parks with their small children if there are too many crows. They cannot tell me why exactly. And surrounding the myriad responses, even among the crow haters, there is nearly always an error of respect—a feeling that crows are, behind their shiny dark eyes, *knowing things*.[248]

Though corvids are omnivores, it is the birds' carrion feeding that has haunted humankind since time out of mind. Even the cave painting of the Lascaux bird-man, that earliest example of Crow Magic, is a tableau of death. While many interpreters, including me, see the prone bird-man as a shaman in a trance state rather than a Paleolithic hunter mortally wounded by his prey, there is no denying that the nearby bison, speared and with its entrails spilling out, is in its death throes. And who's to say that the nearby depiction of an upright staff with a crow-like bird on top is not a totemic tool of the shaman but simply a corvid on a pole waiting to feast on both the dying human and beast? Although, again, the wounded hunter interpretation is not one I share.

Still, the stage was set in the depths of Lascaux by what is one of the earliest artworks known to humankind: if Mr. D—death—shows up, a crow or raven will not be far behind.

As I have noted, humankind's ceaseless wars throughout millennia left corpses scattered across battlefields, providing feasts for crows, ravens, and other carrion-eating animals. John Marzluff and Tony Angell succinctly summarize what I call the shadowy side of corvid history: "Seeing crows scaveng-

---

248 Haupt, *Crow Planet*, 20; italics in original.

ing the dead, people began to draw literary, spiritual, and artistic connections between corvids and death." Unnerved humans began to believe that crows and ravens were "evil harbingers of death, with connections to the supernatural."[249]

As Edward Armstrong writes, the penchant of ravens to feast on battlefield corpses led human imagination "to the assumption that the birds could predict death and doom. ... All over Europe, and also in parts of Africa and Asia, a croaking raven portends death."[250]

In the ancient Norse and Celtic sagas, corvids are inextricably, although not exclusively, bound up in death and mayhem. While I have not seen systems of avian augury quantified by scholars, I can say, somewhat anecdotally, that my investigations of bird-related oracles reveal more crow and raven omens involving death and malevolence than those of other birds.

Ernest Ingersoll, in his *Birds in Legend, Fable, and Folklore*, quotes *The Encyclopedia Londinensis*, a self-proclaimed "universal dictionary of arts, sciences, and literature" published in twenty-four volumes in the early 1800s: "The most inauspicious omens were given by ravens."[251]

Elsewhere Ingersoll notes a legend that says "European crows go down to hell once every year," where they must pay a tribute of feathers to the devil. Because the reputed trip occurs during the crows' real-life summer molting season, Ingersoll playfully wonders if the legend may be true.[252]

As Armstrong observed, the ominous reputation of corvids extends beyond Europe, and indeed one suspects that reputation is as ubiquitous as the birds themselves. Armstrong writes that "all" Semitic peoples believe ravens possess strange powers. Syriac tales of exorcisms say that devils take the shape of ravens when they flee humans' bodies, and those ancient texts likewise relate that evil spirits adopt the guise of "black stinking ravens" to pester the saints. Arabs claim the birds "foretell death and disaster."[253]

Numerous observers have noted that the black color of crows and ravens factors into their malevolent reputation—black being the shade associated with death, evil, and metaphysical darkness. Ingersoll writes:

---

249 Marzluff and Angell, *In the Company of Crows and Ravens*, 289.

250 Armstrong, *The Folklore of Birds*, 77.

251 Ingersoll, *Birds in Legend, Fable, and Folklore*, 213.

252 Ingersoll, *Birds in Legend, Fable, and Folklore*, 166.

253 Armstrong, *The Folklore of Birds*, 77.

In Greece and Italy ravens were sacred to Apollo, the great patron of augurs, who in a pet turned this bird from white to black—and an ill turn it was, *for black feathers make black birds*; and in this blackness of coat lies, in my opinion, the root of their sinister repute.[254]

Lest we believe such unsettling tales can be found only, as Edgar Allan Poe put it, in "many a quaint and curious volume of forgotten lore" from centuries past, a quick tour of modern-era pop culture will prove otherwise.[255]

In Poe's 1845 poem "The Raven," a grieving narrator wonders if he will ever be reunited with his deceased lover, Lenore, and "once upon a midnight dreary" he gets his answer when a creepy raven flies into his study—a talking raven at that, with a one-word vocabulary. Here are the last stanzas of Poe's classic, which was, popularity-wise, sort of the "Stairway to Heaven" of its day:

"Prophet!" said I, "thing of evil!—prophet still, if bird or devil!
By that Heaven that bends above us—by that God we both adore—
Tell this soul with sorrow laden if, within the distant Aidenn,
It shall clasp a sainted maiden whom the angels name Lenore—
Clasp a rare and radiant maiden whom the angels name Lenore."
Quoth the Raven "Nevermore."

"Be that word our sign of parting, bird or fiend!" I shrieked, upstarting—
"Get thee back into the tempest and the Night's Plutonian shore!
Leave no black plume as a token of that lie thy soul hath spoken!
Leave my loneliness unbroken!—quit the bust above my door!
Take thy beak from out my heart, and take thy form from off my door!"
Quoth the Raven "Nevermore."

And the Raven, never flitting, still is sitting, still is sitting
On the pallid bust of Pallas just above my chamber door;

---

254 Ingersoll, *Birds in Legend, Fable, and Folklore*, 168; italics in original.
255 Poe, "The Raven."

And his eyes have all the seeming of a demon's that is dreaming,
And the lamp-light o'er him streaming throws his shadow on the
floor;
And my soul from out that shadow that lies floating on the floor
Shall be lifted—nevermore![256]

In Alfred Hitchcock's 1963 film *The Birds*, based on a 1952 Daphne du Maurier novella of the same title, all sorts of birds run amok, yet perhaps Hitch knew that having a berserk—ahem—murder of crows attack those sweet, innocent, scared-shitless school children would heighten the fear factor.

Likewise the scene of a man's corpse with his eyes pecked out: The crow perpetrator is lying deathly still, with stiff wings flung wide, on a nearby bed. Although many birds are known to feast on the eyes of their prey, Hitchcock chose a crow for this scene, too. One can assume the bird lost its life satisfying its bloodlust, yet anyone who has read the Norse sagas may wonder if this corvid is merely passed out in a drunken, blood-satiated stupor.

A 2016 headline in the *Telegraph*, a British newspaper, read: "Death from above: the ravens slaughtering newborn lambs." A 2019 headline in the *Daily Mail*, another British newspaper, read: "The savage cruelty of a law that lets crows torture and kill lambs," while subheads read "One lamb had its eyes pecked out by a crow while she gave birth and is blind" and "Another had to have its tongue removed after being viciously attacked by crows."

When a friend, Kathleen Phillips, heard I was working on a book about crows and ravens, she shared her personal story with me:

> There were signs from the other side that I ignored eight-plus years ago. There were two incidents that stick out in my mind, but there were probably more. I don't ignore or minimize signs and messages from spirit anymore.
>
> In May of 2008 I visited my mother in Sacramento, California. Had my little doggie Dana with me. Every time I went outside to walk her a large raven followed me everywhere I went. It went from tree to tree and was waiting for me outside the back door.

---

256 Poe, "The Raven."

My mother said, "That bird wants your dog—don't take your eyes off her!"

So, I went to the office of my mother's retirement village and found an employee to discuss the lurking raven. A young woman around thirty was seated at a desk on the computer. She wore an Eskaton badge [the name of the retirement village] with the name Christine. I told her what was going on and that I was concerned for the little doggies on patios in the village. She walked with me back to my mother's place and sure enough the bird was waiting by the main building and followed us back to my mother's place.

Christine came inside with me and my mother served us tea and cookies in the kitchen. She told us of her military service and hung out for a while, talking like an old friend or family member. She followed me to my room—I went to get something—and as I sat on the bed she said: "Did you know that the spirit of a young man is sitting on the bed next to you?" I told her that I didn't and that I couldn't think of a young man that had passed on that would be with me. She told me that someone wouldn't have to be passed on for their spirit to be with me. The raven continued to follow me and wait for me for the remainder of that visit in May of 2008.

My son passed away suddenly on July 15, 2008—three months after this. Next time I was in Eskaton I tried to locate Christine, and no one could figure out who she was.

For those of us who choose—or have been chosen—to practice Crow-Raven Magic, what are we to make of such accounts across the centuries?

The world's religions and spiritual paths—and not just the Pagan ones of the Western esoteric tradition—are populated by what some observers cavalierly or hesitantly call the "dark" goddesses and gods: Kali, Hecate, Lilith, the Cailleach, Baron Samedi, Hades, the Morrigan, the fearsome, demonic-looking "wrathful deities" of Tantric Buddhism. To outsiders who casually encounter such deities and their modern-day devotees, whether in writings or through some sort of personal engagement, such practices may seem befuddling if not disturbing or downright terrifying. After all, such outsiders are thinking, "Isn't a spiritual path about enlightenment and walking toward the light? About raising oneself and all of humanity out of our base instincts and petty behaviors and into an elevated state of higher consciousness and greater good?"

Why, yes, of course. It's just that those who engage the so-called dark deities, or whose practice incorporates some sort of shadow work, have discovered the startling, immense power that such paths can have for personal transformation.

Chapter 23

LESSONS: HEARING THE CALL OF THE MORRIGAN

Cuchulainn, the mythic ancient Irish warrior, hasn't been the only human to be spellbound, plagued, cajoled, befuddled, or seduced (spiritually and/or erotically) by the Morrigan.

If any sort of Crow Magic or Raven Magic can be said to inhabit contemporary Paganism—following in the lineage of the Lascaux shaman, the Roman military commander Marcus Valerius Corvus, the ancient Norse with their Raven banners, the ancient Irish with their shape-shifting battle goddesses, and Native Americans with their Raven tales—then that Corvid Magic is most evident in modern-day manifestations of the Morrigan.

In a July 30, 2017, blog post titled "When You Hear the Call of the Morrigan," author John Beckett writes that his essays on the Celtic, raven-shifting battle goddess generate more reader interest than posts on Lugh, Cernunnos, Danu, Brigid, or Isis. Then, in words that are unnervingly prophetic in hindsight, given the pandemic that would shroud the world in 2020, Beckett adds:

> People are hearing the call of the Morrigan, but they don't know how to respond....
>
> I know many people whose lives have been made better by the presence of the Morrigan—I'm one of them. But I've never had any of them tell me the Great Queen saved them, rescued them, rehabilitated them, or in any other way "fixed" them. I don't know a soul who says she made their lives easier. The Morrigan doesn't

save people. She calls people into her service. What are you being called to do?

A lot of people are called to be warriors…Some people are called to be Ravens, to clean up the aftermath of the battle, to scavenge what can be reused, and to prepare the land for new growth. Unfortunately, I think we're going to need a lot of Ravens in the coming days.[257]

While quantifying contemporary literature about specific Pagan divinities—Odin, Cernunnos, Freya, Oshun, et al.—is difficult, a quick internet perusal reveals as many titles on the Morrigan as any other god or goddess. Likewise an internet search of Pagan visual art and statuary.

While some observers may say that veneration of the Morrigan is Crow-Raven Magic by proxy at best, or not Corvid Magic at all, the view of Wiccan priestess and writer Courtney Weber should be kept in mind:

Often thought of as the raven, but usually referred to as a black bird, the Morrigan as bird is the deity's most iconic guise. This is her signature shape-shifting move, appearing in too many myths to list in one section.…The Morrigan as the bird is a symbol of her most natural self. When we call upon the Morrigan as bird, we are calling on the clearest, most direct aspect of the Morrigan.[258]

But, as Beckett and others have noted, it is often the "Great Queen" who does the calling.

Singer-guitarists Mama Gina and Brian Henke, two bards popular on the Pagan festival circuit, have each written songs by request—at the request—of the Morrigan.

"The Morrigan gave this story to me and I was like, 'Holy Shit!'" says Mama Gina, a Tampa resident who in the mundane world is known as Gina LaMonte. "She always comes as a crow. The Morrigan talks to a lot of us [bards]."[259]

---

257 Beckett, "When You Hear the Call of the Morrigan."

258 Weber, *The Morrigan*, 131.

259 Mama Gina, interview with author, April 15, 2020.

That story became the song "Ruby" on Mama Gina's 2014 album *The Undertaker's Daughter*. "Ruby" opens with a crow cawing over a quiet heartbeat, then LaMonte's acoustic twelve-string guitar strumming sets a folk-rock mood amid subtle synth melodies and the pitter-patter of djembe drumming. Then LaMonte's earthy voice begins the tale of the Morrigan, who in the first verse is retrieving the heart of a fallen warrior.

The song continues with the Morrigan retrieving the heart of a woman who dies in childbirth and then bringing a heart to a child "who was conceived of a violent rape, because that child is going to need a warrior's heart," LaMonte says.[260]

Henke's forlorn ballad, "Morrighan – Queen of Ravens," appears on his 2019 album *Dance with the Fireflies*, his sixth solo album.

"My relationship with the Morrighan is a personal one," Henke says. "I was asked directly by her to be her bard. I misunderstood at first what she was asking and said no. Then after some discussion and mutual recognition and understanding, I said I would write about her, but only the truth that I know and not follow anyone else's dogma."[261]

He wrote "Morrighan – Queen of Ravens" "as a greater and personal truth that is different from what many believe, and not as a universal truth that I feel everyone needs to believe. It is very much my own personal truth from my own point of view."[262] The song honors that dark goddess of the Irish/Celtic pantheon, even as it laments the ways of men.

LaMonte's song "Ravens of the Nine Worlds," from her album *Solitaire*, released in 2015, was inspired by her encounter with two persistent crows as she made a long road trip from Florida to Asheville, North Carolina.

"I kept seeing two crows everywhere I went," says LaMonte, who was named the 2019 Best Female Artist by the International Pagan Music Association. "Two crows. Stop for gas—there would be two crows. Everywhere. It was kind of odd."[263]

---

260 Gina, interview.

261 Brian Henke, interview with author, March 16, 2020.

262 Henke, interview.

263 Gina, interview.

After another stop further down the road, "There were these two crows again, and I went, 'Oh my gosh, that's Hugin and Munin,'" LaMonte says.[264] As she often does after such otherworldly encounters, LaMonte took to the internet to find out more about Odin's ravens. She discovered one source that claimed the traditional translations of their names, Thought and Memory, might be inaccurate—that, instead, one of their names might mean "Desire."

"That was the linchpin for the whole song, adding desire to that thought and memory thing," LaMonte says. "It blew up that whole story of Odin and his ravens for me."[265]

LaMonte says her otherworldly encounters, which have included other deities and entities, "can be very unsettling. It's less unsettling now, but a few years ago, hell, yeah, it shook me up every time something new came through. They are absolutely real, the gods and goddesses and entities that show up. I am a very rational person—I'm like, 'I'm not so sure that's real.' But in the moment of creativity, in the moment of understanding I have to suspend any disbelief I have and I have to live it. I have to listen. I have to be open to it. And it makes a difference in my life, and so that is the proof that it's real.

"So, when the Morrigan comes pecking at the back of my head or when Odin's ravens keep showing up on a long drive—whoever happens to show up, I am open to it and I listen."[266]

Daragh Smyth, in *A Guide to Irish Mythology*, reports—and indeed, *reports* seems like the correct word given his journalistic, just-the-facts-ma'am tone—about the last "recorded" time the Morrigan appeared in Ireland:

> The Morrigan appeared before the battle of Mag Rath in A.D. 637, grey-haired, in the form of a lean, nimble hag, hovering and hopping about on the spears and shields of the royal army who were to be victorious. Her last recorded appearance was at the Battle of Clontarf in 1014.[267]

---

264 Gina, interview.

265 Gina, interview.

266 Gina, interview.

267 Smyth, *A Guide to Irish Mythology*, 127.

Modern-day Pagans in both the Emerald Isle and elsewhere may quibble with Smyth about the last time the Morrigan was sighted. That is one lesson from Crow and Raven, as evidenced in the experiences of Beckett, Weber, LaMonte, Henke, and doubtless many others: the Morrigan, and Crow-Raven Magic, are not just the stuff of ancient myth—they live, and thrive, today.

Also, given corvids' readily observable roles as carrion birds and their resultant reputation as "death birds," that pre-Covid-19 prophecy Beckett delivered in his 2017 *Patheos* blog on the Morrigan is particularly chilling and bears repeating: "Unfortunately, I think we're going to need a lot of Ravens in the coming days." Yet one must take to heart the other side of his keen observation: "Some people are called to be Ravens, to clean up the aftermath of the battle, to scavenge what can be reused, and to prepare the land for new growth."[268]

That, too, is a lesson for today from Crow and Raven: Like the flesh-blood-and-bone ravens and crows that populate Gaia's earth, people who are called to be "Ravens" have their necessary place, shadow side and all, in today's world, just as that Lascaux Cave artist-shaman intuited nineteen millennia ago.

Lesson: the goddesses and gods live!

Lesson: heed your calling.

---

268 Beckett, "When You Hear the Call of the Morrigan."

Chapter 24

GRIMOIRE: CANDLE SHADOW SCRYING

Scrying is a magical technique that involves deep contemplation of an object. It's a simple and effective way to alter one's consciousness and enter non-ordinary reality, and the altered states achieved in scrying are typically used to discern and interpret prophetic messages. However, scrying also is an effective means of achieving self-trance.

This method of candle shadow scrying is really a mash-up of meditation and, one hopes, trance work achieved using basic tools. This type of scrying is yet another exercise in this text that makes use of a visual image—the magic of visual image.

By focusing your intention, you will become a psychonaut—someone who explores altered states of consciousness, but you will have a specific goal: to contact and immerse yourself in Crow-Raven Spirit and thus forge a deeper communion with that aspect of Gaian magic.

WHAT YOU WILL NEED

- One low candle of any preferred color—a jar candle or even a tea light is fine but not a long, slender taper—plus matches
- A small table or stool, from six inches to three feet high
- A darkened, secluded room or space
- A blank, white, 24-x-24-inch gallery-wrapped artist's canvas (for outdoor scrying if desired)

- A crow or raven icon, statuary, talisman, or fetish
- A small, potted, live plant in real dirt (for indoor scrying if desired)

BACKGROUND

Some 19,000 years ago, one of our Paleolithic ancestors descended into the womb of Gaia that is Lascaux Cave in what is modern-day France. With primitive mineral pigments, a rudimentary brush, and some sort of crude torch—perhaps, anthropologists say, a sandstone lamp that burned animal fat—this ancient artist began to paint the famous bird-man shaman.[269]

With the fire's light flickering, this ancient Picasso must have been as enchanted by the image taking shape as we are today when we witness this marvel of cave art, even if we must do so in books or on websites.

Practice candle shadow scrying and you will find yourself time-tripping back to that moment of the world's first instance of Crow Magic, when that Lascaux Cave artist worked in the low, softly dancing glow of firelight amidst the enveloping darkness.

PREPARATION

If you are new to trance work of any sort, consider participating in several group guided meditations before proceeding with a solo session of candle shadow scrying—or any other modality that leads to deep-altered consciousness. Group guided meditations are a staple at almost every Pagan festival I have attended, and metaphysical shops frequently offer such workshops.

The basic techniques of a group meditation will resemble those discussed below. Thus you will become familiar, under the hands-on guidance of an experienced teacher, with the mechanics of journeying from ordinary to non-ordinary realities and back again.

Choosing a Corvid Icon, Statuary, Talisman, or Fetish

You can shadow scry with any statuary or fetish (typically defined as an object imbued with magical powers or inhabited by a spirit) that you so desire. Choose an object that is, well, crow-shaped or strongly associated with corvids, such as a statuette of Odin or the Morrigan. I most often draft Rave, my palm-sized craft-store crow that transmuted himself into one of my fetishes.

---

269 Clottes, "The Lascaux Cave Paintings."

Not surprisingly, those fetishes that represent—possess—a naturally kinetic entity make for the most fruitful candle shadow sessions. In my experience this is not only esoterically/magically so, but also physically/literally so: if a deity or supernatural entity is one that flies or dances, then likely its fetish or statuary will inherently be designed to reflect that motion either spectacularly or subtly, and its kinetic aspect will come alive during shadow scrying.

You will, quite literally, be animating one of your sacred icons, unleashing it from a static perch upon your altar. Recall how our minds casually and giddily seek dragons, bunnies, dogs, wizards, aliens, and all sorts of creatures when we gaze at those fluffy cumulus clouds on a summer day. Similarly, what mystics call your Third Eye, a gate to higher consciousness, will open during candle shadow scrying, and that portal will summon and shape-shift the arcana that has been buried in your inner self. The flickering, dancing candle flame will produce a dancing, kinetic shadow image of your sacred object, and as you gaze and meditate upon that image, it will somersault through your Third Eye and into your subconsciousness, into your Mysti-Intu Brain (Mystical-Intuitive Brain).

Thus will the veil between mundane reality and the hidden realms be parted. You will become a psychonaut, exploring not only your inner self but also the collective unconscious, the universal soul/spirit.[270]

Choosing a Space

Find a darkened room that offers seclusion and has a blank space upon one wall, and a place to set up a small table or stool near the wall. The room doesn't have to be pitch-black, I-can't-see-my-hand dark. The only requirement is that you are able to plainly see shadows cast by the candlelight.

A room with at least two open doorways, or an open door and an open window, is ideal for two reasons: A draft, even a small one, will make for more interesting shadow play—and no, that's not cheating to have a natural breeze, Gaia's breath, be part of your session. And, esoterically and magically, the feel of a room with several gateways will spur the flow of the spiritual energy immanent in nature from both animate and inanimate entities. This is, after all, Crow and Raven Magic, and the bird spirits should—must—feel free to fly in and out at will.

---

270 Boechat, "The Collective Unconscious."

Make sure that your candle, which will be placed on the table or stool along with your corvid fetish, will be burning in a safe spot so that nothing will catch on fire if you trance out and the candle burns down to its base. I always place aluminum foil under any candles used during rituals, scrying, or meditations.

Scrying Outdoors

I have had fascinating, insight-provoking shadow scrying sessions indoors, and I must say that the sight of a crow fluttering on my inside walls infused—and even consecrated—my home with a palpable Crow Spirit that I wasn't expecting. But holding a candle shadow scrying session outdoors can open a portal to an even more powerful enchantment. Crows and ravens, after all, live in the wild, not indoors, and working their magic in their environs will amplify the energy.

Of course, one must be able to work this trance magic with a minimal chance of being disturbed by random sounds or other intrusions. Finding a good spot can be daunting. Attempting to cast a crow shadow against an outer wall of your home, garage, or tool shed will negate the very purpose of being outside—to allow nature (in my case, the wilderness behind my home) and the night sky to compose the mise en scene of your session. I solved the problem by propping up a blank, white, 24-x-24-inch gallery-wrapped artist's canvas (available at arts and crafts stores) on the ground in my backyard, with my candle and crow fetish perched on a six-inch-high foot stool in front of it and the blessed full moon rising above the woods.

While scrying beneath a full moon is stunning, even more mesmerizing for me has been shadow scrying during springtime in North America, with the constellation Corvus the Crow rising in the south after sunset at that time of year. Corvus is not a majestic constellation—it is small and boxy and can be found not far from Spica, the lone bright star in the constellation Virgo. That said, scrying beneath a celestial corvid flying across the dark heavens will unleash a strange brew of Crow Magic, at once furtive and ecstatic.

Scrying Time—Night or Twilight?

I prefer candle shadow scrying at night, when it is easy to create a darkened room, but there is also a magical-esoteric reason: This is, literally, shadow work—and the intensity of sunlight is inimical to shadows, always seeking to blaze and burn them away even as, paradoxically, sunlight creates them. So, no matter how dark you can make an interior room of your home or sanctuary, what I call deep scrying is for the night. (Afternoon or twilight scrying, which may be preferable for some practitioners, is discussed later in the "Grounding" section.)

When your deep scrying session is complete, your psyche and spirit will not want to emerge back into full consciousness accompanied by a sudden, jolting blast of sunlight. Moving slowly from the deep shadow of candlelight to the normal shadow of a low-lit room at nighttime, illuminated by a low-watt lamp, will be not only aesthetically more pleasing but also psychically beneficial. The images and experiences of your session will linger as your consciousness moves through this crucial, quasi-hypnopompic state—the state where magic frequently happens—and you will be able to continue to process what happened … well, what is still happening in those moments.

Also, any Raven spirits, Crow goddesses, DMT elves (without the DMT!), or other spirit beings or entities you may have encountered should be allowed to recede and dissipate gently at their own pace, rather than be shocked into banishment by a burst of intense sunlight from a suddenly opened door or by the flick of a switch of a bright room light.

And don't worry—you will soon enough bring your session formally and magically to a complete close so that you will safely bid adieu to all you have encountered and emerge back into full everyday consciousness.

Staying Connected to Ordinary Reality

As part of your tableau if you are indoors, place a small potted plant behind you and to one side. Any plant will do so long as it grows in actual dirt. You will use this plant to literally and metaphysically ground yourself during your meditation/trance journey, if so desired, and to return to mundane reality at the end of your session. If you are outdoors, make sure you are conducting your scrying session on grass or ground (not on concrete).

Before you begin your psychonaut journey, there is one important consideration to keep in mind—to *keep in mind literally*—and it is explored by Arnold Mindell in his 1993 book, *The Shaman's Body: A New Shamanism for Transforming Health, Relationships, and the Community*. During dream, trance, and vision work, he advises, one must "remember your ordinary self" in any such altered state of consciousness.[271]

---

271 Mindell, *The Shaman's Body*, 85.

You should have your ecstatic experiences and also dis-identify from them. The first step in working on yourself alone is to realize that you are the observer as well as the participant. Choose when to identify with and when to dis-identify with the trip.[272]

It is only through staying connected to your everyday self that the "tools" acquired during an altered state will remain available to you once you return to ordinary reality, Mindell says.[273]

It can be a delicate, difficult dance to maintain that balance between ordinary and non-ordinary reality. What's the point of venturing into the otherworldly realms via dream-trance-vision if you are going to be thinking about the hot dog you had for lunch? As a psychonaut exploring the inner space of your consciousness, you want to be a capable pilot as you launch dream-trance to sail into the Otherworld. Such trips (yes, that Leary-esque term is used intentionally) can be, should be, and will be exhilarating. But if you are a neophyte psychonaut, you may want to leave a trail of popcorn as you go down that rabbit hole so you can reassure yourself that you can find your way back.

How does one maintain a balance between everyday awareness and altered consciousness? How does one "dis-identify"?

Mindell relates the advice of the shaman don Juan Matus to Carlos Castaneda to look at one's hands during an altered state. That simple act has no symbolic or esoteric meaning. Rather, "looking at anything in a dream" is a prompt for a psychonaut to remember one's ordinary self.[274]

Mindell notes "there are many methods for distinguishing yourself from the processes you are working with in order to resist possession."[275] That is, putting aside that scary *P* word for the moment, there are ways for explorers of non-ordinary realties to remember they are the observer and are separate from the observed as they venture into what master psychonaut Robert Anton Wilson, in his memoir *Cosmic Trigger: Final Secret of the Illuminati,* calls "Chapel Perilous"—and yes, there's another scary *P* word.[276]

---

272 Mindell, *The Shaman's Body*, 84–85.

273 Mindell, *The Shaman's Body*, 85.

274 Mindell, *The Shaman's Body*, 84.

275 Mindell, *The Shaman's Body*, 85.

276 Wilson, *Cosmic Trigger*, 6–8.

Remembering your ordinary self during altered states will help you "avoid floating away," to use Mindell's phrase.[277]

Also, staying rooted to your everyday self, to whatever degree, will help you avoid what I call the "Pretty Psychedelic Pictures Syndrome." Yes, it can be fascinating to take a trance journey—whether fueled by scrying, lucid dreaming, or ayahuasca or some other entheogen—and then "Ooo" and "Ahh" at the phantasmagoria that will unfold before your mind's eye and be done with it.

But you are parting the veil to reveal the Mysteries for a reason. Maintaining a degree of connection to the observer—yourself—will not only prevent you from "floating away," but also it will facilitate your ability to connect your visions to your everyday life, not unlike those experienced, adept shamans who journey to the other realms seeking cures or knowledge for healings back in the "real" world.

Grounding

This is where that potted plant, or more specifically the dirt in which it grows, comes into play.

During your scrying session, you may feel you have become lost in the "pretty pictures" or, more unsettling, that you have ventured perilously close to a cliff's edge in your own inner space—and it is *your* inner space, regardless of the other entities who may frolic there. So, if you intuit a need to reconnect to your everyday consciousness, simply caress the soil of your potted plant with the fingertips of one hand, or touch the ground if you are outdoors. Alternately, you can plan before your session to intentionally, periodically touch this ground throughout your trip. Either way, you will be reminding yourself of the "set and setting"—a Timothy Leary term,[278] discussed later—that you established before your journey. Thus you will remind yourself that yes, indeed, you are the observer in the midst of a dream, trance, vision, or deep meditation. Yes, this is an adaptation of the post-ritual grounding technique—to be discussed shortly—favored by many Pagans and Witches, whether at large festivals or small coven sabbats.

If you are skittish and concerned about being consumed by or, to use that scary *P* word deployed by Mindell, "possessed" by deep trance work, or you

---

277 Mindell, *The Shaman's Body*, 85.
278 Hartogsohn, "Constructing Drug Effects."

are concerned about "floating away," or if you are a neophyte to scrying or trance-visioning, then by all means conduct your session in a room with open doors and windows and lit by the natural sunlight of late afternoon, sunset, or very early twilight. It is surprising how much candle shadows can come alive and work their trance magic in such softly lit environs, and I have had quite fruitful sessions in such conditions when I was a neophyte using this technique. Such a setting will almost invariably keep you aware of your ordinary reality and buoy your everyday consciousness while also allowing some, perhaps many, of the benefits of trance scrying to flourish.

Invaluable insight on these matters is offered by Janet Farrar and Gavin Bone in their 2016 book, *Lifting the Veil: A Witches' Guide to Trance-Prophecy, Drawing Down the Moon, and Ecstatic Ritual*. In a segment titled "Dealing with Negative Possessions in Trance-Prophecy Work," they note that some people have approached them expressing concerns that trance work can have adverse effects or even be "dangerous." Such questioners, they write, are actually concerned about "the seer becoming schizophrenic or being possessed by an evil spirit."[279]

Such a mindset, Farrar and Bone note, is a holdover from being raised in a culture that tells us the spirits we can communicate with are evil—a false perception spawned by some mainstream monotheistic churches and propagated by modern-day pop culture in the form of horror films and novels.[280]

"Such statements really say more about the individual asking than the work being undertaken…it is negative emotion that is the biggest danger when working in the world of spirit," Farrar and Bone say.[281]

Some Final Insights Before Scrying

I am tempted to offer a glib "viewer discretion advised" caution concerning trance-visioning, but that may be overstating the case, and indeed perhaps the same can be said of the necessity of Mindell's "dis-identify" provision.

As with any metaphysical path, approach, technique, or ritual, it takes practice to reap its rewards. It is no accident that one "practices" Witchcraft or someone says, "I'm a practicing Pagan" or "I'm a practicing [fill in the blank

279 Farrar and Bone, *Lifting the Veil*, 270.

280 Farrar and Bone, *Lifting the Veil*, 271.

281 Farrar and Bone, *Lifting the Veil*, 271.

with almost any religion]." We become more adept, in both the mundane and metaphysical sense, the further we advance upon our path.

Always remember that adventuring into the otherworldly realms through dream, trance, and vision work is not something to cloak in trepidation. The reason we embark on such a path is to forge a deeper communion with the ensouled, inspirited world of Gaia/nature, with the higher realms, the Other Realms, cosmic consciousness, divinity, the goddesses and gods, Spirit with a capital *S*. In such deeper communion awaits not only wisdom that we can bring back to our daily lives, but also ecstatic joy.

ACTIONS

You have your tools and your place for your scrying session: a short candle; matches; a small table, tray, or stool; a darkened or shadowy room with at least a small blank space upon one wall; a small, potted plant in actual dirt; and some sort of Crow or Raven fetish, icon, statuary, or talisman of your choice.

Set up the scene so that your table or stool is near the wall. Place the candle (contained in a fireproof holder) in front of your Crow-Raven fetish so that the light will cast the bird's shadow upon the wall, or perhaps you are using some other surface.

To begin your session, light your candle, and sit in a comfortable position, preferably a cross-legged Buddha pose but it doesn't have to be so.

Request Crow or Raven to act as a messenger between the realms during a scrying session, tarot reading, or ritual and you will be tapping into a storied, sacred tradition. Begin your session by murmuring an invocation of your own creation, akin to:

> *Crow Spirit, Raven Spirit,*
> *May this light cast upon your wings*
> *Guide you into the Shadowy Realms*
> *And the Other Realms, there and back again*
> *So that you may caw and gronk*
> *Their beautiful arcana to me.*

For this session, your query will take a page from chaos magic and follow the technique of no-technique. That is, simply "burn, scry, and learn" with no specific query or goal in mind. Yes, this is sort of like playing 52-pickup with a tarot deck, in which you take a handful of the cards, toss them on the floor (some landing upright, some landing face down), and use them as a Rorschach test. Only with candle scrying, the dancing shadow will be the Rorschach that your mind will ruminate upon.

Begin the scry by focusing on the candle flame for ten seconds or so, then shift your eyes to your fetish/icon/statuary for ten seconds, then to the dancing shadow for ten seconds, then close your eyes for ten seconds. Repeat this pattern, but don't be in a hurry, and don't be alarmed if your monkey mind intrudes—if so, simply return your concentration to the flame, the fetish, and its shadow.

At some point—your intuition will let you know—you should cease the ten-ten-ten-ten gazing pattern and let your eyes wander where they will, whether it's upon the flame, the fetish, the shadow, or with eyes closed, the inner theater of your mind. More likely, your Third Eye now will be in the pilot's seat, and you will not need to make any conscious decision about where your eyes focus. You will be in an altered state, the dreaming time, Spiritus Mundi, the upper branches of the World Tree, the highways and byways of cosmic consciousness, and/or your own inner space.

If a god, a goddess, or some spirit guide appears, you may be led or desire to engage with them. You may want to request their name or names. Or you may prefer to be a silent witness—an observer—rather than directly engage the visionary stream that you have set in motion. I rarely speak out loud during trance, scrying, or tarot sessions, preferring instead to engage any vision with my thoughts alone.

Time may melt during your session, and indeed that is even desirable. You are not on the clock, nor do you want to be. Along with my writing path, I am also a sitar player and a drum circle enthusiast, and my most powerful visions during those activities have been accompanied by a sense of lost time or rather of being "outside" of time. I will "awake" thinking I have been playing for only twenty or thirty minutes, only to discover three, four, or even five hours have passed. A similar phenomenon may happen during scrying or any trance work.

Ending Your Scrying Session

When you intuit that your session should come to an end, you do not want to leap out of it and directly back into mundane reality. Express your gratitude to any gods, goddesses, or spirit guides that appeared. You also may choose to give thanks to Spiritus Mundi, your ancestors, or what Yeats, in the aftermath of automatic writing sessions with his wife, Georgie, called the "instructors."[282] He even wrote a poem titled "Gratitude to the Unknown Instructors."

To conclude your session, relax your concentration upon the matter at hand. Drift. Allow the monkey mind to resume its chatter, but be aware that insights still may arrive during this stage, which is quite similar to the hypnopompic state as one moves from sleep to awakeness.

Before putting out your flame, ground yourself—metaphysically and literally—by dipping the fingertips of both hands gently into the dirt of your potted plant for 10 or 20 seconds, or longer if you intuit such a need. This mirrors a common technique of grounding oneself to conclude rituals by placing one's palms upon the earth—a technique almost universally used when I have taken part in rituals at the Florida Pagan Gathering, Phoenix Phyre, and coven sabbats. If you indeed are outdoors for this exercise, simply place both your palms upon the ground, again for 10 or 20 seconds, or longer if you feel called to do so. The reverse jolt of energy from "coming back down-to-earth"—again, both metaphysically and literally—can be quite palpable, and oddly satisfying. I have often found the sensations following ritual, trance sessions, and other esoteric adventures to very much resemble the post-orgasmic bliss of sexual intimacy.

GOING FORWARD

These methods detailed in this chapter work for me, but you should feel free to alter, reject, or add to them as your intuition and common sense guide you.

---

282 Yeats, *A Critical Edition of Yeats's A Vision (1925)*, xlviii.

Chapter 25

GRIMOIRE: BE THE CROW

Therianthropy is shape-shifting—the act of a human being metamorphosing into an animal form or a human-animal hybrid. One who does so is a therianthrope. The terms come from two ancient Greek words: *therion*, "wild beast," plus *anthropos*, "man."

Achieving a therianthropic experience can be elusive. A successful result will bring about a deeper communion with corvid kind unlike any other connection. And in the mysteries of that deeper communion, you may discover not only new wisdom to bring back to the mundane world, but also a profound joy to lift your spiritual practice.

WHAT YOU WILL NEED

- An open(ed) mind
- Deep knowledge of corvid kind and experience observing them

BACKGROUND

Once again we return to Lascaux Cave's bird-man shaman: human body, head of a bird that some scholars identify as a corvid. Clearly a therianthrope—and likely humankind's first depiction of such. Did the Lascaux artist *experience* shapeshifting in some manner (via some ancient entheogen or some sort of spontaneous trance-vision), or was that artwork the result of "mere" imagination?

The weltanschauung of animism comes into play here. Animism holds that all natural phenomena, such as earth, sky, forests, animals, sun, moon, thunderstorms, mountains, rivers, wind, etc., are ensouled. That is, they are imbued with some sort of Spirit. Put another way, animism contends that animals and features of the natural environment "are non-human persons with whom we may maintain and develop social relationships. ... Animism, in some form or other, has been the dominant religious tradition across all human societies since our ancestors first left Africa."[283]

That phrase "maintain and develop social relationships," with the ensouled but seemingly alien "others" that share our planet with us, is key. However, a veil separates our mundane work-day existence from the alive, animistic natural (and preternatural) world where Spirit and its many manifestations reside and thrive. So, we embark on our spiritual/metaphysical paths to forge a deeper communion with the ensouled world of Gaia/nature, with the Other Realms, with cosmic consciousness, with divinity, with the goddess and gods.

That veil can be parted via Eliade's shamanic, "archaic techniques of ecstasy" and other methods: music making, Buddhist-like meditation as well as the "walking mediation" espoused by Alan Watts,[284] hermetic deep-woods solitude (see how long you can avoid human contact—it's rather difficult these days), self-induced trance, scrying, automatic writing, tarot, hand drumming (whether solitary or in drum circles), making or contemplating art, chanting, heightened communion with those mystical, intelligent creatures known as corvids, and ... shape-shifting.

Of all the techniques and magical operations one may use to part the veil and alter/altar one's consciousness, therianthropy may remain the most elusive.

Pursue tarot reading, scrying, meditation, trance work, drumming, deep-woods solitude, art, sacred play, etc. and something will happen, even though the results may be seemingly transient and trivial rather than the never-expected but secretly desired seismic shift in one's soul.

Such practices as tarot and scrying are approached with full-tilt intention. However, therianthropy may or may not click during each and every attempt, and even when it does, your goal should be quite different from what you seek via those aforementioned techniques. Among all the consciousness-altering-"altar-ing" practices cited in this book, therianthropy may be the least "practical." Yes, you can pursue a shape-shifting with some sort of knowledge-seeking query

283 Smith, "Animism."

284 Watts, "Zen Bones," 159.

or a deep, esoteric goal in mind, but scrying, tarot, guided meditations, and other trance-vision techniques likely will be more effective for such focused quests.

The Role of Imagination

Read tales about the Norse god Odin and his ravens, Hugin and Munin, Thought and Memory, and you will take wing with those two corvids—in your imagination—and join them as they soar through the skies, high above the hustle and bustle of us earthbound humans. Your soaring will be flights of fantasy, imagination, and daydreaming—same as if you were reading a *Witch World* novel by Andre Norton or adventuring across Barsoom in one of Edgar Rice Burroughs's adventure tales about John Carter of Mars.

Or is this mere daydreaming?

Unlike Eastern cultures, our Western culture tends to assign little or no Third Eye mysticism to the realms of the imagination. In our techno-industrial-soaked society, we have willingly allowed the "military-industrial-entertainment complex," as FBI Agent Fox Mulder once quipped on an episode of *The X-Files*, to commandeer control and exercise of our imaginative powers. *Game of Thrones*, the *Marvel* cinematic universe, and many other uber-teched films, TV shows, and video games are astonishing entertainments, but more and more such creations "do our imagination" for us. These days our mass culture considers imagination to be an ordinary, everyday, and often frivolous thing—we "imagine" what we would buy if we won the mega-millions lotto, or one daydreams about making love to Beyoncé or Idris Elba, then we go back to work and salivate over the fact that the new season of our favorite television show is coming soon.

Nothing wrong with that, but how often do we, especially us adults, take our imagination out for a walk—or a flight with Hugin and Munin? How often do we bypass the thrills of the "military-industrial-entertainment complex," the diversions of electronic media, to go deep or even not-so-deep into our imagination and allow it to conjure something/anything after we have passively contemplated a cloud's shape, a leaf's veins, or a tale of an old god that most of the world considers long dead?

"We are brought up to believe that to imagine something means that we do not perceive the truth," writes modern-day Celticist Mara Freeman.[285]

---

285 Freeman, *Kindling the Celtic Spirit*, 78.

"It's all in your imagination!" is the ultimate devaluing remark. In fact, *imagination is the language of the soul.* The images that appear during reverie, dream, and vision are the interface between ourselves and the invisible inhabitants of the world that lies beyond the five senses. So don't be concerned that you're "making it all up."[286]

The more you give free rein to your imagination in metaphysical exercises and spiritual excursions, Freeman concludes, "the more you will get out of them."[287]

A Quantum Physics Explanation

Iron Feathers, a shaman and self-described "non-native, European mongrel" who studied with shamans in the United States, Mexico, and Peru, said he witnessed a Peruvian shaman turn into a white egret and that a friend watched him transform into a bear. He cited the work of Nobel Prize–winning zoologist and ornithologist Konrad Lorenz, who

> put forth the idea that in the motor cortex is an image of the body, and the body tries to conform to that image. Some would call this body mapping. ... What I believe is that the shaman receives the image of the animal in his motor cortex. From the quantum physics point of view, the body, and all matter, re-creates itself every nanosecond. The energy for this change comes from the electromagnetic field of the universe—the Divine, God, or Universal Life Force. Yogis have talked about this kind of transformation for about 5,000 years. So the shaman has the image of the bear in the motor cortex, and in non-ordinary reality he has the ability to take that image and re-create a new image of a bear.[288]

Sometimes a person may sense they are approaching a shape-shift and are "touching the image" in the motor cortex, but they are "not strong enough to bring it into this reality and maintain it," Iron Feathers said.[289]

---

286 Freeman, *Kindling the Celtic Spirit*, 78; italics in original.

287 Freeman, *Kindling the Celtic Spirit*, 78.

288 Stange, *The Spiritual Nature of Animals*, 61.

289 Stange, *The Spiritual Nature of Animals*, 62.

PREPARATION

For me, shape-shifting entered my repertoire of shamanic techniques rather organically, through evolution rather than revolution, even though the breakthrough was sudden, unforeseen, unexpected, and quite jolting. An outside observer might even say it was unsought, unintended, and therefore "accidental," but I agree with many metaphysical explorers, spiritual seekers, meditation practitioners, occultists, magicians, Pagans, shamans, and travelers to non-ordinary realities that what seems "accidental" is often (always?) the result of groundwork laid down beforehand, both consciously and subconsciously.

Or perhaps I should say that I had not launched into therianthropy with any deliberate, *conscious* intention. Looking back, I am quite certain that I had subconsciously, intuitively laid the groundwork, and then one day I was looking out of my living room window at the crows in the trees in my backyard, and suddenly and somewhat inexplicably, my Third Eye mechanics kicked in and— boom! Like Lord Valiant the alpha crow, my crow body was gliding downward from the top of a slash pine toward my back lawn, and the ground was rushing to greet me as my black wings spread and I pulled up, and that distinctive, palpable roller-coaster queasiness rose in my stomach just before landing.

I was left wondering: *What just happened?*

In the following days and weeks, such spontaneous therianthropy continued happening, but only fleetingly. It was some time before I discovered I could shape-shift into crows, other animals, or trees apart from their immediate physical presence—but only if I had intimately engaged their kind at some point previously, and frequently.

However, such shifts didn't come without effort, and I wasn't able to just "will" them into happening. Sometimes my attempts failed. The "set and setting"—the mental, emotional, social, and physical environment—that Timothy Leary spoke of as proper and necessary preparation for an LSD trip or other psychedelic adventure, didn't seem to apply here. A bucolic niche in the woods might not necessarily lead to a desired shape-shift, while a crow perched on a lamp post in a grocery store parking lot might be motivation for a successful, semi-spontaneous trip.

Pursue shape-shifting or other metaphysical exercises on even a semi-regular basis and you will be reminded that "simple" imagination is not so simple. Rather, it's a latent but powerful tool for venturing into non-ordinary realms. The visions that will come to you, from your subconscious or the astral plane or wherever, will seem surprising and unbidden, leaving you to think, "Where did *that* come from?!" Children naturally know and engage the power of imagination. This faculty often atrophies as we mature into adults.

If your Rat-Prag Brain (Rational-Pragmatic Brain) protests that "It's just your imagination; it's not real!" then remember the discussion earlier: dreams, hallucinations, and, yes, imagination are indeed real, just not in what the rationalists see as a "materialistic" way. Heck, scientists study the faculty of imagination just like they study dreams, phantasms, and all sorts of supernatural phenomena.

Another thing: while our imagination is a common and (seemingly) easily activated Third Eye enterprise, it is the gateway to deeper realms of the Mysti-Intu Brain (Mystical-Intuitive Brain) such as intuition itself, visions, communication with the spirit world, encounters with God/Goddess, the ability to not only recognize but give meaning to synchronicities, and more.

These realms require that we be conversant in their "language," a nonverbal language that is a foreign one to most of us—unless we begin to practice it and exercise it and become familiar with it, which is where imagination comes in.

ACTIONS

While a step-by-step technique is difficult to formulate, here are some guidelines to help cultivate a shape-shifting experience.

Intimacy Is Required

You will never shape-shift into a tiger or a wolf if you are not intimately familiar with their ways, their behaviors, their daily lives. My unbidden shape-shift into Lord Valiant happened only after years of observing him and other crows, as well as educating myself about the ways of crow and raven kind via books and documentaries on television and YouTube.

Don't Just Look—See

So often, as our robot self moves through daily life, we do things by rote. As Colin Wilson says, our robot has its place and its uses: many of our mundane tasks do not require deep engagement or focused attention. But we humans too easily allow the robot to take over the steering wheel. Matters that deserve our focus are glossed over. Encounters that would enhance our emotional well-being are left unengaged, like a concertgoer who allows his monkey mind to chatter about after-show cocktails while the symphony performs Beethoven's Ninth.[290]

It sounds absurdly simple to say *really look at and see* crows and ravens if you desire to pursue therianthropy, but the robot is insidious and may have unknowingly lulled you into less-than-intense engagements with Crow and Raven kind. Indeed, superficial engagement with Spirit is something all seekers must guard against.

Shape-shifting requires close study of corvids' flight and movements. The wingspan of crows in flight will seem disproportionately massive compared to the birds' body size while perched on a limb with wings tucked. I am still surprised by the august span of a crow's wings when I am fortunate to see one flying up close or when I capture one of the birds in flight with my camera. Also, crows' wingtip feathers spread out like fingers when they are flying.

Unlike the nervous, jittery flight of Carolina wrens, cardinals, robins, or other songbirds, crows fly with grace, majesty, deliberation, and intention. After alighting on my Chinese tallow Crow Spirit Tree to partake of the saltine cracker brunch I put out for them, they will depart by wheeling artfully through the nearby slash pines, bluejack oaks, and Florida silver palms. When crows take off from the ground, they will hop once or twice before launching themselves into the air.

Because I have never witnessed ravens beyond glimpses of them during my travels in New Mexico, I cannot shape-shift into one. And so I envy those humans who may shift into a raven and perform the wild, joyous barrel rolls and somersaults they are known to do in flight—a feat crows cannot achieve.

While crows are majestic in flight, their walk upon the ground is almost comical, as their heads bob back and forth like exaggerated chickens.

A crow perched high in a tree won't seem diminutive, especially compared to those aforementioned songbirds. But if that crow alights closer to you, on either a lower branch or the ground, and you are able to see the crow in profile, you will be shocked at its girth—it's as if the crow itself has shape-shifted into a bigger beast.

When crows "come in for a landing," with their wings spread wide and their feet extended for touchdown, their bodies will suddenly halt in flight,

---

290 Wilson, *Super Consciousness*, 86–87.

and for the briefest of moments they are in stasis. Their feet are just inches from the earth but still they reside in the air. They are not merely suspended between the realms of earth and sky—they are magically suspended between worlds: between Asgard, the abode of the Norse gods, and Midgard, the realm of humans; between the realm of the Morrigan, the Irish battle goddess, and the earthly realm of Cuchulainn, the mythic Irish warrior; between the realm of Raven, the Native American trickster, and the lush forests of the Pacific Northwest.

Watch crows in that beautiful moment of stasis, and you may experience that mild, delightfully queasy feeling in your stomach that one gets when riding a tame roller coaster or when a car crests over a hilltop. Experiencing that sensation is one of the alerts that will let you know you may have transcended "mere" imagination and reverie—that you may have shifted.

No Prep Work

To begin a shape-shifting session, or to inadvertently slip into one, you need not do any preparatory breathwork, meditation, or invocation. Such preliminaries may actually be counterproductive

Unlike trance or vision work, the goal of therianthropy (as outlined here) is to become palpably and more deeply engaged with the physical world—the trees, forests, lakes, meadows, farmlands, cityscapes, clouds, deer, dogs, hawks, otters, humans … all that populates the typography of Gaia's flesh and the breath of Nuit, the Egyptian sky goddess.

You will be looking at the world through the eyes of a crow or raven.

Heighten Your Sensory Engagement

Indeed, that's how you begin: Simply imagine you're looking through the eyes of a corvid. Do not close your eyes—you will want to heighten, not diminish, your sensory engagement with your environment. You will know you have shifted, as opposed to experiencing a flight of "mere" imagination, when you begin to experience perhaps subtle but palpable physical sensations: a gasp in your breath, a mild lightheadedness, or butterflies in your stomach—all physiological responses we humans may experience when our bodies are transported skyward, whether by plane, roller coaster, or climbing stairs to gaze from the top of a skyscraper.

Don't Always Solo

When you launch/venture into/assume/stumble into a shape-shift, see if you can join other crows or ravens while in flight.

Fake It 'Til You Make It

Don't be afraid to fake it until you make it. I was flying with Hugin and Munin in simple, imaginative reverie (OK, not-so-simple reverie) long before I experienced shape-shifting. But, you ask, "What's the difference between imagining flights of fancy and shape-shifting?" The glib answer may be, "Not much."

As so often is the case with esoteric/metaphysical matters, our everyday language fails us. The answer "intensity" comes to mind—therianthropy is more vivid, intense, and oddly personal than flights of reverie and, as noted, it will commonly induce physical sensations. Yet one should recall the mantra that Paganism, Wicca, and Witchcraft are not spiritual paths "of the book" but of experience and engagement. Like sex, non-ordinary realities can be described in words, but ultimately one has to experience these things to know their true essence—and then the inadequacy of mere words will be revealed.

GOING FORWARD

Out of all the techniques and practices presented in this book, shape-shifting is the most slippery and elusive, sometimes frustratingly so. Spread a tarot deck into some pattern or engage a scrying session, and the probability is quite high that something is going to happen. Therianthropy—perhaps, perhaps not.

It's important to remember that spellwork or any magical operation—just like any human endeavor that combines head, heart, and hand—is going to be fraught with caprice. NBA legends such as Michael Jordan and Magic Johnson would enter each game with the intention of scoring sixty points and leading their team to victory, but even their mega-skills were not always up to the task. A master chef will prepare the same meal over and over, yet sometimes her culinary delights just seem more exquisitely tasty and at other times not quite as much.

So, don't fret if a shape-shifting session doesn't always take you soaring. At the very least you will have activated simple, everyday imagination—which, it turns out, is not so simple after all. If one never experiences that crossover from reverie to shape-shifting, if you believe you have never gone beyond the "fake it" of reverie, you still will have the benefits of escape, play, and release that come from the exercise of one's imagination—and you also will experience some sort of deeper communion with corvid kind as a result.

But it is therianthropy that will take you to places that seem otherworldly, realms that reside above the forest or desert and below the clouds, places that are strange and wonderful and magical. And then you will realize: "This is not an alien realm. This is not a strange world. This is Gaia's breast. This is Nuit's breath. This is the earth. This is where I live—I've just never perceived or experienced it this way."

And you will look beside you and you will be flying with your fellow crows and ravens, and you will caw and gronk and soar, and you will think, "Life is good."

Conclusion

THE GREATEST LESSON

Was the Lascaux Cave artist a shaman? When that artist took pigments harvested from the minerals of Gaia's flesh and crafted the image of a supine, ithyphallic, crow-human therianthrope with a crow-topped staff nearby, they left evidence of a pivotal moment in history: Humans had become aware of liminal space. Humans had become aware that a threshold exists between the palpable, physical world of clan, fires, hunting, and procreation and that mysterious, unseen realm whose existence they had intuited some time ago, that realm where something "other," something nonhuman, something non-earthly resides.

Whether the Lascaux artist was a shaman, an intentional traveler between the seen and unseen realms, they certainly yearned to cross that liminal divide—and a crow, I surmise, served as that artist's guide.

We can only wonder about that artist's encounters with Crow or Raven kind: The first time they noted some intelligent behavior, perhaps the way that crows or ravens followed the human clan's hunting forays to feast on the remains of a carcass. Or maybe they were awestruck by the way crows talked to each other, or the ways they seemed to recognize and remember human faces.

Corvids, they realized, are of this world, but also possess powers of the beyond-this-world: Crows and ravens must be walkers between worlds! Crows and ravens must talk to the mysterious, unseen entities that exist near but outside the world of hunting and gathering and survival!

Magic, this artist-shaman intuited, is afoot. Crow Magic! Raven Magic!

And so the Lascaux artist invoked that magic, celebrated that magic, and sent a communiqué to their tribe, their kind, and all humankind that would follow: We can cross that liminal divide. We can part the veil to reveal the Mysteries. Crows and ravens do it. We can too. Magic is afoot. Crow Magic. Raven Magic.

Glimpse an image of the Lascaux crow-man and a palpable jolt, spawned 19,000 years ago deep in a cave in France, will reverberate through your soul. An ancestor of the crow you see in your backyard is the very crow that enchanted the Lascaux artist. Crows and ravens are the most intelligent nonhuman creatures that most humans will ever encounter—and they are creatures that humankind will encounter often. They are everywhere, almost, going about their corvid ways and their corvid lives, watching us humans doing the same, and reminding us—well, reminding anyone who bothers to take notice—that there are more things in heaven and earth than are dreamt of in most people's philosophies.

Pursue Crow-Raven Magic and you will be following in the footsteps of that ancient artist, the ancient Norse and Celts, Native Americans, and other cultures. Like each and every one of them, you will find deeper communion with Gaia and her flora and fauna, and you will part the veil, and the mysteries and magic of the goddesses and gods will be revealed.

This is the greatest lesson of Crow and Raven kind: Magic is real. Magic is afoot—and as close as your backyard. Caw! Gronk!

RECOMMENDED READING

ON CROWS, RAVENS, AND CORVIDS

In the Company of Crows and Ravens by John M. Marzluff and Tony Angell
> If there is a "bible" of corvidology, this is it.

Gifts of the Crow: How Perception, Emotion, and Thought Allow Smart Birds to Behave Like Humans by John Marzluff and Tony Angell
> This worthy follow-up to *In the Company of Crows and Ravens* is more oriented to hard science, but it is far from being a dry textbook.

Ravens in Winter by Bernd Heinrich
> A first-person, observational, journal-style account of ravens (and some crows) by an academic field biologist.

Crow Planet: Essential Wisdom from the Urban Wilderness by Lyanda Lynn Haupt
> A first-person, crow-centric account of wildlife, nature, and humans sharing the same space, thus leading the author to beguiling excursions into history, science, pop culture, and the wisdom to be learned from feathered kind.

Crows: Encounters with the Wise Guys of the Avian World by Candace Savage
> A compendium of corvid lore, anecdotes, first-person accounts, and historical oddities, plus photos and illustrations.

BIRDING AND NATURE

Any National Audubon Society field guide specific to your region is an excellent choice. Audubon publishes guides specifically about birds, but choose one that covers all the flora and fauna of your area—you will get a broader, more fascinating look at the world inhabited by corvids.

The American Crow and the Common Raven by Lawrence Kilham

> A hardcore, in-the-field, corvid-centric birding book—exhaustive yet engrossing in its details.

ANIMALS IN SPIRITUALITY

The Way of the Animal Powers by Joseph Campbell

> A wide-ranging exploration of the mythic origins of humankind, with ample excursions into the roles that animals played in the rise of humans' shamanic, animistic, and spiritual practices.

Shamanism: Archaic Techniques of Ecstasy by Mircea Eliade

> Akin to the Campbell book, animals figure prominently in Eliade's exploration of the history of humankind's shamanic and spiritual beliefs.

The Folklore of Birds: An Enquiry into the Origin & Distribution of Some Magico-Religious Traditions by Edward A. Armstrong.

> A pan-cultural tour de force by a British ornithologist. Rare and out of print but worth tracking down for serious students of ornithology.

Animal Speak: The Spiritual & Magical Powers of Creatures Great & Small by Ted Andrews.

> An exhaustive, encyclopedia-style survey of the animal kingdom, replete with science and folklore, plus magical exercises, by a popular metaphysical author who also was a naturalist and licensed wildlife rehabilitator.

Animal Magick: The Art of Recognizing & Working with Familiars by D. J. Conway.

> Another encyclopedia-style work that includes not only legends, myths, science, and magical lore but also rituals, meditations, and chants.

BIBLIOGRAPHY

Abram, Christopher. *Myths of the Pagan North: The Gods of the Norsemen*. New York: Continuum, 2011.

"American Crow." All About Birds. Accessed September 21, 2020. https://www.allaboutbirds.org/guide/American_Crow/lifehistory.

Anderson, Rasmus B. *Norse Mythology; or, The Religion of Our Forefathers, Containing All the Myths of the Eddas, Systematized and Interpreted. With an Introduction, Vocabulary and Index*. 4th ed. Chicago: Scott, Foresman, and Company, 1884.

Armstrong, Edward Allworthy. *The Folklore of Birds: An Enquiry into the Origin & Distribution of Some Magico-Religious Traditions*. Boston: Houghton Mifflin, 1959.

Barker, Ernest. *The Political Thought of Plato and Aristotle*. New York: Russell & Russell, 1959.

"The Battle of Clontarf 23rd April 1014." Battle of Clontarf. Accessed June 20, 2023. https://www.battleofclontarf.net/vacations-ireland/the-battle-of-clontarf-23rd-april-1014/3423.

Beck, Guy L., ed. *Sacred Sound: Experiencing Music and World Religions*. Waterloo, Ontario: Wilfrid Laurier University Press, 2006.

Beckett, John. "When You Hear the Call of the Morrigan." *Under the Ancient Oaks: Musings of a Pagan, Druid, and Unitarian Universalist* (blog), *Patheos*, July 30, 2017. https://www.patheos.com/blogs/johnbeckett/2017/07/hear-call-morrigan.html.

Belarde-Lewis, Miranda. "There Are Many Versions of the Tlingit 'Raven' Story, but Its Truth and Hopeful Message Are Universal." *Seattle Times*. Updated July 12, 2019. https://www.seattletimes.com/pacific-nw -magazine/there-are-many-versions-of-the-tlingit-raven-story-but-its -truth-and-hopeful-message-are-universal/.

Bellows, Henry Adams, trans. *The Poetic Edda, translated from the Icelandic with an introduction and notes*. New York: American-Scandinavian Foundation, 1923.

Best, R. I. "Prognostications from the Raven and the Wren." *Ériu* 8 (1916): 120–26. jstor.org/stable/30005405.

"The Bill Reid Gallery." Bill Reid Gallery of Northwest Coast Art. Accessed Jan. 11, 2020. https://www.billreidgallery.ca/.

Bird, Christopher David, and Nathan John Emery. "Rooks Use Stones to Raise the Water Level to Reach a Floating Worm." *Current Biology* 19, no. 16 (August 25, 2009): 1410–14. https://doi.org/10.1016/j.cub.2009.07.033.

BirdNote. "A Wide World of Crows." January 7, 2023. https://www.birdnote .org/listen/shows/wide-world-crows.

Black Letter Press. "W. B. Yeats - Spiritus Mundi." Accessed November 29, 2023. https://www.blackletter-press.com/product-page /w-b-yeats-spiritus-mundi.

Boarman, William I., and Bernd Heinrich. "Common Raven." Cornell Lab of Ornithology. Accessed November 24, 2023. https://birdsoftheworld .org/bow/species/comrav/cur/introduction.

Boechat, Walter. "The Collective Unconscious." International Association for Analytical Psychology. Accessed November 30, 2023. https://iaap .org/jung-analytical-psychology/short-articles-on-analytical-psychology /the-collective-unconscious-2/.

"The Book Review: Shamans of Prehistory." Bradshaw Foundation. Accessed November 26, 2023. https://www.bradshawfoundation.com/books /shamans_of_prehistory.php.

British Birds. "Obituary: Rev. Edward Allworthy Armstrong." Accessed November 26, 2023. https://britishbirds.co.uk/wp-content/uploads /article_files/V72/V72_N05/V72_N05_P219_221_OB058.pdf.

Buckland, Raymond. *The Witch Book: The Encyclopedia of Witchcraft, Wicca, and Neo-Paganism*. Detroit: Visible Ink Press, 2002.

Calder, James T. *Sketch of the Civil and Traditional History of Caithness, from the Tenth Century*. Glasgow: Thomas Murray and Son, 1861.

Campbell, Alistair, ed. *Encomium Emmae Reginae*. Vol. 72. London: Offices of the Royal Historical Society, 1949.

Campbell, Joseph. *The Way of Animal Powers*. Historical Atlas of World Mythology, vol 1. London: Alfred Van Der Marck Editions, 1983.

———. *Occidental Mythology*. The Masks of God. New York: Penguin Books, 1975.

———. *Primitive Mythology*. The Masks of God. New York: Viking Press, 1969.

Camus, Albert. *The Stranger*. Translated by Stuart Gilbert. New York: Vintage Books, 1946.

Carlin, George. *On Location at USC*. Internet Movie Database. Accessed November 29, 2023. https://www.imdb.com/title/tt0249854/characters/nm0137506.

Casey, Denis. "Battle of Clontarf." Britannica. Updated April 16, 2023. https://www.britannica.com/topic/Battle-of-Clontarf.

Castaneda, Carlos. *Journey to Ixtlan: The Lessons of Don Juan*. New York: Simon & Schuster: 1975.

———. *A Separate Reality; Further Conversations with Don Juan*. New York: Simon & Schuster, 1972.

"Cave Paintings Reveal Use of Complex Astronomy." University of Edinburgh. November 27, 2018. https://www.ed.ac.uk/news/2018/cave-paintings-reveal-use-of-complex-astronomy.

Cicero. *On Old Age. On Friendship. On Divination*. Translated by W. A. Falconer. Loeb Classical Library 154. Cambridge, MA: Harvard University Press, 1923.

Clottes, Jean. "The Lascaux Cave Paintings." Bradshaw Foundation. Accessed May 15, 2023. https://www.bradshawfoundation.com/lascaux/.

Clottes, Jean, and David Lewis-Williams. *The Shamans of Prehistory: Trance and Magic in the Painted Caves*. New York: Harry N. Abrams, 1998.

Cornell, Heather N., John M. Marzluff, and Shannon Pecoraro. "Social learning spreads knowledge about dangerous humans among American crows." *Proceedings Biological Sciences* 279, 1728 (February 7, 2012): 499–508. doi:10.1098/rspb.2011.0957.

"Compared Translations of the Meaning of the Quran – 5:31 al-Ma'idah – The Table, The Table Spread Verse 5 : 31." Internet Mosque. Accessed July 14, 2023. https://www.internetmosque.net/read/english_translation_of_the _quran_meaning/5/31/index.html.

Cristol, Daniel A., Paul V. Switzer, Kara L. Johnson, and Leah S. Walke. "Crows Do Not Use Automobiles as Nutcrackers: Putting an Anecdote to the Test." *The Auk* 114, no. 2 (April 1, 1997): 296–98. https://doi .org/10.2307/4089172.

Criswell. *Criswell's Forbidden Predictions; Based on Nostradamus and the Tarot.* Atlanta: Droke House/Hallux, 1972.

Crawford, Jackson, trans. *The Poetic Edda: Stories of the Norse Gods and Heroes.* Indianapolis: Hackett Publishing Company, 2015.

"The Crow Hop." AAA Native Arts Gallery. Accessed November 30, 2022. https://www.aaanativearts.com/the-crow-hop.

Crowley, Aleister. *Magick in Theory and Practice.* New York: Dover Publications, 1976.

Dasent, George Webbe. *The Story of Burnt Njal; or, Life in Iceland at the End of the Tenth Century. From the Icelandic of the Njals Saga.* Vols 1 and 2. Edinburgh: Edmonston and Douglas, 1861.

Davis, Gareth Huw. "Bird Brains." *The Life of Birds.* Accessed May 9, 2023. https://www.pbs.org/lifeofbirds/brain/index.html.

de Yampert, Rick. "Bang a Gong: Rock Music Rocks Rituals." The Wild Hunt. May 27, 2018. https://wildhunt.org/2018/05/bang-a-gong-rock-music -rocks-rituals.html.

———. "Pagan Artists Present Third Offering at Paganicon." The Wild Hunt. March 11, 2018. https://wildhunt.org/2018/03/pagan-artists -present-third-offering-at-paganicon.html.

Dunlap, David W. "Crows and Ravens Make New York Comebacks to Caw (and Cr-r-ruck) About." *New York Times.* October, 23, 2016. https://www

.nytimes.com/2016/10/24/nyregion/crows-and-ravens-make-new-york
-comebacks-to-caw-and-cr-r-uck-about.html.

Dunn, Joseph, trans. *The Ancient Irish Epic Tale Táin Bó Cúalnge*. London: D. Nutt, 1914.

Dyer, Wayne W. *The Power of Intention: Learning to Co-Create Your World Your Way*. Carlsbad, CA: Hay House, 2004.

Echard, Siân, Robert Rouse, Jacqueline A. Fay, Helen Fulton, and Geoff Rector, eds. *The Encyclopedia of Medieval Literature in Britain*. Hoboken, NJ: John Wiley & Sons, 2017.

Eliade, Mircea. *Shamanism: Archaic Techniques of Ecstasy*. Translated by Willard R. Trask. New York: Penguin, 1989.

Ellis, Hilda Roderick. *The Road To Hel: A Study of the Conception of the Dead in Old Norse Literature*. New York: Cambridge University Press, 1943.

Editors of Encyclopaedia Britannica. "Celt." Britannica. Updated June 21, 2023. https://www.britannica.com/topic/Celt-people.

———. "Natural History." Britannica. Updated Janary 24, 2019. https://www.britannica.com/topic/Natural-History-encyclopedic-scientific-by-Pliny-the-Elder.

Editors of Time-Life Books. *Keepers of the Totem*. The American Indians, edited by Henry Woodhead. Alexandria, VA: Time-Life Books, 1993.

Evans-Wentz, W. Y., *The Fairy-Faith in Celtic Countries*. London: Henry Frowde/Oxford University Press, 1911.

Faraday, Lucy Winifred. *The Cattle-Raid of Cualnge (Táin Bó Cúailnge): an Old Irish Prose-Epic Translated for the First Time from Leabhar na h-Uidhri and the Yellow Book of Lecan by L. Winifred Faraday, M. A.* London: D. Nutt, 1904.

Farrar, Janet. and Gavin Bone. *Lifting the Veil: A Witches' Guide to Trance-Prophesy, Drawing Down the Moon, and Ecstatic Ritual*. Oregon: Acorn Guild Press, 2016.

Faulkner, William. *Requiem for a Nun*. London: Chatto & Windus, 1919.

"Feathers and the Law." U.S. Fish & Wildlife Service. Updated April 17, 2023. https://www.fws.gov/lab/featheratlas/feathers-and-the-law.php.

Feuerstein, Georg. *Holy Madness: The Shock Tactics and Radical Teachings of Crazy-Wise Adepts, Holy Fools, and Rascal Gurus*. New York: Arkana, 1990.

Finlay, Alison, trans. *Fagrskinna, a Catalogue of the Kings of Norway: A Translation with Introduction and Notes*. Translated by Alison Finlay. Boston: Brill, 2004.

Frazer, James George. *The Golden Bough: A Study in Magic and Religion*. New York: Macmillan, 1922.

Freeman, Mara. *Kindling the Celtic Spirit: Ancient Traditions to Illumine Your Life Throughout the Seasons*. San Francisco: HarperSan Francisco, 2001.

Garcia, Brittany. "Romulus and Remus." World History Encyclopedia. April 18, 2018. https://www.ancient.eu/Romulus_and_Remus/.

Giles, Cynthia. *The Tarot: History, Mystery, and Lore*. New York: Paragon House, 1992.

Ginzberg, Louis. *The Legends of the Jews; translated from the German manuscript by Henrietta Szold*. Translated by Henrietta Szold. Philadelphia: The Jewish Publication Society of America, 1909.

Green, Miranda. *Animals in Celtic Life and Myth*. London: Routledge, 1992.

———. *Celtic Goddesses: Warriors, Virgins, and Mothers*. New York: G. Braziller, 1996.

———. *Dictionary of Celtic Myth and Legend*. London: Thames and Hudson, 1992.

———. *Symbol and Image in Celtic Religious Art*. London: Routledge, 1989.

Green, W. C., trans. *The Story of Egil Skallagrimsson: Being an Icelandic Family History of the Ninth and Tenth Centuries*. London: E. Stock, 1893. https://www.sagadb.org/egils_saga.en.

Greene, David H., ed. *An Anthology of Irish Literature*. Vol. 1. New York: New York University Press, 1954.

Guerber, H. A. *Myths of the Norsemen from the Eddas and Sagas*. London: George G. Harrap, 1909.

Guest, Lady Charlotte, trans. *The Mabinogion*. London: T. Fisher Unwin, 1902.

Gwynn, Edward, trans. *The Metrical Dindsenchas*. Royal Irish Academy. Todd Lecture Series. Vol. 8–12. Dublin: Hodges, Figgis, 1903.

Haekel, Josef. "Totemism." Britannica. Updated September 8, 2022. https://www.britannica.com/topic/totemism-religion.

Hansen, Chadwick. *Witchcraft at Salem*. New York: Signet Books, 1969.

Hartogsohn, Ido. "Constructing Drug Effects: A History of Set and Setting."
Sage Journals. January 1, 2017. https://journals.sagepub
.com/doi/10.1177/2050324516683325.

Hjaltalin, Jon A., and Gilbert Goudie, trans. *The Orkneyinga Saga, translated
from the Icelandic by Jon A. Hjaltalin and Gilbert Goudie; edited, with notes and
introduction, by Joseph Anderson*. Edited by Joseph Anderson. Edinburgh:
Edmonston and Douglas, 1873.

Haupt, Lyanda Lynn. *Crow Planet: Essential Wisdom from the Urban Wilderness*.
New York: Back Bay Books, 2009.

Heinrich, Bernd. *Mind of the Raven: Investigations and Adventures with Wolf-Birds*.
New York: Harper Perennial, 2006.

Heinrich, Bernd, and Thomas Bugnyar. "Just How Smart Are Ravens?" *Scientific American*, April 2007.

Hennessy, W. M. "The Ancient Irish Goddess of War." 1870. https://www
.sacred-texts.com/neu/celt/aigw/aigw01.htm.

———. "On the Goddess of War of the Ancient Irish." *Proceedings of the Royal
Irish Academy* 10 (1866): 421, 423–40. www.jstor.org/stable/20489002.

Hollander, Lee M. *Old Norse Poems: The Most Important Non-Skaldic Verse Not
Included in the Poetic Edda*. New York: Columbia University Press, 1936.

"How Raven Brought Fire to the Indians." World of Tales. Accessed January
11, 2020. https://www.worldoftales.com/Native_American_folktales
/Native_American_Folktale_59.html.

"How Raven Stole Crow's Potlatch." Mr. Donn's Site for Kids & Teachers.
Accessed May 9, 2023. https://nativeamericans.mrdonn.org/stories/raven
.html.

Hull, Eleanor. *Cuchulain, the Hound of Ulster*. London: George G. Harrap, 1911.

———. *The Cuchullin Saga in Irish Literature: Being a Collection of Stories Relating
to the Hero Cuchullin*. London: D. Nutt, 1898.

———. *The Northmen in Britain*. New York: Thomas Y. Crowell Company,
1913.

———. "Observations of Classical Writers on the Habits of the Celtic Nations,
as Illustrated from Irish Records." *The Celtic Review* 3, no. 9 (July 1906):
62–76, 138–154.

Ingersoll, Ernest. *Birds in Legend, Fable, and Folklore*. New York: Longmans, Green and Co., 1923.

Jackson, Jake, ed. *Norse Myths*. The World's Greatest Myths and Legends. London: Flame Tree Publishing, 2014.

"John Ferguson McLennan." New World Encyclopedia. Accessed June 6, 2023. https://www.newworldencyclopedia.org/entry/John_Ferguson_McLennan.

Johnson, W. J. *A Dictionary of Hinduism*. New York: Oxford University Press, 2009.

Kaufman, Kenn. "American Crow." Audubon. Accessed June 28, 2019. https://www.audubon.org/field-guide/bird/american-crow.

———. "Common Raven." Audubon. Accessed June 28, 2019. https://www.audubon.org/field-guide/bird/common-raven.

Kilham, Lawrence. *The American Crow and the Common Raven*. College Station, Texas: Texas A&M University Press, 1989.

———. "Sustained Robbing of American Crows by Common Ravens at a Feeding Station." *Journal of Field Ornithology* 56, no. 4 (Autumn 1985): 425–26.

Kramer-Rolls, Dana. "Moon." In *The Encyclopedia of Modern Witchcraft and Neo-Paganism*, edited by Shelley Rabinovich and James Lewis, 160–61. New York: Citadel Press, 2002.

Larson, Kay. *Where the Heart Beats: John Cage, Zen Buddhism, and the Inner Life of Artists*. New York: Penguin Books, 2013.

Laufer, Berthold. "Bird Divination among the Tibetans (Notes on Document Pelliot No. 3530, with a Study of Tibetan Phonology of the Ninth Century)." *T'oung Pao* 15, no. 1 (1914): 1–110. jstor.org/stable/4526388.

Leakey, Richard, and Roger Lewin. *Origins Reconsidered: In Search of What Makes Us Human*. New York: Doubleday, 1992.

Leonard, Pat. "Crows Have a Mob Mentality Toward Ravens." All about Birds. July 4, 2018. https://www.allaboutbirds.org/news/crows-have-a-mob-mentality-toward-ravens/#.

Lévi-Strauss, Claude. *Totemism*. Boston: Beacon Press, 1963.

Link, Russell. "Living with Wildlife: Crows." Washington Department of Fish and Wildlife. Accessed September 22, 2020. https://wdfw.wa.gov/sites/default/files/publications/00611/wdfw00611.pdf.

Livy (Titus Livius). *The History of Rome, Vol. 2.* Translated by George Baker. New York: Peter A. Mesier et al., 1823.

Lorenz, Konrad. *King Solomon's Ring: New Light on Animal Ways.* Translated by Marjorie Kerr Wilson. London: Methuen, 1952.

Lukman, N. "The Raven Banner and the Changing Ravens: A Viking Miracle from Carolingian Court Poetry to Saga and Arthurian Romance." *Classica et Mediaevalia* 19 (1958): 133–51.

Lysaght, Patricia. *The Banshee: The Irish Death Messenger.* Boulder, CO: Roberts Rineheart, 1986.

Mac Cana, Proinsias. *Celtic Mythology.* Feltham, London: Hamlyn, 1970.

MacKendrick, Paul. *The Dacian Stones Speak.* Chapel Hill, NC: University of North Carolina Press, 2000.

MacKillop, James. "Washer at the Ford." In *A Dictionary of Celtic Mythology.* Oxford: Oxford University Press, 1998. https://www.oxfordreference.com/view/10.1093/oi/authority.20110803121134488.

MacLeod, Sharon Paice. *Celtic Myth and Religion: A Study of Traditional Belief, with Newly Translated Prayers, Poems and Songs.* Jefferson, NC: McFarland, 2012.

MacRae, Fiona. "Why You're More Likely to Have Weird and Wonderful Dreams When There's a Full Moon." *Daily Mail*, March 27, 2014. https://www.dailymail.co.uk/sciencetech/article-2590317/Dark-moon-Why-youre-likely-weird-wonderful-dreams-certain-nights.html.

Malin, Edward. *Totem Poles of the Pacific Northwest Coast.* Portland: Timber Press, 1986.

Maple, Eric. "Wands." In *Man, Myth & Magic: An Illustrated Encyclopedia of the Supernatural*, edited by Richard Cavendish, 2985–87. New York: Marshall Cavendish, 1970.

Marvell, Andrew. "To His Coy Mistress." Poetry Foundation. Accessed November 28, 2023. https://www.poetryfoundation.org/poems/44688/to-his-coy-mistress.

Marzluff, John M., and Tony Angell. *In the Company of Crows and Ravens*. New Haven: Yale University Press, 2005.

———. *Gifts of the Crow: How Perception, Emotion, and Thought Allow Smart Birds to Behave Like Humans*. New York: Free Press, 2012.

May, Rollo. *The Courage to Create*. New York: W.W. Norton, 1975.

McGowan, Kat. "Meet the Bird Brainiacs: American Crow." *Audubon Magazine*, March–April 2016. https://www.audubon.org/magazine /march-april-2016/meet-bird-brainiacs-american-crow#.

McGowan, Kevin. "Frequently Asked Questions about Crows." Cornell Lab of Ornithology. Updated November 9, 2010. https://www.birds.cornell .edu/crows/crowfaq.htm#roost.

McGowan, Kevin, and Karen Rodriguez. "Caw vs. Croak: Inside the Calls of Crows and Ravens." Bird Academy. Accessed May 21, 2019. https:// academy.allaboutbirds.org/caw-vs-croak-inside-the-calls-of-crows -and-ravens/.

Mindell, Arnold. *The Shaman's Body: A New Shamanism for Transforming Health, Relationships, and the Community*. San Francisco: HarperSanFrancisco, 1993.

Montanari, Shaena. "We Knew Ravens Are Smart. But Not This Smart." *National Geographic*, July 13, 2017. https://news.nationalgeographic .com/2017/07/ravens-problem-solving-smart-birds/.

Montgomery, Sy. "Crow." Britannica. Accessed November 25, 2023. https:// www.britannica.com/animal/crow-bird.

Mortensen, Karl. *A Handbook of Norse Mythology*. Translated by A. Clinton Crowell. Mineola, NY: Dover Publications, 2003.

National Audubon Society. "The Migratory Bird Treaty Act, Explained." Audu- bon. Accessed May 24, 2023. https://www.audubon.org/news /the-migratory-bird-treaty-act-explained.

Ní Mhaonaigh, Máire. "The Date of *Cogad Gáedel re Gallaib*." *Pertitia* 9 (1995): 354–77. https://doi.org/10.1484/J.Peri.3.255.

Nijhuis, Michelle. "Friend or Foe? Crows Never Forget a Face, It Seems." *New York Times*, August 25, 2008. https://www.nytimes.com/2008/08/26 /science/26crow.html.

Nisker, Wes "Scoop." *The Essential Crazy Wisdom*. Berkeley: Ten Speed Press, 1990.

Ó Corráin, Donncha. *Ireland before the Normans*. Gill History of Ireland. Dublin: Gill and Macmillan, 1972.

Ó hÓgáin, Daithi. *Myth, Legend & Romance: An Encyclopedia of the Irish Folk Tradition*. New York: Prentice Hall Press, 1991.

"One for Sorrow ... Magpie Nursery Rhyme." Bird Spot. Accessed June 23, 2023. https://www.birdspot.co.uk/culture/one-for-sorrow-magpie-nursery-rhyme.

"One for Sorrow (Nursery Rhyme) about Magpies." Birdfact. Updated April 19, 2022. https://birdfact.com/articles/one-for-sorrow-nursery-rhyme-about-magpies#alternativeVersionsOfOneForSorrow.

O'Neill, Brian. "The Battle of Clontarf." Your Irish Culture. Updated March 2, 2020. https://www.yourirish.com/history/medieval/battle-of-clontarf.

Ovid. *The Metamorphoses*. Translated by A. S. Kline. London: Poetry in Translation, 2000.

Pálsson, Hermann, and Paul Edwards, trans. *Orkneyinga Saga: The History of the Earls of Orkney*. New York: Penguin, 1981.

Peterson, Roger Tory. *A Field Guide to the Birds: A Completely New Guide to All the Birds of Eastern and Central North America*. 4th ed. Boston: Houghton Mifflin, 1980.

Pliny the Elder. *Pliny's Natural History in Thirty-Seven Books. A translation on the basis of that by Dr. Philemon Holland, ed. 1601, with Critical and Explanatory Notes*. Vol. 1, bk. 7, 10. Translated by Jonathan Couch and edited by the Wernerian Club. London: George Barclay, 1847–49.

Poe, Edgar Allan. "The Raven." Poetry Foundation. Accessed November 30, 2023. https://www.poetryfoundation.org/poems/48860/the-raven.

Radin, Paul. *The Trickster: A Study in American Indian Myth*. New York: Schocken Books, 1956.

Reck, David. *Music of the Whole Earth*. New York: Da Capo Press, 1997.

Reid, Sian Lee. "Tools of the Art." In *The Encyclopedia of Modern Witchcraft and Neo-Paganism*, edited by Shelley Rabinovich and James Lewis, 272–74. New York: Citadel Press, 2002.

"Rock Art Theories V." Bradshaw Foundation. May 8, 2015. http://www
.bradshawfoundation.com/news/index.php?id=Rock-art-theories-V.

"Rock Art Theories VI." Bradshaw Foundation. May 12, 2015. https://www
.bradshawfoundation.com/news/index.php?id=Rock-art-theories-VI.

Ross, Anne. *Druids: Preachers of Immortality*. Stroud, Gloucestershire: The
History Press, 2013.

———. *Pagan Celtic Britain: Studies in Iconography and Tradition*. Chicago: Academy Chicago Publishers, 1996.

Rutherford, Ward. *Celtic Lore: The History of the Druids and Their Timeless Traditions*. London: Aquarian Press, 1993.

Ryan, Robert E. *The Strong Eye of Shamanism: A Journey into the Caves of Consciousness*. Rochester, VT: Inner Traditions, 1999.

Sandars, N. K., trans. *The Epic of Gilgamesh: An English Version with an Introduction*. Revised edition. New York: Penguin, 1972.

Savage, Candace. *Crows: Encounters with the Wise Guys of the Avian World*. Vancouver: Greystone Books, 2015.

Schoepperle, Gertrude. "The Washer of the Ford." *The Journal of English and
Germanic Philology* 18, no. 1 (January 1919): 60–66.

Shakespeare, William. *Hamlet*. Edited by Barbara A. Mowat, Paul Werstine,
Michael Poston, and Rebecca Niles. Washington, DC: Folger Shakespeare
Library. https://www.folger.edu/explore/shakespeares-works/hamlet
/read/.

Smith, Tiddy. "Animism." Internet Encyclopedia of Philosophy. Accessed June
13, 2023. https://iep.utm.edu/animism/.

Smith, William, ed. "Augur, Augurium." In *A Dictionary of Greek and Roman
Antiquities*, 174–79. London: John Murray, 1875. http://penelope.uchicago
.edu/Thayer/E/Roman/Texts/secondary/SMIGRA*/Augurium.html.

Smyth, Daragh. *A Guide to Irish Mythology*. Dublin: Irish Academic Press, 1996.

Society for Northern Research. *Saga-Book of the Viking Club*. Vol. 6. Proceedings. London: printed by the author, 1908–9.

Stange, Karlene. *The Spiritual Nature of Animals: A Country Vet Explores the
Wisdom, Compassion, and Souls of Animals*. Novato, CA: New World Library,
2017.

Stevenson, William Henry, ed. *Asser's Life of King Alfred, Together with the Annals of Saint Neots Erroneously Ascribed to Asser, edited with an introduction and commentary by William Henry Stevenson.* Oxford: Clarendon Press, 1904.

Stevenson, Joseph, trans. *The Church Historians of England.* Vol. 2, Part 2. London: Seeleys, 1854.

Stewart, C. Nelson. "Talismans." In *Man, Myth & Magic: An Encyclopedia of the Supernatural,* edited by Richard Cavendish, 2772–75. New York: Marshall Cavendish, 1970.

Stokes, Whitley, ed. "Cuchulainn's Death [abridged from the Book of Leinster, ff. 77, *a* 1 – 78, *b* 2]," *Revue Celtique* 3 (1876–1878): 175–185, 152.

———. "The Destruction of Dá Derga's Hostel." *Revue Celtique* 22 (1901): 9–61, 165–215, 282–329, 390–437.

———. *The Destruction of Dá Derga's Hostel.* New York: P. F. Collier & Son, 1910.

———. "The Prose Tales in the Rennes Dindshenchas." *Revue Celtique* 15 (1894): 418–84.

———. "The Second Battle of Moytura." *Revue Celtique* 12 (1891): 52–130, 306–8.

Sturluson, Snorri. *The Prose Edda, by Snorri Sturluson, translated from the Icelandic with an introduction by Arthur Gilchrist Brodeur.* New York: The American-Scandinavian Foundation, 1916.

Summers, Montague. *The Geography of Witchcraft.* New York: University Books, 1958.

Sweatman, Martin B., and Alistair Coombs. "Decoding European Paleolithic Art: Extremely Ancient Knowledge of Precession of the Equinoxes." *Athens Journal of History* 5, no. 1 (January 2019): 1–30.

Swift, Kaeli. "FAQs about Crows." *Corvid Research* (blog). https://corvidresearch.blog/.

Tanabe, Jennifer. "Totemism." New World Encyclopedia. Updated May 28, 2015. https://www.newworldencyclopedia.org/p/index.php?title=Totemism&oldid=988394.

Teit, James. "Traditions of the Lillooet Indians of British Columbia." *The Journal of American Folklore* 25, no. 98 (October–December 1912), 287–371.

Todd, James Henthorn, trans. *Cogadh Gaedhel re Gallaibh.The War of the Gaedhil with the Gaill; or, The Invasions of Ireland by the Danes and Other Norsemen.* London: Longmans, Green, Reader, and Dyer, 1867.

Turville-Petre, E. O. G. *Myth and Religion of the North; The Religion of Ancient Scandinavia.* Westport, CT: Greenwood Press, 1964.

Upham, Charles Wentworth. *Salem Witchcraft; with an Account of Salem Village, a History of Opinions on Witchcraft and Kindred Subjects.* Vol. 1. Boston: Wiggin and Lunt, 1867.

Valiente, Doreen. *An ABC of Witchcraft: Past and Present.* Custer, WA: Phoenix Publishing, 1988.

———. *Witchcraft for Tomorrow.* Custer, Washington: Phoenix Publishing, 1978.

Vonnegut, Kurt. "Address to Graduating Class at Bennington College." James Somers. Accessed June 9, 2023. https://jsomers.net/vonnegut-1970 -commencement.html.

Walker, Benjamin. "Moon." In *Man, Myth & Magic: An Illustrated Encyclopedia of the Supernatural,* edited by Richard Cavendish, 1876–82. New York: Marshall Cavendish, 1970.

Watts, Alan. *The Tao of Philosophy.* Boston: Tuttle Publishing, 1995.

———. "Zen Bones." In *Eastern Wisdom, Modern Life: Collected Talks 1960–1969,* 151–165. Novato, California: New World Library, 2006.

Weber, Courtney. *The Morrigan: Celtic Goddess of Magick and Might.* Newburyport, MA: Weiser Books, 2019.

Wei-Haas, Maya. "40,000-Year-Old Cave Art May Be World's Oldest Animal Drawing." *National Geographic.* November, 7, 2018. https://www .nationalgeographic.com/science/2018/11 /news-oldest-animal-drawing-borneo-cave-art-human-origins/.

"What Is a Native American Pow Wow? – The Meaning of Pow Wows." Pow Wows. Accessed November 30, 2022. https://www.powwows .com/what-is-a-pow-wow/.

Whitford, David M. *The Curse of Ham in the Early Modern Era: The Bible and the Justifications for Slavery.* Surrey, England: Ashgate, 2009.

Wilde, Lady. *Ancient Cures, Charms, and Usages of Ireland; Contributions to Irish Lore*. London: Ward and Downey, 1890.

Wilson, Colin. *Super Consciousness: The Quest for the Peak Experience*. London: Watkins Publishing, 2009.

Wilson, Robert Anton. *Cosmic Trigger: Final Secret of the Illuminati*. Las Vegas, Nevada: Falcon Press, 1989.Trigger

Woolf, Virginia. *Mr. Bennett and Mrs. Brown*. London: The Hogarth Press, 1924.

Yates, James. "Amuletum." In *A Dictionary of Greek and Roman Antiquities*, edited by William Smith, 91. 2nd edition. Boston: Little, Brown, and Company, 1859.

Yeats, William Butler. "Adam's Curse." In *The Collected Poems of W. B. Yeats*. Definitive Edition, With the Author's Final Revisions, 78–79. New York: Macmillan, 1956."

———. *A Critical Edition of Yeats's A Vision (1925)*. Edited by George Mills Harper and Walter Kelly Hood. London: Macmillan, 1978.

———. "Gratitude to the Unknown Instructors." In *The Collected Poems of W. B. Yeats*. Definitive Edition, With the Author's Final Revisions, 249. New York: Macmillan, 1956.

———. "If I Were Four-and-Twenty." In *Explorations*, 263–70. London: Macmillan, 1962.

———. "The Lake Isle of Innisfree." In *The Collected Poems of W. B. Yeats*. Definitive Edition, With the Author's Final Revisions, 39. New York: Macmillan, 1956.

Zakroff, Laura Tempest. *Visual Alchemy: A Witch's Guide to Sigils, Art & Magic*. Woodbury, MN: Llewellyn Publications, 2022.

Zell, Oberon. "Biography." Oberon Zell. Accessed March 21, 2020. https:// oberonzell.com/biography/.

Zimmerman, Larry J. *The Sacred Wisdom of the Native Americans*. New York: Chartwell Books, 2016.

Zorich, Zach. "New Dates for the Oldest Cave Painting." *Archaeology*, July/August 2016. https://www.archaeology.org/issues/221-1607/trenches/4551-trenches-france-chauvet-dating.

INDEX

G

H

I

J

K

L

M

N

O

P

Q

R

S

Y

Z

NOTES